D1344099

HARDEN'S

London
Restaurants
1997

Where to buy Harden's guides
Harden's guides are on sale in most major bookshops
in the UK, and many major bookshops in the US.
In case of difficulty, call Harden's Guides on
0171-839 4763.

Customised editions –
the ideal corporate gift
Harden's London Restaurants is available in specially
customised corporate gift formats. For information,
please call 0171-839 4763.

mail@hardens.com
We now have an e-mail address. You may use it to
register for the updates or to send us any other
communications.

© Harden's Guides, 1996

ISBN 1-873721-10-2

British Library Cataloguing-in-Publication data:
a catalogue record for this book is available from
the British Library.

Printed and bound in Finland by
Werner Söderström Osakeyhtiö

Harden's Guides
29 Villiers Street
London WC2N 6ND

Distributed in the United States of America by
Seven Hills Book Distributors,
49 Central Avenue, Cincinnati, OH 45202

The contents of this book are believed correct
at the time of printing. Nevertheless, the publishers
can accept no responsibility for errors or changes in
or omissions from the details given.

No part of this publication may be reproduced or
transmitted in any form or by any means, electronically
or mechanically, including photocopying, recording or
any information storage or retrieval system, without
prior permission in writing from the publishers.

CONTENTS

Ratings & prices

	Page
From the Editors	**8**
Survey results	
Most mentioned	10
Nominations	11
Highest ratings	12
Top special deals	**16**
The restaurant scene	**18**
Openings and closings	**20**
Directory	**24**
Indexes	
Breakfast	162
Brunch menus	163
Business	163
BYO	164
Children	165
Entertainment	167
Late	169
No-smoking areas	170
Outside tables	172
Private rooms	175
Romantic	178
Rooms with a view	179
Vegetarian menus	179
Cuisine lists	**180**
Area overviews	**194**
Maps	**222**

1 – London overview
2 – West End overview
3 – Mayfair, St James's & West Soho
4 – East Soho, Chinatown & Covent Garden
5 – Knightsbridge, Chelsea & South Kensington
6 – Notting Hill & Bayswater
7 – Hammersmith & Chiswick
8 – Islington, Camden Town & Hampstead
9 – The City
10 – South London (and Fulham)

RATINGS & PRICES

Ratings

Our rating system is unlike those found in other guides (most of which tell you nothing more helpful than that expensive restaurants are, as a general rule, better than cheap ones).

What we do is to compare each restaurant's performance with other restaurants in the same price-bracket.

This system has the advantage that it helps you find – whatever your budget for any particular meal – where you will get the best "bang for your buck".

The following qualities are assessed:

> **F** — Food
> **S** — Service
> **A** — Ambience

The rating indicates that, *in comparison with other restaurants in the same price-bracket*, performance is …

> **❶** — Exceptional
> **❷** — Very good
> **❸** — Good
> ④ — Mediocre
> ⑤ — Disappointing

Prices

The price shown for each restaurant is the cost for one (1) person of an average three-course *dinner* with half a bottle of house wine and coffee, any cover charge, service and VAT. Lunch is often cheaper. With BYO restaurants, we have assumed that two people share a £5 bottle of off-licence wine.

Telephone numbers – only '0181' numbers are prefixed; all others are '0171' numbers.

Map reference – shown immediately after the telephone number.

Last orders time – the first entry in the small print (Sunday may be up to 90 minutes earlier).

Opening hours – unless otherwise stated, restaurants are open for lunch and dinner seven days a week.

Credit and debit cards – unless otherwise stated, Mastercard, Visa, Amex and Switch are accepted.

Dress – where appropriate, the management's preferences concerning patrons' dress are given.

Smoking – cigarette smoking restrictions are noted. Pipe or cigar smokers should always check ahead.

FROM THE EDITORS

This is the sixth edition of our annual guide to London's restaurants, designed to help you find the right place for any particular occasion and then, as briefly as possible, to tell you everything you need to know about it.

The Survey

This year, the guide has been compiled with the help of the 1,500 reporters who took part in our annual survey – roughly twice the number who participated last year. We are very grateful to all those who have taken part in the survey, and who have helped us to expand it by introducing friends and colleagues.

Reporters eat out, on average, 3.6 times a week. Thus the survey reflects the experiences of over 250,000 meals eaten in the preceding 12 months.

We have ourselves visited every restaurant, or chain, listed in this book – always anonymously and at our own expense. We believe that this combination of our own personal experience with the views of hundreds of other people enables the production of a guide that is of unequalled reliability.

Restaurants are getting bigger, and it is no particular surprise that many of the new "mega-brasseries" have difficulty in achieving consistent standards. For a guide, the question, more than ever, is not "what can the chef do on a good day", but rather "how well do the legions of chefs in the kitchen actually work together most of the time?" This question can only be answered by reference to the views of a number of diners – the views of a single investigator, however perceptive, just cannot answer the point.

Where the 500 most commented-upon restaurants are concerned, we almost always accept the verdict dictated by a numerical analysis of the ratings given by reporters in the survey. On the occasions where we feel that we can add something by noting dissent from the "average" view, we do so in the text. Our own opinions are, of necessity, more to the fore in reviews of newly opened places and smaller 'locals' which attract fewer comments.

Changes this year

As always, we have tried to incorporate improvements to make the guide easier to use.

Rating system – Perhaps the most shocking change for regular readers will be the introduction of a 5-point rating scale. Under the old 4-point system, we had progressively felt that the distinction between 'good' and 'fair' in the middle ranks was too crude. The new middle grade enables us to distinguish the better performers in the middle ground from the more mediocre places.

Comparing the London restaurant scene now with that when we published our first guide five years ago, it is just so much, well, bigger – and also more widely spread – than it used to be. This edition reflects this in two ways:

New maps – Not one but two maps have been added – one covering the Mayfair/St James's dining zone, and the other the burgeoning scene around Hammersmith and Chiswick. By so doing we have, at last, been able to introduce the improvement most frequently requested by readers: maps now show the names of restaurants, rather than irritating little reference numbers.

Greater coverage – By changing to a new paper stock, we have been able to increase the number of reviews by about 10%, while actually reducing the bulk of the book and maintaining its handy slimline format.

Help us to help you

This book is to an unusual extent a partnership between readers and publishers. For our part, we try to offer a service which we do not believe is matched by any other restaurant guide in the world – including free updates and newsletters about developments in the restaurant scene (see below).

And for your part? If you register for the free updates you will be invited, in the summer of 1997, to take part in our next survey. **If you take part in the survey, you will, on publication, receive a complimentary copy of *Harden's London Restaurants 1998*.**

Richard Harden   **Peter Harden**

FREE UPDATES

To receive your free updates to *Harden's London Restaurants 1997* (published in February and June 1997), please complete and return the detachable, reply-paid card from the back of the guide. You will then also be registered to take part in the next survey.

Alternatively you may register by e-mail: just send your details to mail@hardens.com.

SURVEY – MOST MENTIONED

These are the restaurants which were most frequently mentioned by reporters. (Last year's position is given in brackets. An asterisk* indicates a first appearance in the list of a recently opened or re-launched restaurant.)

1	Mezzo*
2	Quaglino's (1)
3	The Ivy (2)
4	Le Pont de la Tour (4)
5	Bibendum (3)
6	L'Odéon*
7	The Criterion*
8	Le Caprice (6)
9	Aubergine (9=)
10	Rules (13=)
11	Coast*
12	Kensington Place (5)
13	Le Palais du Jardin (22=)
14	The River Café (8)
15	Belgo Centraal (-)
16	La Tante Claire (11)
17=	Blue Elephant (15)
17=	Daphne's (7)
19	Fifth Floor at Harvey Nichols (24=)
20	The Avenue*
21	Restaurant Marco Pierre White (16=)
22	Wagamama (16=)
23	Atlantic Bar & Grill (21)
24	Vong*
25	Simpsons-in-the-Strand (12)
26	The Greenhouse (24=)
27	The Canteen (9=)
28=	Fulham Road (13=)
28=	Savoy Grill (20)
30=	Christopher's (34)
30=	Savoy River Room (18)
32=	Le Gavroche (-)
32=	The People's Palace (-)
34	Chez Nico at Ninety (39)
35	The Collection*
36=	The Brackenbury (31)
36=	Clarke's (19)
38=	Launceston Place (26=)
38=	Orso (28)
40	Chutney Mary (-)

SURVEY – NOMINATIONS

Ranked by the number of reporters' votes for:

Best meal of the year

1   Aubergine (2)
2   La Tante Claire (1)
3   Bibendum (3)
4   Restaurant Marco Pierre White (5)
5   Le Gavroche (-)
6   Le Pont de la Tour (7)
7   Chez Nico at Ninety (6)
8   The River Café (8)
9   The Criterion*
10 The Ivy (-)

Favourite

1   The Ivy
2   Le Caprice
3   Aubergine
4   La Tante Claire
5   Bibendum
6   Le Pont de la Tour
7   Le Palais du Jardin
8= Andrew Edmunds
8= The River Café
10 Kensington Place

Best for business

1   Le Pont de la Tour
2   Savoy Grill
3   The Ivy
4   The Square
5= Bibendum
5= Le Caprice
7   City Brasserie
8   Langan's Brasserie
9   Gladwins
10 Mezzo

Best for romance

1   La Poule au Pot
2   Julie's
3   Launceston Place
4   Odette's
5   Blue Elephant
6   Aubergine
7   Blakes Hotel
8= Andrew Edmunds
8= Le Caprice
8= The Criterion

SURVEY – HIGHEST RATINGS

Rankings are determined from reporters' average ratings:

Money no object (£50+)

Food	Service
1 Aubergine	1 Oak Room
2 Tatsuso	2 Connaught
3 La Tante Claire	3 Le Gavroche
4 Chez Nico at Ninety	4 La Tante Claire
5 Le Gavroche	5 Aubergine

Expensive (£40-£49)

Food	Service
1 Clarke's	1 Dorchester Grill
2 The River Café	2 Matsuri
3 Halcyon Hotel	3 Le Caprice
4 Poissonnerie de l'Av.	4 The Heights
5 Vong	5 The Ivy

Upper mid-price (£30-£39)

Food	Service
1 Jason's	1 Oslo Court
2 Chez Bruce	2 Odin's
3 L'Oranger	3 Beoty's
4 Livebait	4 Chez Moi
5 La Dordogne	5 Euphorium

Lower mid-price (£20-£29)

Food	Service
1 Mandarin Kitchen	1 La Pomme d'Amour
2 Inaho	2 Cappadoccia
3 Two Brothers	3 Blues
4 The Stepping Stone	4 The Stepping Stone
5 Café Spice Namaste	5 S&P Patara

Budget (£19 or less)

Food	Service
1 Lahore Kebab House	1 Kastoori
2 Shree Krishna	2 Tokyo Diner
3 Moshi Moshi Sushi	3 Pizzeria Condotti
4 Kastoori	4 Wagamama
5 Poon's, Lisle Street	5 The Place Below

Ambience

1 The Ritz
2 Blakes
3 Café Royal Grill Room
4 Lanesborough
5 Savoy River Room

Overall

1 Aubergine
2 La Tante Claire
3 Le Gavroche
4 Oak Room
5 Connaught

Ambience

1 The Lindsay House
2 Blue Elephant
3 Le Caprice
4 The Ivy
5 Halcyon Hotel

Overall

1 Le Caprice
2 The Ivy
3 Halcyon Hotel
4 Dorchester Grill
5 Blue Elephant

Ambience

1 Mr Wing
2 Julie's
3 The Belvedere
4 Tate Gallery
5 Odin's

Overall

1 Oslo Court
2 L'Aventure
3 Odin's
4 L'Oranger
5 Chez Bruce

Ambience

1 Naked Turtle
2 Pizza Pomodoro SW3
3 Blues
4 Rebato's
5 Jimmy Beez

Overall

1 Blues
2 Naked Turtle
3 The Stepping Stone
4 O'Conor Don
5 Little Italy

Ambience

1 Simpson's of Cornhill
2 Grenadier
3 Pâtisserie Valerie
4 La Rueda
5 Windsor Castle

Overall

1 Kastoori
2 Fox & Anchor
3 Tokyo Diner
4 Moshi Moshi Sushi
5 The Place Below

SURVEY – HIGHEST RATINGS

Highest average ratings by cuisine

These are the restaurants which received the best average food ratings, listed by cuisine. (A few equally deserving restaurants are excluded because they are too little known to generate a sufficient number of reports.)

Each section is divided into '£30 and over', and 'under £30'. Within each section, restaurants are ranked by rating.

Modern British

£30 and over
1 Clarke's
2 Chez Bruce
3 Halcyon Hotel
4 Le Caprice
5 The Square
6 Stephen Bull
7 Euphorium
8 The Canteen
9 The Sugar Club
10 The Heights

Under £30
1 The Stepping Stone
2 Tabac
3 Alastair Little, W11
4 The Mason's Arms
5 Ladbroke Arms

Traditional British

£30 and over
1 The Greenhouse
2 Connaught
3 Dorchester Grill

Under £30
4 Fox & Anchor

East/West

£30 and over
1 Vong

Steaks & Grills

£30 and over
1 The Rib Room

French

£30 and over
1 Aubergine
2 La Tante Claire
3 Chez Nico at Ninety
4 Le Gavroche
5 Four Seasons
6 L'Oranger
7 Interlude de Chavot
8 La Dordogne
9 L'Aventure
10 Capital Hotel

Italian/Mediterranean

£30 and over
1 The River Café
2 Riva
3 Al San Vincenzo
4 Zafferano

Under £30
1 Del Buongustaio
2 The Red Pepper
3 The Eagle

Fish & seafood

£30 and over
1 Jason's
2 Livebait
3 Poissonnerie de l'Avenue

Under £30
1 Chez Liline
2 Bibendum Oyster Bar

Fish & chips

Under £30
1 Two Brothers
2 Seashell
3 Geale's
4 Upper Street Fish Shop

Pizza

Under £30
1 Pizzeria Castello
2 Eco
3 Calzone
4 Delizia

Spanish

Under £30
1 Rebato's

Russian

£30 and over
1 Kaspia

Vegetarian

Under £30
1 The Gate
2 The Place Below

Snacks

Under £30
1 Pâtisserie Valerie

Chinese

£30 and over
1 Dorchester, Oriental
2 Fung Shing
3 Zen Central

Under £30
1 Mandarin Kitchen
2 Poon's, Lisle St
3 Mao Tai
4 Royal China W2
5 Harbour City

Japanese

£30 and over
1 Tatsuso
2 Shogun
3 Matsuri

Under £30
1 Inaho
2 Moshi Moshi Sushi
3 Ikkyu
4 Tokyo Diner
5 Wagamama

Indian

£30 and over
1 Bengal Clipper

Under £30
1 Lahore Kebab House
2 Shree Krishna
3 Kastoori
4 Café Spice Namaste
5 Standard Tandoori
6 Khan's of Kensington

Thai

Under £30
1 Bedlington Café
2 Churchill

TOP SPECIAL DEALS

Menus are included in the following lists which give you the chance to eat in the restaurants concerned at a significant discount compared to the evening à la carte prices.

The price in brackets is calculated in accordance with our formula (ie three courses with house wine, coffee and tip).

Special menus are by their nature susceptible to change – please call ahead to check that they are still available.

Weekday lunch

Ajimura *(£14)*
Arisugawa *(£14)*
Atlantic Bar & Grill *(£25)*
Aubergine *(£33)*
Aykoku-Kaku *(£19)*
Beach Blanket
  Babylon *(£17)*
Belgo Centraal *(£15)*
Busabong Tree *(£15)*
Bombay Brasserie *(£25)*
Byron's *(£15)*
Café des Arts *(£16)*
Café Royal Grill *(£36)*
Chiaroscuro *(£21)*
Cibo *(£26)*
Connaught *(£42)*
Dorchester,
  Oriental *(£33)*
English House *(£23)*
The Establishment *(£20)*
La Fontana *(£21)*
Frederick's *(£20)*
Galicia *(£12)*
Garbo's *(£16)*
Le Gavroche *(£38)*
Inaho *(£15)*
L'Incontro *(£33)*
Khyber Pass *(£12)*
The Lanesborough *(£31)*
Launceston Place *(£25)*
Lemonia *(£13)*
Leonardo's *(£17)*
Leith's *(£35)*
Lindsay House *(£24)*
Lobster Pot *(£22)*
Lou Pescadou *(£17)*
Maggie Jones's *(£21)*
Mandeer *(£10)*
Le Mercury *(£11)*
Mezzonine *(£16)*

Mon Plaisir *(£20)*
Monkeys *(£24)*
Montpeliano *(£24)*
Nayab *(£14)*
Odette's *(£19)*
Olivo *(£13)*
Orso *(£19)*
Pasha *(£11)*
Le P'tit Normand *(£16)*
Phoenicia *(£17)*
Pied à Terre *(£40)*
La Porte des Indes *(£22)*
La Poule au Pot *(£23)*
Red Fort *(£20)*
Restaurant MPW *(£52)*
The Ritz *(£37)*
Royal China *(£16)*
San Frediano *(£22)*
Santini *(£31)*
Singapore Garden *'(£15)*
The Sugar Club *(£22)*
Le Suquet *(£20)*
Thai on the River *(£17)*
Thierry's *(£19)*
Toff's *(£14)*
Turner's *(£24)*
Veeraswamy *(£24)*
Vegia Zena *(£17)*
Verbanella *(£19)*
Walton's *(£24)*
Wódka *(£19)*

Pre/post theatre

Ajimura *(£20)*
Alba *(£21)*
L'Altro *(£22)*
Archduke Wine Bar *(£19)*
Atelier *(£25)*
The Avenue *(£26)*
Blues *(£23)*
Boudin Blanc *(£17)*

Café des Arts *(£15)*
Café du Jardin *(£22)*
Café Med *(£20)*
Café Royal Grill *(£41)*
Caffe Graffiti *(£17)*
Chiswick *(£19)*
L'Estaminet *(£18)*
The Gaucho Grill *(£20)*
Hujo's *(£17)*
Lindsay House *(£32)*
Magno's Brasserie *(£23)*
Mezzo *(£24)*
Mezzonine *(£16)*
Mon Plaisir *(£17)*
Mr Wing *(£24)*
Nicole's *(£29)*
Orsino *(£23)*
The Pen *(£22)*
Quaglino's *(£24)*
Red Fort *(£26)*
Savoy Grill *(£45)*
Savoy River Room *(£46)*
Sheekey's *(£29)*
Sol e Luna *(£23)*

Sunday lunch

The Abingdon *(£23)*
Albero & Grana *(£31)*
Buchan's *(£19)*
Byron's *(£17)*
Chutney Mary *(£24)*
The Cross Keys *(£24)*
English Garden *(£29)*
Four Seasons *(£38)*
Garbo's *(£17)*
The Green Olive *(£22)*
Greenhouse *(£29)*
Jim Thompson's *(£16)*
Kensington Place *(£26)*
Mezzo *(£24)*
Noughts 'n' Crosses *(£22)*
Le P'tit Normand *(£19)*
Phoenicia *(£19)*
Savoy River Room *(£40)*
Simpsons-in-
  the-Strand *(£27)*
Sonny's *(£23)*
Le Soufflé *(£36)*
The Stepping Stone *(£23)*
The Tenth *(£27)*
Walton's *(£27)*
Ziani *(£24)*

SIZE ISN'T EVERYTHING

Why are these big new restaurants so bad?

The 1990s have seen the emergence of London as a recognised world centre of excellence on the gastronomic front.

The same period has also seen the rise of upmarket restaurants on a scale that had seldom been attempted previously, such as Mezzo, L'Odéon and the Oxo Tower.

It is easy to assume that the rise in the general level of quality is somehow linked with, or perhaps even driven by, the mega-restaurant phenomenon. In fact, the most striking result of our survey of 1,500 regular London restaurant-goers is just how poorly almost all of these vast diners are thought to perform.

Take the five 200+ seaters from our most notable newcomers selection, opposite – The Avenue, The Collection, The Criterion, L'Odéon and La Porte des Indes*. Given the prices they charge, only two of them were reckoned by the punters to provide acceptable cooking (and not a single one of them was thought to provide reliable service).

Or consider the list of most-mentioned restaurants (page 10), and compare it with the list of favourite restaurants (page 11). Four very large restaurants are among the top ten most-mentioned: Mezzo (1st), Quaglino's (2nd), L'Odéon (6th) and The Criterion (7th). None of them makes it into the top ten favourites list.

There is no mystery in this. It is hardly surprising if the food in a very large restaurant has a "factory" quality about it, or if the service is impersonal or disjointed.

However, people expect mass-produced products to come at mass-produced prices, and almost all of the mega-restaurants are pitching their prices at levels which induce a level of customer expectations which realistically just cannot be met.

This leads to the paradox that, while there is no doubt that the general culinary level in London has leapt ahead, the restaurants whose very names are taken as emblematic of the great advance are, in fact, those where good value cooking and service are relatively unlikely to be found.

In the short term, the message is clear. If you are happy to pay a premium for the privilege of dining with a couple of hundred other people, this month's new mega-venue may be for you. If, on the other hand, you are just looking for good value cooking and agreeable, efficient service, you are very likely to fare better elsewhere.

* The Oxo Tower opened too late for reporters to comment on it.

THE RESTAURANT SCENE

There is more money pouring into the London restaurant business now than at any time since the Second World War (and probably ever). Activity is frenzied at all levels. Chains multiply and proliferate. Theme-diners throng around Leicester Square. Banks, airline offices, tailors' premises and court-rooms are all converted to provide more catering capacity.

It is now taken for granted that many areas of London (especially the residential areas to the south and west) possess a range of quality restaurants which would have seemed amazing even five years ago. We therefore concentrate, for this brief review, on the West End.

Despite all the activity, there are disappointments (apart from the concerns voiced opposite). Much of the "action" in the West End is in the £35-£45 price range – a section of the market surely risking saturation – with relatively few 'covers' being added either side of this price-bracket. There must be demand both for more £45+ restaurants with **real** gastronomic ambitions, and for more central all-rounders in the £25-£35 range.

The ongoing staff crisis does not help. The trade press is awash with stories of the difficulty of recruiting sufficient staff at all skill levels (perhaps going some way to explain the predictable line-up of dishes on far too many menus). From outside the trade, it remains rather depressing, in comparison with the attention lavished on concept and design, how little money and management skill sometimes seems to be directed towards getting the basic product right

A year ago, restaurateurs and pundits alike were speculating on the capacity of the London dining out market to absorb the new Mezzo. In fact, there have been no notable closures over the past year, and it is still often impossible to get a booking at many of the more popular venues on the day. The problem today is not excess supply, but excess demand.

The 'top ten' notable newcomers

In each edition of the guide, we present what appear to us to be the ten most significant openings of the past twelve months. This year, our selection is as follows:

The Avenue	L'Odéon
Café Spice Namaste	L'Oranger
The Collection	Oxo Tower
The Criterion	La Porte des Indes
Livebait	Vong

Early signs suggest that next year's crop will be just as interesting.

OPENINGS

Afghan Kitchen *(N1)*
Al Sultan *(W1)*
Alastair Little,
  Lancaster Road *(W11)*
Anglesea Arms *(W6)*
The Apprentice *(SE1)*
Assaggi *(W2)*
Aurora *(W1)*
The Avenue *(SW1)*
Babe Ruth's *(E1)*
Balans West *(SW5)*
The Bank *(SW11)*
Bank *(WC2)*
Barcelona Tapas *(EC3)*
Bellinis *(SW13)*
Beyoglu *(SW11)*
Blakes *(NW1)*
Blenheim Bis *(W11)*
Blues *(W1)*
Boiled Egg &
  Soldiers *(SW11)*
Le Bon Choix *(SW10)*
Browns *(W1)*
Café on the
  Common *(SW4)*
Cappadoccia *(SW10)*
Cento 50 *(W11)*
Chelsea Ram *(SW10)*
Christoph's *(SW10)*
Ciabatta *(SW3)*
The Collection *(SW3)*
The Cook House *(SW15)*
The Crescent *(SW3)*
The Cross Keys *(SW3)*
Detroit *(WC2)*
Diverso *(W1)*
Drones *(SW1)*
East One *(EC1)*
81 *(SW1)*
Epicuria *(W1)*
Euten's *(WC2)*
Exxo *(W1)*
Fables *(SW6)*
Fashion Café *(W1)*
Football Football *(SW1)*
The Foundation *(SW1)*
The Fulham Tup *(SW10)*
Gastro *(SW4)*
Gladwins *(EC3)*
The Green Olive *(W9)*
Gresslin's *(NW3)*
The Havelock
  Tavern *(W14)*

Hollihead *(W1)*
I-Thai *(W2)*
The Lancers *(W1)*
Little Italy *(W1)*
Livebait *(SE1)*
Luna *(NW1)*
Maison Novelli *(EC1)*
Malabar Junction *(WC1)*
Mandalay *(W2)*
Maze *(W1)*
Mondo *(W1)*
L'Odéon *(W1)*
Oliveto *(SW1)*
L'Oranger *(SW1)*
Osteria Le Fate *(SW3)*
Oxo Tower *(SE1)*
Phoenix Bar &
  Grill *(SW15)*
Pizza Metro *(SW11)*
La Porte des Indes *(W1)*
Princess of Wales *(SW3)*
Randall & Aubin *(W1)*
Rupee Room *(EC2)*
Le Sacré-Coeur *(N1)*
Saint *(WC2)*
Sarastro *(WC2)*
755 *(SW6)*
Sol e Stella *(W1)*
Sotheby's Café *(W1)*
Springbok Café *(W4)*
Sri Thai *(EC4)*
The Stamford *(W6)*
The Tenth *(W8)*
Thai Bistro *(W4)*
Tusc *(SW5)*
Twenty two degrees
  south *(W1)*
Valhalla *(SW11)*
Vincent's *(SW15)*
Vingt-Quatre *(SW10)*
Vong *(SW1)*
Young Turks *(EC2)*

CLOSINGS

Al Gallo Doro
Arts Theatre Café
Avenue West Eleven
  (now a bar)
Baboon
Benkei
Bistro Vino
Bloom's E1
Café des Fleurs
Café Météor
Café Poppy
La Chiave
L'Epicure
Gopal's in the City
Grahame's Seafare
Jason's SW11
Johnny Rocket's
Jones
Lalbag
M Fish
Ma Cuisine
Meson Doña Ana
Overton's
Planet Poppadom
Pontevecchio
Red Pepper SW3
Sabor y Salsa
Sec's and Checks
The Studio
Uma
Up All Night
Upstairs at the
  Basil Street

DIRECTORY

Comments in "double quotation-marks" were made by reporters.

Establishments which we judge to be particularly notable have their NAME IN CAPITALS.

A Tavola NW8 £ 28 ④⑤❷
7 St John's Wood High St   586 4776   8–3A
Disappointing, given that it's "got lots of potential" – although this "fun", characterful, rustic Italian in St John's Wood has its followers, the promising cooking here tends to be bland and service is erratic in the extreme; it "could be cheaper", too.
/ 11 pm; no credit cards.

Abeno NW9 £ 19 ❸❷④
Yaohan Plaza, 399 Edgware Rd   0181-205 1131   1–1A
If you can't afford the air fare to Tokyo, take the Northern Line to Colindale, and Europe's only okonomi-yaki restaurant (situated on the first floor of a huge and rather amazing Nipponese shopping centre) – the pizza/omelette hybrid staple seems highly authentic, though it may not be to all tastes; more culinary/cultural adventures are to be found in the ground floor food hall (see Yaohan Plaza). / 11 pm.

The Abingdon W8 £ 30 ❸❷❸
54 Abingdon Rd   937 3339   5–2A
"Very enjoyable", "relaxed" and stylish Kensington local, of a type in surprisingly short supply thereabouts; the brasserie cooking is very sound – and some go further in their praise – but it is the "attention paid to diners" which scores most highly. / 11 pm.

L'Accento Italiano W2 £ 26 ❸④④
16 Garway Rd   243 2201   6–1B
Bayswater "favourite neighbourhood venue", which strikes some as being "like an Italian family meal" – "authentic", "good value" cooking, rather "sloppily served"; the set menus are especially worth considering. / 11.30 pm; no Amex; smart casual.

Adams Café W12 £ 20 ❷❷④
77 Askew Rd   0181-743 0572   7–1B
Shepherd's Bush "greasy spoon" which moonlights as a "cheap and cheerful" Tunisian café, where "great cous-cous" is the attraction; the setting is more atmospheric at the front than at the rear. / 11 pm; D only; no Amex.

Afghan Kitchen N1 £ 11 ❶④④
35 Islington Gn   359 8019   8–3D
Tiny and basic Islington café serving a small selection of very cheap, extremely tasty Afghan dishes in plentiful portions; it's far from being fast food, at least in our experience; licensed, but you can BYO. / Midnight; closed Mon & Sun; no credit cards.

Ajimura WC2 £ 34 ❸④④
51-53 Shelton St   240 9424   4–2C
Though it's "perhaps somewhat tired", this Covent Garden Japanese (Britain's longest established) continues to offer some "very fresh" and carefully prepared food, and prices are "reasonable". / 10.30 pm; closed Sat L & Sun; no Switch; no smoking area.

Al Basha W8 £32 ❸❸❸
222 Kensington High St   938 1794   5–1A
*Smart Holland Park-side Lebanese which, though a touch
"overpriced", consistently offers quality food and attentive
service. / Midnight.*

Al Bustan SW1 £39 ❷❷❸
27 Motcomb St   235 8277   2–4A
*"Very good" Belgravia Lebanese; with its "flexible" service and
agreeably unglitzy premises, in a pretty street, it deserves to
be rather better known. / 11 pm; smart casual.*

Al Hamra W1 £33 ❷⑤⑤
31-33 Shepherd Mkt   493 1954   3–4B
*This long-established Shepherd Market Lebanese always
provides good quality, if slightly pricey, food, and on
a summer's day few rendezvous are better than its pavement
tables; inside, though, the naff décor really could do with
a make-over; service perennially disappoints. / 11.30 pm;
no Switch.*

Al San Vincenzo W2 £39 ❶❷④
30 Connaught St   262 9623   6–1D
*If the Borgonzolo family's tiny Bayswater Italian could seat
a few more people, surely it would be better known, as it
serves "incredible food" with "some of the freshest tastes"
in town; the "cramped" conditions do inhibit the
atmosphere, though. / 10 pm; closed Sat L & Sun; no Amex & no Switch.*

Al Sultan W1 £27 ❷❸❸
51-52 Hertford St   408 1155   3–4B
*Top quality Lebanese newcomer in Shepherd Market, whose
understated premises are quite brightly lit but otherwise very
comfortable; prices, by Mayfair standards, are reasonable.
/ 11.30 pm.*

Al's EC1 £18 ❷❸❸
11-13 Exmouth Mkt   837 4821   8–4D
*"Spangly, funky City-fringe hang-out", which serves "super-
huge portions" of "good, cheap scoff" – it's especially popular
for brunch; expansion into the basement, to include a bar and
music venue, is scheduled. / 11 pm, Sat & Sun 8 pm.*

Alastair Little W1 £34 ❸④⑤
49 Frith St   734 5183   4–2A
*The food is "getting better" at Soho's seminal modern British
restaurant, where Juliet Peston has now taken over the stove;
even those who note "exceptional" cooking, however, can
find the overall experience "unpleasant", thanks to unduly
"sparse" surroundings and sometimes "dreadful" service.
/ 11.30 pm; closed Sat L & Sun.*

Alastair Little, Lancaster Road W11 £29 ❷❸❸
136a Lancaster Rd   243 2220   6–1A
*"A great improvement on the Frith Street original" – the
"simple cooking" at Mr Little's new venture (just west of
Ladbroke Grove tube) "rarely disappoints", and the setting is
positively luxurious compared to Soho; service is "courteous",
too, and overall it's "a bargain" – "will he keep it up?" / 11 pm;
closed Sun.*

Alba EC1 £29 ❸❷④
107 Whitecross St   588 1798   9–1B
*A "City place not filled with City types", this "friendly" modern
Italian – in the wasteland surrounding the Barbican – is an
oasis for culture-vultures and a destination for those who
appreciate its "lovely", "unusual" food, with Piedmontese
specialities; "blandness" of cuisine can be noted, however,
and some find the décor "clinical". / 11 pm; closed Sat & Sun.*

Albero & Grana SW3 £44 ④④❷
89 Sloane Ave   225 1048   5–2C
*Opinions divide sharply on this modern Chelsea Hispanic;
some find "seriously good food" – even if it "seems very
un-Spanish" – in a "stylish" and vibrant venue; others say
it's an "awful place" with "strange" cooking, "appalling"
service and a "completely pretentious" atmosphere.
/ 11 pm; smart casual.*

Albero & Grana
Tapas Bar SW3 £22 ❷❸❶
89 Sloane Ave   225 1048   5–2C
*"Sometimes it's too overcrowded", but this stylish Chelsea
bar gets a much clearer thumbs-up than the adjacent
restaurant; the tapas are "good", and it is "great fun" –
if you like a frenzied Eurocrush, that is. / Midnight; D only ex Sat,
when open all day.*

Alfred WC2 £30 ❷❸⑤
245 Shaftesbury Ave   240 2566   4–1C
*Hipster Fred Taylor's minimalist, modern British establishment
(in a "pretty dreadful location", on a busy intersection near
the British Museum) is praised for its "very tasty", "inventive"
cooking, but not for its non-atmosphere; an "interesting drinks
list" is a feature. / 11.30 pm; closed Sat L & Sun.*

Ali Baba NW1 £18 ❷❸④
32 Ivor Pl   723 5805   8–4A
*Entered through a take-away behind Marylebone Station,
this tiny Egyptian feels like a brightly-lit, Middle Eastern family
dining room; very good and inexpensive cooking, and you can
BYO too. / 11.30 pm; no credit cards.*

All Bar One £19 ❸❸❷

3-4 Hanover St, W1   485 2216   3–2C
36-38 Dean St, W1   287 4641   4–1D
48 Leicester Sq, WC2   839 0972   4–3C
587-591 Fulham Rd, SW6   385 6668   5–4A
197-199 Chiswick High Rd, W4   0181-742 3338   7–2A
1 Liverpool Rd, N1   278 5906   8–3D
60 St John's Wood High St, NW8   722 6144   8–3A
42 Mackenzie Walk, E14   512 3435   1–3D
44-46 Ludgate Hl, EC4   248 1356   9–2A

Amazing – a mega-corporate (Bass) concept that actually works!; "extremely well presented", "fresh and flavourful" bar food from a "tantalizing menu", efficiently served in uncluttered surroundings, keeps this new chain's twenty-something followers very happy indeed. / Mon-Thu 10 pm, Fri-Sun 9 pm; Hanover St, City and E14 branches close part of weekend; no booking.

All Saints W11 £31 ❸⑤❸

12 All Saints Rd   243 2808   6–1B

Groovy and "interesting" Portobello hang-out, where if the staff were more laid-back they'd risk unconsciousness; the "imaginative", modern British food still has its moments, but complaints of "so-so" cooking were more common this year. / 11.30 pm; Mon-Fri D only, closed Sun D; no Amex.

Alma SW18 £22 ④④❸

499 Old York Rd   0181-870 2537   10–2B

In spite of rather iffy grub, this well known, very atmospheric Wandsworth pub remains popular (but can be "spoilt by the rugby crowd"); the separate dining section is agreeable. / 10.30 pm.

Alounak W14 £12 ❶❸④

72 Russell Rd   371 2350   7–1D

"We are talking really CHEAP!", and in the ultimate recherché location – a Portakabin by the Olympia railway tracks (you go into the car park, sharp right); the attraction of "very tasty, fresh, simple" Iranian fare draws a surprisingly well-heeled crowd; BYO. / 11.30 pm; no credit cards.

L'Altro W11 £36 ❸④❸

210 Kensington Pk Rd   792 1066   6–1A

"Consistently great – but not cheap – grilled fish and pasta" are served at this small but "really pretty" Portobello Italian, decorated in operatic stage-set style; staff can seem "painfully inexperienced". / 11.30 pm.

Alwaha W1 £26 ④❸④

20 Shaftesbury Ave   437 0411   3–3D

Large Lebanese, just by Piccadilly Circus; even if it's not somewhere you might actively seek out, it offers a useful refuge from the Theatreland mêlée, and – given its tourist-trap location – OK value. / 1 am, summer 3 am; no Switch; no smoking area.

Andrew Edmunds W1 £ 22 ❸❷❶
46 Lexington St   437 5708   3–2D
*"Still an all-time favourite" for many, this "lovely, cosy,
intimate" Soho townhouse has a "romantic" atmosphere
that "can't be beaten" – especially as the place "always
offers good value"; the modern British grub may not be out to
win any awards, but it is "tasty" and "interesting", and the
intelligent wine list is reasonably priced. / 10.45 pm.*

Anglesea Arms W6 £ 23 ❸⑤④
35 Wingate Rd   0181-749 1291   7–1B
*"Vaguely Boho" Brackenbury Village pub newcomer, offering
simple and "intriguing" modern British dishes, and at very
keen prices; conditions are not comfortable, though, and the
"feeble" service has "ruined" more than one meal here –
the kitchen is "so, slow ... so, so, slow". / 10.30 pm;
no Amex; no booking.*

Anglo Asian Tandoori N16 £ 18 ❷❸❷
60-62 Stoke Newington Ch St   254 9298   1–1C
*"Dishes spiced to the hilt in romantic surroundings" –
an unlikely combination, perhaps, but it makes this low-lit
Stoke Newington Indian a superior local. / 11.45 pm, Fri & Sat
12.30 am; no Switch.*

Anna's Place N1 £ 26 ❷❷❸
90 Mildmay Pk   249 9379   1–1C
*"Good news for Islingtonians"; Anna "continues to serve
superb Swedish food" – "reliably good, occasionally
excellent" – at this "friendly" institution, located in an
atmospheric townhouse. / 10.45 pm; closed Mon & Sun; no credit cards.*

Antipasto e Pasta SW4 £ 30 ❸❸❸
31 Abbeville Rd   0181-675 6260   10–2D
*Stylish if cramped Clapham trattoria; its satisfying fare may
be in a rather old-fashioned mould, but attracts a steady
following, in spite of prices which are well up to
Chelsea levels. / 11.30 pm; no Switch.*

The Apprentice SE1 £ 20 ❷④④
31 Shad Thames   234 0254   9–4D
*Trainee chefs get the chance to experiment on human
guinea pigs at the dining room of the new Butler's Wharf
school; the only real drawback is the "stark", "corridor-like"
setting – the modern British food, if "slightly haphazard", is
"excellent value", and service is "so desperate it's hilarious".
/ 8.30 pm; closed Sat & Sun; no Amex.*

Archduke Wine Bar SE1 £ 24 ⑤④❸
Arch 153, Concert Hall Appr.   928 9370   2–3D
*"A good pre-South bank meeting place", perhaps, but this
wine bar set in the arches of Hungerford railway bridge is
"not trying hard enough", and the menu "could do with
updating"; "good wines", though. / 11 pm; closed Sat L & Sun.*

Arirang W1 £24 ❸❷④
31-32 Poland St   437 6633   3–1D
*London's oldest Korean lurks behind an anonymous façade,
just south of Oxford Street; it's a pleasant enough place,
offering a warm welcome and carefully prepared food.*
/ 10.45 pm; closed Sun D; no Switch.

Arisugawa W1 £35 ❸❷④
27a Percy St   636 8913   2–1C
*Comfortable if unexciting basement Japanese, just off
Tottenham Court Road, offering consistently good
quality cooking. / 10 pm, Sat 9.30 pm; closed Sat L & Sun.*

The Ark W8 £25 ④❸④
122 Palace Gdns Ter   229 4024   6–2B
*"Like an old friend"; devotees of this dated 'Alpine ski lodge',
off Notting Hill Gate, keep coming back for its "sensible"
cooking, warm welcome and low prices; to some, though,
it's just "unimaginative and boring". / 11 pm; closed Sat L & Sun;
no smoking area.*

L'Artiste Assoiffé W11 £39 ❸⑤❷
122 Kensington Pk Rd   727 4714   6–1B
*The arrival of chef Mark Broadbent (ex Avenue West Eleven,
which is now a bar only) – just as we go to press – has vastly
improved the previously awful cooking at this "romantic",
"rambling" '60s survivor, whose "very good atmosphere is
great for a 'special' evening"; the interesting modern British
food hardly comes at a bargain price, however, and to say
that, on our visit, it arrived at a snail's pace would be a slur
on gastropods everywhere. / 11.30 pm.*

L'Artiste Musclé W1 £21 ④④❷
1 Shepherd Mkt   493 6150   3–4B
*"A little French bistro transported to England" – this Shepherd
Market corner site does receive praise for its "good value",
but, as service is "chaotic" and the food really nothing special,
it is the "very Gallic feel" which is the prime attraction.
/ 11.15 pm; winter closed Sun L; no Switch.*

Ashtons EC3 £37 ④❸❸
13-15 Leadenhall Mkt   929 2022   9–2D
*That this Leadenhall Market seafood parlour is "still a
good bet in the area" speaks volumes about the quality of
the competition in the City lunching market; admittedly it is
a pleasant place, though, with attentive staff. / L only; closed Sat
& Sun; no Switch.*

Ask! Pizza £ 14 ❸❷❸

121 Park St, W1   495 7760   2–2A
48 Grafton Way, W1   388 8108   2–1B
345 Fulham Palace Rd, SW6   371 0392   10–1B
Gloucester Arcade, SW7   835 0840   5–2B
221 Chiswick High Rd, W4   0181-742 1323   7–2A
Bus' Design Ctr, Upper St, N1   495 7760   8–3D
216 Haverstock Hill, NW3   433 3896   8–2A
Expanding chain of pizzerias, of varying quality, but whose best performers are very good indeed; the Chiswick branch is particularly appealing – "bright and airy" in design, and with cooking well up to the standards of the leading chain competitors. / 11.30 pm.

Assaggi W2 £ 30 ❷❸④

39 Chepstow Pl   792 5501   6–1B
'Wait till you see it – eeezzz wonderful', is how the maître d' seems to introduce every dish at this much-hailed, Italian newcomer, above a pub on the Bayswater/Notting Hill divide; the interesting, artfully simple food lived up to its billing on our visit, but prices are high, and the interior (with its gaudy Rothko-lookalikes) is not especially comfortable. / 11 pm; closed Mon & Sun D.

Atelier W1 £ 32 ❷❸④

41 Beak St   287 2057   3–2D
Soho ad-land lunching haunt, offering carefully prepared modern British cooking, sometimes rather slowly; we agree with those who think it's a "good space", but others find it "precious" and note a lack of atmosphere, especially in the quieter evenings; the pre-theatre menu is a "bargain". / 10.45 pm; closed Sat L & Sun.

Atlantic Bar & Grill W1 £ 38 ④④❷

20 Glasshouse St   734 4888   3–3D
The "heady", "happening" atmosphere is now the only real attraction of this vast, once mould-breaking basement, just off Piccadilly Circus – the service was always "sloppy", but the once-good modern British cooking is now at best only "acceptable"; book for a late table if you want to make it past the velvet rope. / Midnight, bar food until 2.30 am; closed Sat L & Sun L.

Atrium SW1 £ 30 ⑤⑤④

4 Millbank   233 0032   2–4C
Antony Worrall Thompson's incursion into Westminster is roundly condemned – a "terrible venue" with "badly thought out", "bland" 'Brirish' – that's British/Irish – cooking and "breathtakingly poor service"; how does it survive? – "there's nothing else in the area". / 10 pm; closed Sat & Sun; no smoking area.

Au Bon Accueil SW3 £25 ④❶❷

19 Elystan St   589 3718   5–2C
*The "old fashioned Italian/French" fare served, with charm,
in this Chelsea backwater may be "really out of date", but
"it must be healthy", as "the regular customers never seem
to die". / 11.30 pm; closed Sat L & Sun.*

Au Jardin des Gourmets W1 £38

5 Greek St   437 1816   4–2A
*At the time of going to press, change is afoot at this Soho
stalwart; the downstairs brasserie is already gone, to be
replaced by a wine bar; upstairs, the very traditional French
restaurant continues to attract few reports; such as it is,
the word is positive however, so perhaps some new sense
of direction has at last been found. / 11.15 pm; closed Sat L & Sun;
smart casual; no smoking area.*

AUBERGINE SW10 £56 ❶❷❷

11 Park Wk   352 3449   5–3B
*"A truly great eating experience"; in only three years,
Gordon Ramsay has overtaken all the established competition,
and made this "impeccable" Chelsea spot, offering "excellent,
contemporary interpretations of French classics", London's
gastronomic champion; service, too, is "superb, and with
a smile"; a reporter with a gift for understatement notes
"some difficulty in booking". / 11 pm; closed Sat L & Sun.*

Aurora W1 £17 ❷❸❸

49 Lexington St   494 0514   3–2D
*Light and refreshing café where stylish Soho chicks pick at
rabbit food (though more solid fare is available) so as to leave
space for the sinful puds; till now it has been lunchtime only,
but evening opening is on the cards as we go to press; at the
rear, there is an unusually nice courtyard. / 4 pm, snacks till 7 pm;
closed Sun; no Switch.*

L'Aventure NW8 £37 ❷❷❶

3 Blenheim Ter   624 6232   8–3A
*No one has a bad word to say about this St John's Wood
spot, the epitome of an "intimate" (if "quite formal") and
"authentic" restaurant du quartier; there are few better
choices for romance, especially on the terrace in summer.
/ 11 pm; closed Sat L and, in Winter, Sun; no Switch.*

The Avenue SW1 £39 ④④❸

7-9 St James's St   321 2111   3–4D
*"Trying a bit too hard to be Manhattan", perhaps, but this
large and "showy", new St James's space is praised by many
for its "buzzing atmosphere"; on the flipside, though, it isn't
at all cheap, and both the modern British cooking and the
service are consistently inconsistent; the recent arrival of
ace-greeter Marian Scrutton may be a positive sign. / 11.45 pm.*

Aykoku-Kaku EC4   £ 43   ❸④④
9 Walbrook   248 2548   9–3C
*Dated Japanese whose basement setting lacks atmosphere;
that said, the cooking is good, if predictably pricey, and the
set lunch (served in a separate canteen area) makes a fair
spot for an informal City rendezvous. / 10 pm; closed Sat & Sun;
no booking for inexpensive lunches.*

B Square SW11   £ 28   ❸❸❸
8 Battersea Sq   924 2288   5–4C
*"They continue to try hard" at this "stylish" yearling, in the
heart of Battersea Village; "somehow the place fails to inspire
enthusiasm", however, which is a shame as the modern
British food, in particular, gets favourable reviews. / 11 pm.*

Babe Ruth's E1   £ 26   ④❸❷
172-176 The Highway   481 8181   1–2D
*"Just what Wapping needs" – this large, purpose-built theme-
restaurant/sports bar (on the aptly named 'Highway') is one
of the first decent restaurants in Docklands, and though
"excellent for children", it's not just a stop for families; the
rather predictable American fare "won't leave you hungry",
but is somewhat "expensive". / 11.30 pm; no smoking area;
no booking.*

Bahn Thai W1   £ 26   ❸⑤⑤
21a Frith St   437 8504   4–2A
*"What a dump – saved only by the tasty food", this Soho
Thai gives an impression of being hell-bent on offering ever-
declining standards; it's a shame, as the "impressive range of
dishes" is still widely praised. / 11.15 pm; smart casual.*

Balans W1   £ 21   ④❸❸
60 Old Compton St   437 5212   4–3A
*"Very jolly, if you like Old Compton Street life" – probably
"too gay", if you don't – this active-all-hours brasserie has
become a linchpin of the cruisiest part of town. / Mon-Thu 4 am,
Fri & Sat 6 am, Sun 1 am; no Amex.*

Balans West SW5   £ 21   ❸❷❷
239 Old Brompton Rd   244 8838   5–3A
*"A welcome addition to Earl's Court", this corner brasserie –
refurbished in 'My Beautiful Launderette' style – is most
popular either for brunch or as a late place; beware though –
"the waiters do tend to flirt with your boyfriend". / 1 am;
no Amex.*

Bangkok SW7   £ 24   ❷❸④
9 Bute St   584 8529   5–2B
*"As a customer of 24 years' standing, I always enjoy
London's original Thai restaurant" is the sort of comment
which epitomises the loyalty inspired by this South Kensington
stalwart; the food is emphatically not, as some claim, "still
the best", but it is very good; the canteen-style setting is
certainly "unpretentious". / 11 pm; closed Sun; no Amex; smart casual.*

Bangles SW11   **£13**   ❷❸④
124 Northcote Rd   924 3566   10–2C
"Very cheap, vegetarian Indian tapas, all freshly made and delicious", make this "unprepossessing Clapham bistro bar" a "neat" choice for an economical dinner. / 10.30 pm; Mon-Fri, closed L.

The Bank SW11   **£27**   ❸❸❸
35-37 Northcote Rd   223 1154   10–2C
"Trying really hard", this "fairly basic bank-conversion" near Clapham Junction offers "imaginative, modern Mediterranean fare" from a "varied, different" and "well priced" menu.
/ 11 pm, Fri & Sat 11.30 pm.

Bank WC2   **£35**
1 Kingsway   379 9797   2–2D
Christian Delteil – whose former Battersea restaurant, L'Arlequin, was blessed by the men from the tyre company – returns to the metropolis as head chef of this ambitious 200-seater, on the fringe of Covent Garden; it is scheduled to open around our publication date. / Midnight.

Banners N8   **£23**   ④④❷
21 Park Rd   0181-348 2930   1–1C
A particular hit for brunch, this laid back Crouch End hangout has a singularly mellow atmosphere; the eclectic cooking is haphazard. / 11.30 pm; no Amex & no Switch.

Bar Central   **£28**   ④❸❸
316 King's Rd, SW3   352 0025   5–3C
3-5 Islington High St, N1   833 9595   8–3D
131 Waterloo Rd, SE1   928 5086   9–4A
11 Bridge St, TW9   0181-332 2524   1–4A
The modern British fare may be no particular attraction, but these fashionable bar/diners offer quite a 'scene', and the SW3 branch is hailed as "the most happening place on the King's Road"; the large new branch at Richmond overlooks the river. / SE1 10.45 pm, SW3 11.15 pm.

Bar Etrusca EC4   **£22**   ❸④❸
41 Bow Ln   329 6364   9–2C
Basic but fun City basement pizzeria, which thrives in spite of "staff who should be taught English, and how to smile before being let loose on the public". / 10 pm; closed Sat & Sun.

Bar Gansa NW1   **£18**   ❷❸❷
2 Inverness St   267 8909   8–3B
Energetic, younger-scene Camden Town tapas bar which delivers good, affordable food in a cheerful, quite stylish setting. / 11.30 pm; no Amex & no Switch.

Bar Italia W1 £ 5 ④④❶
22 Frith St   437 4520   4–2A
*Famed, all-night Italian café in Soho, beloved of Italians
watching football and clubbers watching MTV; the coffee is
the "best in London", but the snacks are not (though dishes
from Little Italy, next door, are now also available). / 5 am, Fri &
Sat 24 hours; no credit cards; no booking.*

Bar Madrid W1 £ 23 ④❸❸
4 Winsley St   436 4649   3–1D
*The tapas are utterly beside the point at this large bar-
nightclub, north of Oxford Street (though they could be
much worse); for eager younger twentysomethings, though,
this remains one of the best pick-up joints in town. / 2.30 am;
D only; closed Sun; smart casual.*

Barcelona Tapas EC3 £ 17 ❷❸❸
1 Beaufort Hs, St Botolph St   377 5222   9–2D
*New sibling of the Petticoat Lane tapas bar (see next);
smarter, if a touch less characterful, than the original it
may be, but it too offers some of the City's best light meals;
the entrance is on Middlesex Street. / 10 pm; closed Sat & Sun D.*

Barcelona Tapas Bar E1 £ 17 ❷❸④
1a Bell Ln   247 7014   9–2D
*"Tasty traditional tapas, served by Spaniards" maintain the
popularity of the more recherché original Barcelona, in
a basement off an East End street market. / 10.30 pm;
closed Sat & Sun D; no booking.*

Basil St Hotel SW3 £ 33 ❸❸❷
8 Basil St   581 3311   5–1D
*A "time-warped" "cocoon", this "delightful and relaxing"
hotel, a short step from Harrods, offers "a real escape in
London"; breakfast and the "excellent Sunday lunch" are
the highlights – at other times it is a touch expensive;
the wonderful 'Upstairs', which used to do the best value
nosh in SW3, is sadly no more. / 10 pm; jacket & tie.*

Battersea Barge Bistro SW8 £ 17 ④❷❷
Nine Elms Ln   498 0004   10–1D
*To get away from it all, head for this "very cosy bistro"
occupying a Thames-side barge (moored down a lane
opposite New Covent Garden market); "the formula works
well" – especially as a romantic or party venue – even if the
food is no particular attraction. / 11 pm; closed Sun D; no credit cards.*

Battersea Rickshaw SW11 £ 23 ❸❸❸
1-16 Battersea Sq   924 2450   5–4C
*"Reliable, comfortable and friendly, but never outstanding"
Battersea Indian, which "may be too bright and clean for
some curry fans". / 11.30 pm.*

Beach Blanket Babylon W11 £ 32 ⑤⑤❷
45 Ledbury Rd   229 2907   6–1B
*Foodwise, "brunch is the only time to go" to this
"pseudo-trendy" Notting Hill hang-out, whose "overblown",
"weird and wonderful" setting is its key attraction, and whose
bar is still "great" (even if now largely "overrun by out-of-
towners"); the Mediterranean food "has not changed –
it was always awful". / 10.45 pm.*

Beauchamp's EC3 £ 47 ④❸④
23-25 Leadenhall Mkt   621 1331   9–2D
*Some City chaps commend Captain Beauchamp Blackett's
fish-parlour – appropriately located above a Leadenhall
Market seafood shop; those who find "the best of a bad
bunch" have got it about right. / L only; closed Sat & Sun.*

Bedlington Café W4 £ 19 ❶④④
24 Fauconberg Rd   0181-994 1965   7–2A
*"Fabulous Thai food" at prices which are "SO cheap" make
this Chiswick "greasy spoon" – it's a workers' caff by day –
"a real bargain", even taking into account the off-hand service
and cramped conditions (and that's after the refurbishment);
it's so well known that it's "difficult to get into"; BYO. / 10 pm;
no credit cards; no smoking area.*

Belgo Centraal WC2 £ 28 ④④❷
50 Earlham St   813 2233   4–2C
*"Fun" and "different", say fans of this large Covent Garden
moules and frites emporium; the striking restaurant, though,
"has much better atmosphere than the beer hall" (in which
"you'd better like the other people, as you sit very close");
given the prices, many find the food "mediocre" and service
poor, so good advice is to "get trashed on the scrummy
Trappist beers, so you're past caring". / 11.30 pm.*

Belgo Noord NW1 £ 29 ❸④❷
72 Chalk Farm Rd   267 0718   8–2B
*The original Belgo continues to outperform its central sibling,
and its "wonderful" setting still wins praise as a venue for
a fun night out; as at Centraal, though, the package of
mussels, Belgian beers and waiters clad as monks does not
seem quite as radical as once it did, and the wise advise that
for value you should "stick to the set menus". / 11.30 pm.*

Bellinis SW13 £ 14 ❸❸❷
2-3 Rocks Ln   0181-255 9922   10–1A
*"One up on PizzaExpress", claims a supporter of this
"friendly" Barnes spot, whose décor does indeed seem to
bear definite similarities to a well known pizza chain's;
foodwise the place is not bad, but for our money no rival to
the original, the best, the most wonderful of groups. / 11.30 pm.*

Belvedere W8 £34 ④❸❶

Holland Hs, off Abbotsbury Rd 602 1238 7–1D
*A "glorious Holland Park setting", a "beautiful building" and
an "interesting interior" make a potent combination, well
suited to romance or some special occasion; of course, they
then spoil it all with British cooking which can "miss by
a long way". / 11 pm; closed Sun D.*

Ben's Thai W9 £19 ❷❸❸

93 Warrington Cr 266 3134 8–4A
*"Good food – very cheap" still makes for "great value" at
the surprisingly grand, lofty dining room on the first floor of
Maida Vale's monumental Warrington Hotel (which is,
of course, a pub); this year, however, enthusiasm has
somewhat dimmed all round. / 10 pm; D only; no Switch;
no smoking area.*

Bengal Clipper SE1 £32 ❶❷❸

Shad Thames 357 9001 9–4D
*"Very tasty and unusual dishes", served by "immaculate"
and usually very "attentive" staff make this grand South Bank
Indian (behind Conran's restaurant row) quite possibly the
best in town. / 11.30 pm.*

Benihana £44 ④④❸

37-43 Sackville St, W1 494 2525 3–3D
77 King's Rd, SW3 376 7799 5–3D
100 Avenue Rd, NW3 586 9508 8–2A
*"Juggling with knives" is the chefs' party-piece at these
smart, "very Americanised" orientals; "good fun" but – for
fare which "has nothing to do with Japanese food" – they can
seem "twice as expensive as they ought to be". / W1 11 pm Thu-
Sat midnight, SW3 10.45 pm, NW3 midnight; NW3 closed Mon L.*

Bentley's W1 £35 ❸❸❸

11-15 Swallow St 734 4756 3–3D
*"No big surprises, but consistent all round", this "very civil,
old-fashioned" fish and seafood restaurant, a stone's throw
from Piccadilly Circus, offers particularly good value if you
stick to the set menus (always available). / 11.30 pm; closed Sun;
smart casual.*

Beotys WC2 £30 ④❶❷

79 St Martin's Ln 836 8768 4–3B
*"Not much changed since last visit 20 years ago", is one
reporter's summary of this dated Theatreland bastion –
"a cross between a gentlemen's club and a grand hotel";
the "old style service" is "charm itself", but the food – a mix
of solid dishes of French and Greek inspiration – provokes
little enthusiasm. / 11.30 pm; closed Sun; no Switch; smart casual.*

Bersagliera SW3 £24 ③②④

372 King's Rd 352 5993 5–3B

It is utterly undistinguished from the outside, but, year-in year-out, this "fun", family-run World's End trattoria provides "fresh and imaginatively cooked" dishes and "excellent pasta"; it can be noisy and smoky though. / Midnight; closed Sun; no Amex.

Bertorelli's £31 ④④④

19-23 Charlotte St, W1 636 4174 2–1C

44a Floral St, WC2 836 3969 4–2D

This Covent Garden Italian has a following which notes its convenience, and says it "delivers good, light food quickly"; the general impression, though, is now of a "characterless" Theatreland joint serving "disappointing" dishes in an "off-hand" way – perhaps it's the distraction of preparing for the Autumn '96 opening of a new Fitzrovia offshoot. / 11.30 pm; WC2 closed Sun.

Beyoglu SW11 £14 ①③④

50 Battersea Pk Rd 627 2052 10–1C

Excellent, new, cheap and cheerful Battersea Turk (on the site of the now defunct Jason's); for simple Middle Eastern nosh, few places offer better value. / 11 pm; closed Sun; no credit cards.

BIBENDUM SW3 £55 ②③②

81 Fulham Rd 581 5817 5–2C

"Bright, modern and alive", Conran's Brompton Cross flagship remains the "top overall experience" for many reporters; the whole is, in truth, rather greater than the sum of the parts, for no longer is any aspect outstanding – the direct modern French cooking can be "good, but not great", the atmosphere, especially in the evening, may fail to excite, and service is far from unimpeachable. / 10.30 pm.

Bibendum Oyster Bar SW3 £29 ①②②

81 Fulham Rd 589 1480 5–2C

"Excellent", "fresh" seafood and "helpful" service combine to make this airy, tiled bar, just off the foyer of the Michelin Building, possibly the best, reasonably affordable rendezvous in the environs of trendy Brompton Cross. / 10.30 pm; no booking.

Bice W1 £37 ④④⑤

13 Albemarle St 409 1011 3–3C

"Unexceptional food, average service, and indifferent ambience" make a thoroughly underwhelming combination at this "overpriced" Mayfair Italian – part of the allegedly glamorous Milan, NY, etc, etc chain. / 10.45 pm; closed Sat L & Sun; smart casual.

Big Easy SW3 £28 ④❷❷
334 King's Rd   352 4071   5–3C
Rowdy Chelsea 'crab-shack', with a "fun atmosphere"
(that's especially "great with the kids") and which keeps
busy till late; prices may be "reasonable", but reports of the
burgers and seafood menu are too often lacklustre. / Midnight,
Fri & Sat 12.30 am; no Switch; no smoking area; Fri pm & Sat pm, no booking.

The Big Night Out NW1 £30 ❸④❸
148 Regent's Pk Rd   586 5768   8–3B
This clean-lined Primrose Hill three-year-old has never quite
lived up to its initial promise; true, people often like the food,
but many feel it is "very pricey for what you get", and it is
served – too variably – in "squashed" conditions. / 11 pm; closed
Mon L; no Amex; no smoking area.

Billboard Café NW6 £21 ❸❸④
280 West End Ln   431 4188   1–1B
The move from Kilburn to more salubrious West Hampstead
has unsettled reports on this popular Italianate restaurant,
with some noting "a disappointing transfer" while others
"love the new premises". / 11 pm, Fri & Sat 11.30 pm;
Mon-Fri closed L.

Bistrot 190 SW7 £29 ❸④❸
189-190 Queen's Gt   581 5666   5–1B
The "relaxed atmosphere" and "some very good dishes"
keep this once pre-eminent Mediterranean brasserie, situated
in a characterful South Kensington townhouse, popular with
a good number of reporters; service, as ever, is quite "poor".
/ 12.30 am; no booking.

Blah! Blah! Blah! W12 £20 ❷❸❸
78 Goldhawk Rd   0181-746 1337   7–1C
"Inventive" Shepherd's Bush veggie drawing a surprisingly
trendy crowd to that unlovely quarter; it offers good value,
and modest but acceptable comfort; BYO. / 11 pm; closed Sun;
no credit cards.

Blakes NW1 £22 ❷④❷
31 Jamestown Rd   482 2959   8–3B
New, trendily converted Camden Town boozer – in
a challenging location – whose first-floor dining room serves
"very acceptable", inventive modern British dishes; the setting,
though atmospheric, verges on basic and, though our service
was fine, a regular says it can be "appalling". / 11 pm, Fri & Sat
midnight.

Blakes Hotel SW7 £81 ❸④❶
33 Roland Gdns   370 6701   5–2B
"Pricey, but so intimate and suggestive", murmur supporters
of this "seductive" South Kensington hotel's dated but "sexy"
basement dining room, which remains a strong "romantic"
favourite; the eclectic cooking "is actually quite good", but
comes at "absurd prices". / Midnight.

Bleeding Heart EC1 £27 ❷❷❷

Bleeding Heart Yd, Greville St   242 8238   9–2A
*This "bleeding good" basement, off a small yard near
Holborn, is "worth seeking out" – and not just because
it's the only place in the area; the "wine bar is probably
a better package" than the slightly pricier restaurant, but
both combine "efficient service", "cramped" charm and
"good, solid", "traditional French" fare; it seems a winter
venue to some, though in summer you can sit out in the yard.
/ 10.30 pm; closed Sat & Sun.*

The Blenheim NW8 £27 ④❸④

21 Loudon Rd   625 1222   8–3A
*To its supporters, this fancily converted St John's Wood pub
is "enjoyable", and serves "consistent" modern British
cooking; our vote, however, is with the dissidents who decry
a "pretentious, overblown" place, serving "overpriced" and
too often "mediocre" fare. / 11 pm; closed Mon L; no smoking area.*

Blenheim Bis W11 £22 ❸④④

37 Kensington Pk Rd   243 0666   6–1A
*Basically converted modern British bistro newcomer (formerly
Meson Doña Ana) in Notting Hill's trendy restaurant strip;
one senses some spark in the kitchen, but by no means
everything is good; service is friendly, but hopelessly undrilled.
/ 11 pm; no credit cards.*

BLUE ELEPHANT SW6 £40 ❷❸❶

4-6 Fulham Broadway   385 6595   5–4A
*"Brilliant atmosphere" and "good food" ("getting better
again") continue to make a huge success of London's best
known and most spectacular ethnic; the Thai fare "may be
pricey", but "it's an experience" to sit in the "beautiful
setting" (and "very romantic by the pond", apparently); one
self-confessed snob rails against the "suburban" ambience
and the "celebratory smiles all around", but such sentiments
are those of a small minority. / 12.30 am, Sun 10.30 pm; closed Sat L;
no Switch; smart casual.*

Blue Jade SW1 £23 ❷❸④

44 Hugh St   828 0321   2–4B
*Pimlico back street Thai, which serves "delicate" cooking in
a comfortable if slightly undercharged setting; "nothing
extraordinary, but quite pleasant". / 11 pm; closed Sat L & Sun.*

Blue Print Café SE1 £35 ❸❸❷

Design Mus, Butler's Whf   378 7031   9–4D
*"Magnificent all around", say fans of the Design Museum's
first-floor restaurant, where the Tower Bridge view is
"spectacular", and whose balcony "is hard to beat" on
a summer day; complaints about "disappointing" service are
fewer this year, and verdicts on the light, modern British
cooking vary from "delicious" to "average". / 11 pm; closed Sun D.*

Blues W1 £29 ❸❷❷
42 Dean St   494 1966   4–2A
*Our initial visit to this "fresh", "spacious" Soho newcomer
found a very good buzz and "attentive staff with a sense of
humour"; we thought the modern British cooking "mediocre",
but there are quite a number of supporters who proclaim an
"excellent new restaurant". / 11.30 pm, Thu-Sat 12.45 am; closed Sun.*

Boiled Egg & Soldiers SW11 £16 ❸❹❸
63 Northcote Rd   223 4894   10–2C
*New "upmarket greasy spoon", which is "reminiscent of the
café in 'Neighbours'" (odd, considering its gentrified environs,
near Battersea Rise); it's "always popular", despite service
which "could be better", and prices that are a fraction
too high. / 6 pm; no booking.*

Boisdale SW1 £33 ❸❸❷
15 Eccleston St   730 6922   2–4B
*"A little gem", this restaurant-cum-wine bar, in the thin
area near Victoria Station, is a cosy, characterful place which
retains a band of loyal regulars; the international fare is
"inexpensive", and there is quite a serious wine list.
/ 10.30 pm; closed Sat L & Sun.*

Bombay Bicycle Club SW12 £28 ❷❸❸
95 Nightingale Ln   0181-673 6217   10–2C
*A continuing south London success story, this Wandsworth
"nouvelle" Indian almost invariably pleases with its light,
carefully prepared food and its "airy feel"; its "exceptional"
new take-away service, at 28 Queenstown Road SW8,
is already doing a roaring trade. / 11.30 pm; closed Sun.*

Bombay Brasserie SW7 £39 ❸❸❷
Courtfield Clo, Glouc. Rd   370 4040   5–2B
*This South Kensington Indian – for long London's leading
large-scale subcontinental – has "gone off" somewhat; it's still
an impressive place (with the conservatory still a venue
favoured by many), but feelings that it's "rather expensive",
as well as "dull" and "presumptuous", are becoming
more prevalent. / Midnight; no Amex & no Switch; smart casual.*

Bombay Palace W2 £30 ❸❷❸
50 Connaught St   723 8855   6–1D
*"Fabulous Indian food", if at a hefty price, wins renewed
support for this "consistent", rather grand Bayswater spot,
whose atmosphere is spoilt for some by the "overbright"
lighting. / 11.15 pm; no smoking area.*

Le Bon Choix SW10 £24 ❸❸⑤
196 Fulham Rd   352 7757   5–3B
*We had good Gallic nosh at this undercharged (because
it's too often "empty") Chelsea newcomer, but the limited
commentary from reporters is very mixed indeed. / 11.30 pm;
closed Sun D; no credit cards.*

Bonjour Vietnam SW6 £24 ④④❸
593-599 Fulham Rd   385 7603   5–4A
Certainly it's no gourmet experience, but most still find this quite stylish Fulham Chinese is basically "good value", on account of the all-you-can-eat policy and the wide choice it offers; it's "the sort of place you go when nobody really cares or remembers". / 11.30 pm.

La Bouchée SW7 £27 ❸④❶
56 Old Brompton Rd   589 1929   5–2B
"Crowded", "very French" South Kensington bistro whose "good value for money" – especially the pre-8pm menu – ensures that it is "always busy"; the food is "simple and homely" and can be "delicious", but, like the service, it's "erratic". / 11 pm; no Amex & no Switch.

Le Bouchon Bordelais SW11 £25 ❸④②
9 Battersea Rs   738 0307   10–2C
The "excellent atmosphere", say fans, is the particular attraction of this "fun" and "noisy" Battersea bistro; the seafood-and-more menu does not always satisfy, however, and service can be erratic. / 11 pm.

Le Bouchon Lyonnais SW8 £25 ④④❸
38 Queenstown Rd   622 2618   10–1C
Like the other Bouchon, this Battersea spot is a local favourite; the simple Gallic menu "rests on its laurels". / 11 pm; 8+ to book.

Boudin Blanc W1 £26 ❷④❸
5 Trebeck St   499 3292   3–4B
"Good value" (particularly from the lunch and pre-8pm menu) ensures a strong following for this Shepherd Market bistro; it's not perfect – the food is sometimes "ordinary", the "cosy" setting is "very crowded", and service "can be tardy" – but, even for detractors, it "oozes enough Gallic charm to keep it on the standby list". / 11 pm.

La Bouffe SW11 £28 ❸❸❸
13 Battersea Rs   228 3384   10–2C
"Quality is on the up" at this "friendly", tightly packed Clapham bistro whose "rustic" cuisine is generally now thought to offer "good value". / 11 pm.

Boulevard WC2 £25 ❸②②
40 Wellington St   240 2992   4–3D
Large, unpretentious, "friendly", Covent Garden brasserie, whose "basic" fare is decent value – for a pre/post theatre bite you could do very much worse. / Midnight.

The Bow Wine Vaults EC4   £24   4③③

10 Bow Church Yd   248 1121   9–2C
*Even though it's inexpensive, the school-dinners-quality
cooking of the ground floor bistro left us with little desire to
explore the basement restaurant at this refurbished City
establishment; the outside tables, nestling under the bulk of
St Mary-le-Bow, are undoubtedly charming on a sunny day.
/ L only; closed Sun.*

Boyd's W8   £34   ❷①③

135 Kensington Ch St   727 5452   5–1A
*"Reliable" and "delicious" modern British fare, and the
"friendly" service, win a reasonable following for Boyd
Gilmour's Kensington restaurant; if there is a fault it is that
the setting is rather low key for some tastes. / 11 pm; closed Sun;
no Switch.*

The Brackenbury W6   £23   ❷③③

129-131 Brackenbury Rd   0181-748 0107   7–1C
*A regular reports "surprises of late" at this famous
Shepherd's Bush wine bar/restaurant, whose ratings this
year were depressed by concerns that it's "not living up to Its
name"; a visit just before going to press, however, confirmed
the quality of the "first class" and "excellent value" modern
British cooking, giving some cause to hope that the patch of
turbulence is now at an end. / 10.45 pm; closed Mon L, Sat L & Sun D.*

Brady's   £16   ❷④④

696 Fulham Rd, SW6   736 3938   10–1B
513 Old York Rd, SW18   0181-877 9599   10–2B
*Wandsworth and Fulham micro-chain "serving deliciously
fresh fish, chunky chips and morish desserts which keep the
multitude of punters happy" – indeed, some fear that the
places are "getting too popular". / 10.45 pm; Apr-Sep
closed Sun D; no credit cards; no booking.*

Brahms SW1   £14   ④④③

147 Lupus St   834 9075   5–3D
*"For the price", this basic French-inspired Pimlico spot makes
a thoroughly "good cheapie restaurant"; no one, though,
would pretend it's art. / 11.45 pm; no credit cards.*

La Brasserie SW3   £29   ④④❷

272 Brompton Rd   584 1668   5–2C
*The "archetypal brasserie", this long-established, atmospheric
standby is at its best for a weekend breakfast or brunch;
everyone agrees that it's "good fun", but, unsurprisingly
given its Brompton Cross location, it's on the "expensive" side.
/ Midnight.*

Brasserie du Marché W10 £29 ❷❷❷
349 Portobello Rd   0181-968 5828   6–1A
New owners have put a traditional Gallic slant on this atmospheric North Kensington brasserie; standards remain high, with attractions including "good rural cuisine" (with "lots for veggies") and "charming young French waiters". / 11.30 pm; closed Mon; no Amex.

La Brasserie Highgate N6 £31 ❷❸④
1 Hampstead Ln   0181-348 7440   8–1B
New management has made strides with this spacious spot; the Italian cooking is of a surprisingly consistent high quality, but, for us, the glam-going-on-naff setting takes the edge off the experience. / 10.15 pm; no smoking area.

Brasserie Rocque EC2 £34 ④④❸
37 Broadgate Circle   638 7919   9–2D
With a tranquil location, by the Broadgate complex's ice rink, this stylish brasserie is "always packed at lunch" and, thanks to its outside tables, "excellent in summer"; some praise "honest endeavour" in the kitchen, but the general view is that this is a (predictably) "expensive City lunch venue". / brasserie 8 pm; closed Sat & Sun; book only in restaurant.

Brasserie St Quentin SW3 £34 ❷❷❷
243 Brompton Rd   589 8005   5–2C
"Top quality food in a genuinely Parisian atmosphere" maintains the popularity of this grand and glittering Knightsbridge brasserie; thanks to its "reliable" standards, "it's often overcrowded". / 11.30 pm.

Brick Lane Beigel Bake E1 £3 ❷❷⑤
159 Brick Ln   729 0616   1–2D
"Excellent at 3am", this famous 24-hour East End institution is known for the best beigels in town, and they could not really be much cheaper. / 24 hr; no Switch.

Brinkley's SW10 £27 ④❸❸
47 Hollywood Rd   351 1683   5–3B
John Brinkley's much reformatted Chelsea institution has its supporters, but the standards of the modern British fare are still far from the level which once made the place celebrated; that said, it is "excellent for summer", when the garden dining-room comes into its own. / 11 pm; D only; closed Sun.

Brown's Hotel W1 £18 ❸❸❷
Dover St   493 6020   3–3C
This "very English", divinely creaky Mayfair hotel is reckoned by numerous connoisseurs as the "best for afternoon tea". / Tea daily 3 pm-5 pm; no booking.

Browns £24 ⑤⑤❸
47 Maddox St, W1   491 4565   3–2C
82-84 St Martin's Ln, WC2   497 5050   4–4B
*This famous provincial chain finally made its first major
metropolitan incursion in 1996, with a Mayfair opening that
has been a complete let-down – "flavourless grub", and an
atmosphere "not as good as the other branches"; let's hope
for better from the newly converted court-room premises
in Theatreland.* / 11.30 pm.

Bruno Soho W1 £27
63 Frith St   734 4545   4–2A
*Bistrot Bruno, as was, is being enlarged and re-launched in
the autumn of 1996 with an emphasis on the cuisines of the
southern and eastern fringes of the Med – Morocco, Egypt,
Lebanon, Turkey, Greece, and so on.* / 11.30 pm; closed Sat L & Sun.

Bu San N7 £19 ❷❸④
43 Holloway Rd   607 8264   8–2D
*"Very superior Korean cooking", at modest cost, is the draw
to this cheap and cheerful spot, just around the corner from
Highbury & Islington tube; the décor, though, could use
a revamp.* / 11 pm; no Amex.

Bubb's EC1 £38 ❷❸❸
329 Cent Mkts, Farringdon Rd   236 2435   9–2A
*Old-fashioned, "very French" establishment, on a corner of
Smithfield Market; its the sort of place which is "good, for
business" – but not if you have to take any very important
decisions later that afternoon.* / L only; closed Sat & Sun.

Bucci SW3 £27 ❷❸❷
386 King's Rd   351 9997   5–3B
*"Good, wholesome Italian", with "pleasant" modern
farmhouse décor, just by the kink in the King's Road; "in the
early evening", it makes a "good place to take the family".*
/ 11.30 pm; no Amex.

Buchan's SW11 £26 ④❸④
62-64 Battersea Br Rd   228 0888   5–4C
*Bright Scottish-themed wine bar cum restaurant (just to the
south of Battersea Bridge); some admirers find it "jolly good",
but too many speak of "pretentiously described" and
"badly cooked" food.* / 10.45 pm.

Buona Sera SW11 £20 ❷❸❷
22 Northcote Rd   228 9925   10–2C
*"Go with your ear plugs" to this highly popular café-style
Italian, which is "always lively", "friendly" and "good value";
they serve "great pizza" and other "simple" dishes.*
/ Midnight; no Amex.

Busabong Too SW10   £26   ②❸④
1a Langton St 352 7414 5–3B
"Consistently good" World's End Thai, with "friendly, helpful service"; its only real drawback is that the "atmosphere can be bland". / 11.15 pm; D only.

Busabong Tree SW10   £26   ②❸④
112 Cheyne Walk 352 7534 5–4B
Despite its rather no man's land Embankment-side location, this Chelsea Thai has survived where others have failed by offering a high quality, standard 'package' (with a few "amazingly good dishes") in surroundings which, if not hugely atmospheric, are comfortable enough; large summer garden. / 11.15 pm; smart casual.

The Butlers Wharf Chop-house SE1 £40   ④④❸
36c Shad Thames 403 3403 9–4D
Conran's riverside chop house has a "fine location" (with Tower Bridge views), and its "light, airy" interior generally finds favour as an "alternative City lunch venue"; results from the "expensive" English menu are too often "so-so", however – perhaps the newly installed chef will raise the perennially lacklustre standards here. / 11 pm; closed Sat L & Sun D.

Byron's NW3   £28   ❸④❸
3a Downshire HI 435 3544 8–2A
It could be delightful, but this "pretty" Hampstead townhouse, just off Rosslyn Hill never quite seems to live up to its potential; even so, most find a "good experience", with acceptable modern British cooking. / 11 pm; no smoking area.

Café 209 SW6   £14   ④❸❸
209 Munster Rd 385 3625 10–1B
A "cheap and cheerful" BYO, Thai standby in a thinly provided area of deepest Fulham; the young local crowd can be deafening. / 10.30 pm; closed Sun; no credit cards.

Café Bohème W1   £28   ④❸②
13 Old Compton St 734 0623 4–2A
Prominently situated on a busy Soho corner, this atmospheric bar-café-restaurant gets very "crowded" with younger folk – it's the kind of place where you can have just a drink or a full meal, and one of the few 'proper' places open 24 hours; to say that "only its location keeps it going" is a little harsh, but allegations of "poorly prepared" fare are hardly uncommon. / 2.45 am, Thu-Sat open 24 hours, Sun 11.30 pm.

Café de Colombia
Museum of Mankind W1   £20   ❸❸⑤
6 Burlington Gdns   287 8148   3–3C
*"Not so good these days" – the café off the foyer of Mayfair's
Museum of Mankind is now in need of some investment
(such as ditching the grubby seat covers); a shame, as it still
offers a pleasant light lunch (salads and cakes) in potentially
stylish surroundings, and the terrace in front of the museum
makes a nice summer spot from which to watch the world
go by.* / L only, Sun pm cakes only; no smoking; no booking.

Café de la Place SW11   £20   ❸⑤❸
11/12 Battersea Sq   978 5374   5–4C
*"It's always busy, and the food's good" at this unpretentious
but welcoming all-day Battersea Village bistro, whose
drawback is "appalling" service.* / 11 pm; closed Sun D; no Amex.

Café Delancey NW1   £25   ④⑤❷
3 Delancey St   387 1985   8–3B
*"Location and ambience are the greatest strengths" of this
large, "very relaxed" Camden Town brasserie known for being
"the best Sunday morning venue"; the food is just about OK,
but it's the "appalling service which lets the place down".*
/ 11.30 pm; no Amex.

Café dell'Ugo SE1   £32   ④④❸
56-58 Tooley St   407 6001   9–4C
*This "casual", "airy" place, built into the arches beneath
London Bridge Station, is "not bad" – but it does miss its
potential; the eclectic fare (though "decent" to some) can
"sound better than it tastes", and service is "not
very professional".* / 11 pm; closed Sat L & Sun.

Café des Amis du Vin WC2   £25   ❸④❸
11-14 Hanover Pl   379 3444   4–2D
*Once well-known Gallic brasserie, in a potentially charming
location in an alley by the side of the Royal Opera House,
which is at last showing signs of coming back from the dead –
perhaps it will once again establish itself as a favourite
central rendezvous.* / 11.30 pm; closed Sun.

Café des Arts NW3   £29   ④❸❷
82 Hampstead High St   435 3608   8–2A
*A rambling, "romantic" bistro in the centre of Hampstead;
most find "good value" from its modern British menu, that
always has something "new and interesting", but there's been
a bit of a consistency problem this year, depressing the
food rating.* / 11.30 pm; no smoking area.

Café du Jardin WC2   £31   ❸❸❸
28 Wellington St   836 8769   4–3D
*"Light and bustling", tightly packed Covent Garden corner
spot, widely praised as a "slick and reliable place for lunch or
a pre-theatre dinner"; as to the main evening menu, however,
the verdict is "nice food, but overpriced"; a major revamp is in
progress at the time of going to press. / Midnight.*

Café du Marché EC1   £30   ❷❷❶
22 Charterhouse Sq   608 1609   9–1B
*A "reliable" "oasis" west of the Barbican, whose rustic
warehouse setting has a "wonderful", "relaxed" atmosphere;
"authentically French" cooking and "friendly" service ensure
that it's "always difficult to get in"; lunchtime is business-
dominated, but the evenings much less so. / 10 pm; closed Sat L
& Sun; no Amex.*

Café Emm W1   £18   ❸❸④
17 Frith St   437 0723   4–2A
*Welcoming, deservedly popular, candle-lit, budget Soho bistro;
the food has no particular pretensions, but comes in "good
helpings" and offers "great value", especially for the heart
of town; "excessively loud music" makes it one for
the younger-at-heart. / 10.30 pm; Fri & Sat 12.30 am; closed Sat L
& Sun L; no Amex; book L only.*

Café Fish SW1   £30   ④④④
39 Panton St   930 3999   4–4A
*Many do recommend the "beautifully prepared, fresh fish"
at this large but tightly-packed Theatreland establishment; it's
certainly "convenient", but others share our view that the
menu is rather "overpriced", and that, at "hectic" times, the
place has all the charm "of a railway station". / 11.30 pm;
closed Sat L & Sun; no smoking area.*

Café Flo   £22   ④④❸
13 Thayer St, W1   935 5023   2–1A
51 St Martin's Ln, WC2   836 8289   4–4C
676 Fulham Rd, SW6   371 9673   10–1B
26 Chiswick High Rd, W4   0181-995 3804   7–2B
127 Kensington Ch St, W8   727 8142   6–2B
334 Upper St, N1   226 7916   8–3D
205 Haverstock Hl, NW3   435 6744   8–2A
*A reasonably genuine "French café ambience" ("they never
push you out, no matter how long you stay") is the particular
attraction of these all-day bistros; their cooking is at least
"adequate", putting them some way ahead of the other
Gallic chains. / 11.30 pm, Sun 11 pm.*

Café Grove W11 £16 ③④②
253a Portobello Rd   243 1094   6–1A
*"When the sun shines, nothing is better" than "hanging out
with the Notting Hillbillies", on the large terrace overlooking
Portobello Market; by day they serve omelettes, salads, and
so on – on summer nights, there is a more extensive menu
(for details, call ahead).* / winter 5 pm, summer 10.30 pm; winter L only
– summer, closed Sat D & Sun D; no credit cards; no booking.

Café Japan NW11 £22 ③②③
626 Finchley Rd   0181-455 6854   1–1B
*A cheery grunt of welcome greets diners at this unusually jolly
Golder's Green Nipponese, just across from the tube station;
it offers good grub at ungreedy prices, with the set menu
offering particular value.* / 10.30 pm; D only, closed Sun; no Amex;
no booking on Fri.

Café Jeune SW9 £21 ③③③
24 Clapham Rd   793 0770   10–1D
*An oasis in the "depressing area" near Oval tube, this
neighbourhood café makes a relaxing hang-out, with outside
terraces front and back for the summer; we found the staples
and other more eclectic dishes satisfying, if a touch variable,
but a local foodie tips "a new cook who really knows
his stuff".* / 11 pm.

Café Lazeez SW7 £29 ③③②
93-95 Old Brompton Rd   581 9993   5–2C
*Rising prices at this "jazzed up" South Kensington Indian
are beginning to engender a sense of "disappointment";
it's a shame, because the stylish design and live music create
a "good atmosphere", and many still find the 'evolved' style of
cooking "delicious" and "not too oily".* / 12.30 am, Sun 10.30 pm;
smart casual; no smoking area.

Café Med W11 £28 ④②②
184a Kensington Pk Rd   221 1150   6–1A
*"Good atmosphere" is at the root of the success of this
accommodating Notting Hill brasserie (which is to form
the basis of a chain to be 'rolled out' during 1997); the fare
is "well executed", but at the price you might hope for
something a little more culinarily demanding than the likes
of (admittedly good) "steak and chips".* / 11.30 pm.

Café Montpeliano SW3 £23 ③③②
144 Brompton Rd   225 2926   5–1C
*A haven for shopping ladies-who-lunch, this "upmarket",
"attractive" café-pâtisserie, a couple of minutes walk from
Harrods, delivers simple Italian dishes, pasta and sandwiches
"at not too hefty a price".* / 11 pm; closed Sun D.

Café Nico
Grosvenor House Hotel W1 £39 ⑤④④

Grosvenor House Hotel, 90 Park Ln 409 1290 3–3A
Why Nico Ladenis associates his name with the brasserie/restaurant adjacent to his Mayfair temple of haute cuisine is a mystery; the two reporters unlucky enough to venture in this year found, as we ourselves did a year ago, a "dreadful experience" – "poor", "expensive" food, and "awful" service. / 10 pm; smart casual; no smoking area.

Café O SW3 £27 ❷❷❷

163 Draycott Ave 584 5950 5–2C
"No plate-smashing or Zorba impersonations here"; this "chic Greek", near Brompton Cross, is "appealing, in a cool, minimalist way", and its "modern Hellenic cuisine" puts that country's food "on a new level" (at least so far as London is concerned). / 11.30 pm; closed Sun D.

Café on the Common SW4 £18 ❸❸④

2 Rookery Rd 498 0770 10–2C
The team from Battersea's Fungus Mungus (RIP) have now transferred to this "quirky" shed in the middle of Clapham Common; as you might expect, it makes a "funky discovery", but the veggie fare is generally satisfying; BYO – there is no neighbouring off-licence. / 11 pm; no credit cards.

Café Pacifico WC2 £25 ❸❷❷

5 Langley St 379 7728 4–2C
The "bartenders deserve special praise" at this raucous and long standing Covent Garden Mexican cantina, which is "fun, but not daft or naff"; that it is possibly the best place of its type is eloquent testimony to the dismal standards of Mexican fare in London. / 11.45 pm; no smoking area; book pre 6.30 pm only.

Café Pasta £19 ④❷❸

184 Shaftesbury Ave, WC2 379 0198 4–2B
2-4 Garrick St, WC2 497 2779 4–3C
270 Chiswick High Rd, W4 0181-995 2903 7–2A
229-231 Kensington High St, W8 937 6314 5–1A
8 Theberton St, N1 704 9089 8–3D
200 Haverstock Hl, NW3 431 8531 8–2A
"Straightforward pasta meals in friendly surroundings" make these conveniently located spots useful for shopping lunches and the like; they are "good with babies", too. / 11.30 pm; no Amex; some have no smoking area; book L and early eve only.

Café Rouge   **£ 23**   ⑤④④

15 Frith St, W1   437 4307   4–2A
46-48 James St, W1   487 4847   3–1A
34 Wellington St, WC2   836 0998   4–3D
27-31 Basil St, SW3   584 2345   5–1D
390 King's Rd, SW3   352 2226   5–3B
855 Fulham Rd, SW6   371 7600   10–1B
102 Old Brompton Rd, SW7   373 2403   5–2B
31 Kensington Pk Rd, W11   221 4449   6–1A
Whiteleys, W2   221 1509   6–1C
227-229 Chiswick High Rd, W4   0181-742 7447   7–2A
158 Fulham Palace Rd, W6   0181-741 5037   7–2C
98-100 Shepherd's Bush Rd, W6   602 7732   7–1C
2 Lancer Sq, Kensington Ch St, W8   938 4200   5–1A
30 Clifton Rd, W9   286 2266   8–4A
6 South Grove, N6   0181-342 9797   8–1B
38-39 High St, NW3   435 4240   8–1A
120 St John's Wood High St, NW8   722 8366   8–3A
Hay's Galleria, Tooley St, SE1   378 0097   9–4D
147 St John's Hill, SW11   924 2112   10–2C
39-49 Parkgate Rd, SW11   924 3565   5–4C
248 Upper R'mond Rd, SW14   0181-878 8897   10–2A
200 Putney Br Rd, SW15   0181-788 4257   10–2B
40 Abbeville Rd, SW4   0181-673 3399   10–2D
140 Fetter Ln, EC4   242 3469   9–2A
Hillgate Hs, Limeburner Ln, EC4   329 1234   9–2A
*"We are being overwhelmed" by this "ghastly French chain" –
with its "tacky décor, inedible food and amateurish service" –
whose continuing growth baffles and irritates many reporters
in equal measure; perhaps Whitbread, the new owner,
will introduce quality-control – a concept apparently
unknown hitherto. / 11 pm.*

Café Royal Grill Room W1   **£ 59**   ❸❷❶
68 Regent St   437 9090   3–3D
*The "outrageously splendid" gilt-and-cherubs décor of this
famous dining room, a short step from Piccadilly Circus,
makes a "relaxing and decadent" backdrop for a meal;
the quality of the classic French cooking – if not truly great –
is far above the tourist tat which many locals seem to
assume, and this remains a sadly under-appreciated venue.
/ 10.30 pm; closed Sat L & Sun; jacket & tie.*

Café Sofra   **£ 14**   ❸④④
10 Shepherd Mkt, W1   495 3434   3–4B
33 Old Compton St, W1   494 0222   4–2A
15 Catherine St, WC2   240 9991   4–3D
101 Fleet St, EC4   583 6669   9–2A
*A "good choice" of inexpensive Turkish fare in a "modern
setting" makes this growing budget chain an ideal standby for
inexpensive snack meals; "the meze are great" (and you can
BYO). / Midnight, EC4 9 pm; no credit cards; no smoking area; no booking.*

Café Sogo SW1   **£ 22**   ❸②④

39-45 Haymarket 333 9036 4–4A

Though it is not particularly cheap, this sushi bar (adjoining a Piccadilly Circus department store) offers quality food and a pool of calm in a frenzied area. / 9.30 pm; closed Sun L

Café Spice Namaste E1   **£ 26**   ❶②❸

16 Prescot St 488 9242 1–2D

Cyrus Todiwala's unusually "interesting" – "creative, fresh, different" – Indian cooking brings followers from far and wide to these large but obscurely located City-wasteland premises; the reporter, though, who finds the new place "good, but not as good as before it moved" has our support. / 10.30 pm; closed Sat L & Sun; no smoking area.

Café Tabac SW15   **£ 20**   ④❸❸

30 Putney High St 0181-788 8668 10–2B

It "wouldn't impress the discerning", but this "attractive, cod-Gallic" Putney bistro is a useful cheap standby in a not over-provided area. / 11 pm; closed Sun D, Aug closed Sun; no Amex.

Caffe Graffiti NW3   **£ 26**   ❸②❸

71 High Street 431 7579 8–2A

"A comfortable room and interesting food" make a continuing success of this "not too pricey", cheerfully decorated, if tightly packed, brasserie in the centre of Hampstead. / 11 pm; no Amex.

Caffe Uno   **£ 23**   ❸❸④

28 Binney St, W1 499 9312 3–2A
5 Argyll St, W1 437 2503 3–1C
64 Tottenham Court Rd, W1 636 3587 2–1C
24 Charing Cross Rd, WC2 240 2524 4–3B
37 St Martin's Ln, WC2 836 5837 4–4C
106 Queensway, W2 229 8470 6–1C
11 Edgware Rd, W2 723 4898 6–1D
9 Kensington High St, W8 937 8961 5–1A
62 Upper St, N1 226 7988 8–3D
4 South Grove, N6 0181-342 8662 8–1B
40-42 Parkway, NW1 428 9124 8–3B
122 St John's Wood High St, NW8 722 0400 8–3A
375 Lonsdale Rd, SW13 0181-876 3414 10–1A

"Bright, friendly" chain, which is "trying hard"; it "knocks spots off the competition", say its supporters, by offering "plenty of choice" of "reasonably priced, good food" – pizza, pasta and more – "quickly and cheerfully"; the only real gripe is the uninspired design concept. / Midnight; some branches have no smoking areas.

La Cage Imaginaire NW3   £27   ④❶④
16 Flask Wk   794 6674   8–1A
*The décor is a touch suburban, the "food is nothing to write
home about", and it's a little "pricey", but this small Gallic
establishment, in an impossibly cute Hampstead backwater,
has a certain romantic charm, and the staff are
"very welcoming". / 11 pm, Sat 11.30 pm; closed Mon.*

Calabash WC2   £19   ❸④⑤
38 King St   836 1976   4–3C
*The basement restaurant at the Africa Centre offers a
degree of luxury not far above that found in the bush;
still, if you want to go on a culinary safari, the rough and
ready cooking (much of it spicy) is certainly interesting.
/ 10.30 pm; closed Sat L & Sun; no Switch.*

Caldesi W1   £27   ❸❷④
15-17 Marylebone Ln   935 9226   3–1A
*Very consistent Italian cooking – in a fairly old-fashioned style
– makes this chichi spot popular with traditionalists and
Wigmore Hall concert-goers. / 10.30 pm; closed Sat L & Sun;
smart casual; no smoking area.*

Calzone   £19   ❷❶❸
335 Fulham Rd, SW10   352 9797   5–3B
2a Kensington Pk Rd, W11   243 2003   6–2B
35 Upper St, N1   359 9191   8–3D
66 Heath St, NW3   794 6775   8–1A
*"Busy, cheerful, moderately priced", small chain that serves
"excellent pizzas and salad" – "thoroughly enjoyable food in
a cool setting". / Midnight, SW10 Fri & Sat 12.45 am; no Amex; booking
only at N1.*

Cambio de Tercio SW5   £27   ④❸④
163 Old Brompton Rd   244 8970   5–2B
*"Attentive" staff win a loyal following for this ambitious, quite
stylish South Kensington tapas bar/restaurant; in our opinion,
its prices have always discouraged the level of custom which
it would otherwise have garnered. / 11.30 pm.*

Camden Brasserie NW1   £27   ❷❷❷
216 Camden High St   482 2114   8–2B
*The name says it all, and "very reliable cooking", "speedy
and attentive service" and the "busy, lively" atmosphere now
make this a place back on very consistent overall form.
/ 11.30 pm; no Amex.*

The Canteen SW10   £36   ❷❸❷
Chelsea Harbour   351 7330   5–4B
*Though now adopting a lower profile than when Marco
Pierre White was behind the scenes, this Chelsea Harbour
"all-rounder" still offers "better than competent" modern
British cooking in a stylish setting which has "a real sense of
occasion"; service seems to have improved since the great
man's departure. / 11 pm, Fri & Sat midnight; closed Sat L & Sun D.*

Cantina del Ponte SE1 £ 30 ⑤⑤④
36c Shad Thames   403 5403   9–4D
*To say that no one has a nice word to say about Conran's
Tower Bridge-side Italian would be unfair – some think it's
"OK for business", that the pizza is "good" and that the
outside tables are "great in summer"; for too many, though,
the place fails comprehensively, thanks to service that is
"always disappointing", and cooking which is "boring"
and "lacking direction".* / 11 pm; closed Sun D.

La Capannina W1 £ 29 ❸❷④
24 Romilly St   437 2473   4–3A
*The style is hardly à la mode, but this long-established
Soho trattoria continues to do what it has always done –
simple nosh, quite well cooked, and professionally served in
cosy, if worn, surroundings.* / 11.30 pm; closed Sat L & Sun.

Capital Hotel SW3 £ 62 ❷❸❸
22-24 Basil St   589 5171   5–1D
*The "more soothing and stylish" décor, installed a year ago,
has rejuvenated the atmosphere of this small, "elegant but
pricey" Knightsbridge hotel dining room, and Philip Britten's
modern French cooking continues generally to please;
service is not quite as it was.* / 11.15 pm; no Switch; jacket & tie.

Cappadoccia SW10 £ 20 ❸❶❸
438 King's Rd   351 4118   5–3B
*"Hospitable service" and pleasant, if "anodyne", surroundings
make for a soothing experience at this new Chelsea-fringe
Turk; a few have encountered "bland, bland, bland" cooking,
but we were among the lucky ones whose visit was good
all round.* / 11.30 pm, Fri & Sat midnight; no Amex.

LE CAPRICE SW1 £ 40 ❷❶❶
Arlington Hs, Arlington St   629 2239   3–4C
*"Utterly professional", "100% reliable" St James's brasserie –
the epitome of a "slick", "well-oiled", metropolitan machine",
but with a "personal" touch that delights celebs and mortals
alike; although it's no longer reporters' favourite restaurant –
having been displaced by its sibling, the Ivy – it remains
"impossible to book".* / Midnight.

Caraffini SW1 £ 30 ❸❷❸
61-63 Lower Sloane St   259 0235   5–2D
*"Less trattoria-like and noisy" than Como Lario (from which it
is a 'break-away'), this nonetheless "cheerful" Italian, a couple
of minutes from Sloane Square, attracts consistent support –
"not a gastronomic experience, but good fresh food".*
/ 11.30 pm; closed Sun.

Caravan Serai W1   £27   ❸❸❷
50 Paddington St   935 1208   2–1A
"Even the banisters are carpeted", at this rug-filled, "fun"
Marylebone Afghan, where the cooking (India meets Persia)
is done with care; it's a sad sign of economic recovery that the
fabulous value set lunch is no more. / 11 pm, Fri & Sat 11.30 pm;
no Switch; no smoking area.

Carnevale EC1   £21   ❷❷❸
135 Whitecross St   250 3452   9–1B
"Very small but charming" vegetarian, north of the Barbican,
whose "delicious" cooking makes it worth a detour. / 10.30 pm;
closed Sun; no credit cards.

Casale Franco N1   £31   ❸④❸
134-137 Upper St   226 8994   8–3D
"Tucked away" down an alleyway, this family-run Islington
Italian is well known for its pizzas and other "lovely",
"medium-priced" food – the queue is something of an
institution; "sniffy" or "unfriendly" staff can take the edge
off the experience. / 11.30 pm; closed Mon, D only Tue-Thu; no Amex;
no smoking area; book L only.

Cave W1   £40
161 Piccadilly   409 0445   3–3C
Reservations about the "slightly bleak" former dining room
at the Caviar House seafood emporium – whose lack of
atmosphere has always been its most obvious drawback –
seem finally to have been recognised by its management;
as we go to press, an entirely new concept is being
hammered out, for a late-1996 re-launch. / 10.30 pm;
closed Sun; smart casual.

Cecconi's W1   £55   ④④④
5a Burlington Gdns   434 1509   3–3C
As ever, "prices are verging on ridiculous" at this grandiose
Mayfair Italian, which is a "great place for people watching"
and, er..., that's it. / 11.30 pm; closed Sat L & Sun; jacket.

Cento 50 W11   £28   ⑤④⑤
150 Notting Hill Gate   221 2442   6–2B
"What are they trying to achieve?", at this large, new,
modern, rustic Italian, whose feel – "like a shopping-mall
theme restaurant" – grates in fashionable Notting Hill Gate;
reports on all aspects of the operation are very mixed indeed.
/ 11.45 pm.

Chaba SW10   £21   ❷❸④
206 Fulham Rd   352 8664   5–3B
A "Thai restaurant tucked away in the basement of a Chelsea
shop", which continues to serve up "delicious" fare at prices
which, especially for that part of town, are very reasonable.
/ 11.30 pm; closed Sat L & Sun L

FSA

Chada SW11 £27 ❸❷❸
208-210 Battersea Pk Rd   622 2209   10–1C
"Upmarket", "consistently good" Battersea Thai offering
"a greater level of comfort" than the norm, and "friendly",
"proper" service; the food is enjoyable going on "ordinary".
/ 11 pm, Fri & Sat 11.30 pm; closed Sat L; smart casual.

Le Champenois EC2 £41 ④❸❸
10 Devonshire Sq   283 7888   9–2D
"A safe choice", "ideal for business", this "slick and
professional" City basement offers "lots of space"; its French
cooking is competent but definitely best enjoyed on expenses.
/ L only; closed Sat & Sun; jacket & tie.

Charco's SW3 £30 ❷❸④
1 Bray Pl   584 0765   5–2D
"Good neighbourhood food" is served in the basement
restaurant of this long-established Chelsea wine bar; service is
occasionally over-stretched, but we blame the dated décor for
the fact that it "can be underpopulated". / 10.30 pm; closed Sun.

Chelsea Bun Diner SW10 £14 ❸④❸
9a Lamont Rd   352 3635   5–3B
"Cheerful" World's End diner "full of trendy or sporty types
trying to look cool", offering "good food at a great price",
and especially well known as a breakfast spot; the new
Battersea offshoot (70 Battersea Bridge Rd, tel 738 9009)
seems a rather soggy effort – presumably as a result of
crossing the river. / 11.30 pm; no credit cards.

Chelsea Kitchen SW3 £11 ❸❸❸
98 King's Rd   589 1330   5–2D
This '60s survivor continues to provide "exceptional value"
for somewhere a short step from Sloane Square; it churns out
"reliable, cheap", international fodder in a canteen setting.
/ 11.45 pm; no credit cards; no smoking area.

Chelsea Ram SW10 £23 ❸❸❸
32 Burnaby St   351 4008   5–4B
Prettily gentrified pub-conversion in the back streets near
Chelsea Harbour; it offers good, but not inexpensive, modern
British fare in relaxing surroundings. / 10 pm, Sun 9 pm; no Amex.

Cheng Du NW1 £28 ❸❷❸
9 Parkway   485 8058   8–3B
Smart Camden Town Chinese recommended for its quality
cooking and service that is "very attentive without being
overbearing"; some feel it smacks of the "expensively
ordinary". / 11.30 pm.

Chez Bruce SW17 £33 ❶❶❷
2 Bellevue Rd   0181-672 0114   10–2C
*This "fabulous restaurant" – benefiting from Bruce Poole's
very "imaginative" and "good value" modern French cooking
– easily justifies a journey even unto Wandsworth Common;
the "warm" and "friendly" service comes in for scarcely less
praise, and the rather unusual décor "manages a sense of
occasion without overpowering"; still, for our money, one of
the best deals in town.* / 10.15 pm; closed Sun D.

Chez Gérard £25 ❸❸④
31 Dover St, W1   499 8171   3–3C
8 Charlotte St, W1   636 4975   2–1C
119 Chancery Ln, WC2   405 0290   2–2D
45 East Ter, Covent Gdn, WC2   379 0666   4–3D
*"Dependable" chain, "good for steak/frites" (the speciality) or
the varied fixed-price menu, and popular for informal business
entertaining; generally, there are complaints of "squashed"
accommodation, but one site they have definitely improved is
the re-launched Opera Terrace – "a welcome addition to
Covent Garden".* / 10 pm-11.15 pm; Charlotte St closed Sat L, Dover St
closed Sun L, Chancery Ln closed Sat & Sun; no smoking area.

Chez Liline N4 £29 ❶④④
101 Stroud Green Rd   263 6550   8–1D
*Sylvain Ho Wing Cheong may now be better known for
Jason's, but it was in this unlovely Finsbury Park location that
he first established himself; "fab, fresh fish" with "inspired"
and sometimes very spicy Mauritian flavours certainly make
a detour here worthwhile, but service can be
"extremely slow".* / 10.30 pm; closed Sun.

Chezmax SW10 £36 ❷❸④
168 Ifield Rd   835 0874   5–3A
*After the untimely death of one of the Renzland brothers,
there is now no family involvement in the Earl's Court
basement whose fame they established; 'their' restaurant
carries on under the care of one of the non-family partners,
and the standards of the "wonderfully French", "slightly
heavy" cooking have held up well; it's a "shame about the
basement" setting, which many find cramped.* / 11 pm; closed
Mon L, Sat L & Sun.

Chez Moi W11 £37 ❸❶❸
1 Addison Ave   603 8267   6–2A
*Loyal supporters of this Holland Park stalwart continue to
vaunt as "exceptional" the traditional-with-a-twist cooking
here – though to others it just seems as "ordinary" as ever;
it's the "discreet", "attentive" and "friendly" service which
really makes the place, though, helping to create a "warm"
and "cosy" atmosphere.* / 11 pm; closed Sat L & Sun; no Switch;
smart casual.

CHEZ NICO AT NINETY
GROSVENOR HOUSE HOTEL W1 £73 ②③④
90 Park Ln   409 1290   3–3A
*Nico Ladenis's "excellent but cold" Mayfair shrine to haute
cuisine generates a hymn of praise for its "faultless" and
"outstanding" cooking; as to the atmosphere, however,
"very relaxing" is about as positive as anyone can get,
with many just finding it "stifling" or even "morgue-like" –
perhaps a result of attracting "too many Michelin-devotees".
/ 11 pm; closed Sat L & Sun; jacket & tie.*

Chiang Mai W1 £27 ③⑤⑤
48 Frith St   437 7444   4–2A
*"Distinct flavours", some unusual dishes and a "very good
vegetarian selection" keep this Soho Thai on the culinary
map; unfortunately, the package also includes "off-hand"
service and an "uncomfortable" setting. / 11 pm; closed Sun L;
no Switch.*

Chiaroscuro WC1 £34 ②③④
24 Coptic St   636 2731   2–1C
*Most people are very up on the "innovative combinations"
and "well presented" modern British cooking at this updated
townhouse, near the British Museum; atmosphere, though,
can be found a little lacking. / 11.45 pm; closed Sat L & Sun D;
smart casual; no smoking area.*

Chicago Pizza Pie Factory W1 £19 ③②④
17 Hanover Sq   629 2669   3–1C
*Even those who think this dated theme-diner near Oxford
Circus "painfully scruffy and outmoded" say that "the quality
of the pizzas almost makes up"; "a fun place with kids".
/ 11.30 pm, Fri 1 am; no smoking area.*

Chicago Rib Shack SW7 £24 ④④④
1 Raphael St   581 5595   5–1C
*Just off Knightsbridge, this well-known spot offers a themed
all-American package growing more dated by the year;
still, it's a "nice buzzy place to take children" – "they are
definitely not considered an irritation". / 11.45 pm;
no smoking area; no booking Sat.*

Chimes SW1 £19 ⑤③④
26 Churton St   821 7456   2–4B
*No one disputes that "the cider selection is very good" at this
"friendly" Pimlico pie 'n' scrumpy house; overall, though, it can
seem an "average place", with cooking likened by its critics to
"the most expensive Fray Bentos pies in London". / 10.15 pm;
no smoking area.*

China City WC2   £21   ❸❸❸
25a Lisle St   734 3388   4–3A
Entered via quite a cute courtyard (complete with naff fountain), this large Chinatown establishment is, for the area, a good all-rounder, with competent cooking, "quick, friendly" service and a "relaxed" and spacious atmosphere. / 11.30 pm; no smoking area.

China Court W1   £26   ❸④❸
10 Wardour St   434 0108   4–4A
Safe but boring Chinese, in the Swiss Centre; it offers a suitably sanitised vision of the true Chinatown, which it borders. / 11.30 pm.

China Jazz NW1   £26   ④④❸
29-31 Parkway   482 3940   8–3B
Some still find this stylish-going-on-tacky Camden Town venue an "entertaining place" with "excellent food"; to others, it's just a lame Peking duck. / Midnight; closed Sat L; smart casual; no smoking area.

Chinon W14   £36   ❶④④
23 Richmond Way   602 4082   7–1C
Jonathan Hayes's "imaginatively prepared and presented" modern French cooking is tipped by some as the "best value food in London"; to sample it, though, you have to trek to an obscure Shepherd's Bush location which has "little atmosphere" and notoriously eccentric service. / 10.30 pm; D only, closed Sun; smart casual.

Chiswick Restaurant W4   £28   ❸④④
131-133 Chiswick High Rd   0181-994 6887   7–2B
Fans of this Chiswick yearling – sister restaurant to the Brackenbury – say it is capable of "outstanding" modern British dishes, and has "fair" prices to boot; others say the cooking is "ordinary", and find the minimalist interior "cramped", "noisy" and "smoky". / 11.30 pm; closed Sat L & Sun D.

Chokdee SW5   £19   ❸❸④
233b Earl's Ct Rd   244 6060   5–2A
"Always a friendly welcome" and "consistent, cheap Thai food" make this comfortable but unpretentious Earl's Court basement a standby worth remembering. / 11.30 pm; D only; no Switch.

Christoph's SW10   £31   ❷❷❸
7 Park Wk   349 8866   5–3B
It's early days for this understated Chelsea spot, whose modern British fare is inspiring to some but "missing something" to others (ourselves included); you would never know that the "predictable" décor is the work of a much vaunted interior designer, but the "attentive" service is an undoubted attraction. / 11 pm; closed Sun D.

Christopher's WC2   £42   ④④❷
18 Wellington St   240 4222   4–3D
*No one disputes the "fashionable" and "sophisticated" aura
of this Covent Garden American, whose menu majors in steak
and seafood; however, "complacent" service and "toppish"
prices lead too many to stigmatise the whole experience as
"very disappointing" and "over-hyped" (making its popularity
with "half of London's PR brigade" all the more appropriate).
/ 11.45 pm; closed Sun D; smart casual.*

Chuen Cheng Ku W1   £21   ❸④④
17 Wardour St   437 1398   4–3A
*It is "for dim-sum from trolleys" that this landmark Chinatown
behemoth is known; other offerings are more standard.
/ 11.45 pm.*

Churchill W8   £11   ❷④❷
119 Kensington Ch St   792 1246   6–2B
*"The secret's out" – it has been for years – about this
"great Thai" in the cheerful annex of a pub, not far from
Notting Hill Gate; it's all "a bit chaotic" and "smoky", but
"delicious" and "cheap" too. / 9.30 pm; closed Sun D; no Amex.*

Chutney Mary SW10   £33   ❷❸❸
535 King's Rd   351 3113   5–4B
*Many reporters now find "marvellous" cooking at this rather
themed Chelsea Anglo-Indian, and praise a menu with "more
variety" and "less predictability" than at most subcontinentals;
the "superb" buffet lunches come in for particular support.
/ 11.30 pm; smart casual; no smoking area.*

Chutneys NW1   £14   ❷⑤④
124 Drummond St   388 0604   8–4C
*"Excellent value" is on offer at this 'little India' veggie –
particularly during the lunchtime and all-day Sunday all-you-
can-eat buffets; "surly service" can be a drawback. / 11.30 pm;
no Amex & no Switch.*

Ciabatta SW3   £14   ❸④❸
356 King's Rd   352 0595   5–3C
*Chelsea offshoot of north London's A Tavola, which shares the
same "lazy", if "friendly", service; the homely setting makes it
an agreeable standby, though, and the pizza (cooked in
a wood burning oven) wins praise. / Midnight; no credit cards.*

Cibo W14   £40   ❸❸④
3 Russell Gdns   371 6271   7–1D
*Sometimes "exquisite" and "innovative" modern Italian fare
can be had at this "pricey" Olympia Italian; some wonder
whether "the staff and atmosphere could be more friendly",
though, and those who say the place is "nothing to write
home about" are gaining ground. / 11 pm; closed Sat L & Sun D;
smart casual.*

City Brasserie EC3 £ 45 ④④❸

Plantation Hs, Mincing Ln 220 7094 9–3D

Q: If a restaurant charges "over £100 for two with nothing to make it different", does that mean it's 'overpriced'?; A: as absolutely everyone in this large, "vibrant" City basement is on expenses, who cares? / L only, ex bar 9 pm; closed Sat & Sun; smart casual; no booking in bar.

City Miyama EC4 £ 53 ❸❸④

17 Godliman St 489 1937 9–3B

This "great Japanese" is "No 1 in the City" – certainly if you want a grand setting for a non-teppan-yaki meal; it's a little "clinical" and, unsurprisingly, prices are rather toppish. / 10 pm; closed Sat D & Sun.

Claridges Restaurant W1 £ 55 ④❷❷

Brook St 629 8860 3–2B

Verdicts on the food at Society's favourite hotel sometimes reach the dizzy heights of "average" – others just say that "it all tastes boiled, possibly in the same pan"; still, the real attractions are the "superb '30s décor" and the "impeccable" service; weekend dinner-dances have been a welcome innovation. / 11.15 pm; jacket & tie.

CLARKE'S W8 £ 42 ❶❸❸

124 Kensington Ch St 221 9225 6–2B

As ever, Sally Clarke's "beautifully cooked and presented", Cal-Ital food and the "excellent" service win practically unanimous plaudits for this slightly low-key Kensington spot (those with romance in mind should try for a table on the ground floor); at dinner, the no-choice menu allows "full attention to be given to the wine and company". / 10 pm; closed Sat & Sun; no smoking area.

The Clerkenwell EC1 £ 26 ❶❸④

73 Clerkenwell Rd 831 7595 9–1A

"Powerful flavours in a modish setting ought to pack out" this modern British spot in Clerkenwell; "sadly, the location is appalling" but, if you brave it, "an excellent foodie experience" awaits. / 10.45 pm; closed Sat & Sun; smart casual.

Clifton E1 £ 15 ❷❸❸

126 Brick Ln 247 2364 1–2D

"Friendly" establishment, on the East End's 'street of a thousand curries', tipped as "a cut above the others in the area" – "the food is sophisticated, and you don't pay a premium for it". / 1 am, Thu-Sat 2.30 am.

Coast W1 £ 40 ③④③

26b Albemarle St 495 5999 3–3C
*"Deeply trendy", converted Mayfair car showroom, whose
hard-edged décor strikes some as too "cold" and "noisy";
Steven Terry's modern British cooking draws similarly mixed
views – there is a high degree of consensus, though, that
prices are "elevated", and that service can be "vague" and
"snotty"; "take a table downstairs only on condition that
they pay you".* / Midnight.

The Collection SW3 £ 30 ④④②

264 Brompton Rd 225 1212 5–2C
*Our visit to Mögens Thölströp's new "fun, young, glam"
sibling to Daphne's was in line with those who find it
"surprisingly good" – a "beautiful" and most unusual space,
with "absolutely delicious", "Asian-slant" food and "warm
and attentive" service; the ratings are dragged down by a very
vociferous minority who thought the experience an all-round
turn-off – perhaps a reaction to the meat-market which is the
large ground-floor bar.* / 11.30 pm.

Como Lario SW1 £ 32 ③④④

22 Holbein Pl 730 2954 5–2D
*To its admirers this long-established Chelsea trattoria,
near Sloane Square, is "always busy and fun"; the food is
"reliable", if "slightly expensive".* / 11.30 pm; closed Sun;
smart casual.

CONNAUGHT W1 £ 67 ③①②

Carlos Pl 499 7070 3–3B
*"An institution, frozen in time" – the Edwardian panelled
dining room at this "very English" Mayfair hotel offers
a wonderful, if extremely "expensive", visit to "a world
gone by"; the "time-warp" menu may be satisfying rather
than startling, but service remains, for many, the best in town.*
/ 10.45 pm; no Switch; jacket & tie; "appreciated if guests try to refrain
from smoking".

Conrad Hotel SW10 £ 35 ②③③

Chelsea Harbour 823 3000 5–4B
*The "great value" champagne buffet brunch at this "out of
the way" and somewhat "sterile" Chelsea Harbour hotel
provides an "enormous spread", of a kind "seldom seen
outside the USA".* / 11.30 pm; no Switch; smart casual.

The Cook House SW15 £ 29 ③③④

56 Lower R'mnd Rd 0181-785 2300 10–1A
*Modern British Putney newcomer, likened to "a dinner party"
at which the menu "sounds confident" but whose execution
"lacks finesse"; the real drawback, however, is that "you BYO,
and end up paying £25 a head", and beware – "the noise
level rises as the vino is consumed".* / 11 pm; closed Mon & Sun;
no Amex.

F Cooke & Sons E8 £ 8 ④❸❷
41 Kingsland High St 254 2878 1–1C
Amazingly, one reporter does proclaim the main dish
"delicious", at London's most famous pie and eel shop;
we ourselves have never acquired the taste, but a trip to
this impressively tiled Dalston establishment offers a true
East End experience – at very modest cost – and you can
always opt for the steak and kidney pie instead. / Mon-Wed
7 pm, Thu 8 pm, Fri & Sat 10 pm; closed Sun; no credit cards; no booking.

Coopers Arms SW3 £ 17 ❸❷❸
87 Flood St 376 3120 5–3C
"Great pub food", of above average variety and interest,
makes this sparsely decorated but clubby Chelsea hostelry of
ever wider repute – "it may be a good 'local', but in fact
many people seem to drive to it". / L only; closed Sat D & Sun D;
book Sun L only.

Cork & Bottle WC2 £ 23 ④④❸
44-46 Cranbourn St 734 7807 4–3B
Even the many supporters of this "lovely, cosy, central
watering hole", conveniently located next to a Leicester
Square sex shop, admit that the grub is "expensive" for what
it is, and that a visit can be "a bit gruesome if you can't get
a table"; the crush, though, attests to the fact that the nosh is
"completely reliable", and there is a "marvellous wine list".
/ Midnight.

Cosmo NW3 £ 22 ❸❷④
4 Northways Pde, Finchley Rd 722 1398 8–2A
Unswayed by modern culinary fashions, this comfortable old
South Hampstead trooper provides satisfying international
grub (with German specialities); the adjoining café does
good breakfasts. / 10.45 pm.

Costa's Fish Restaurant W8 £ 13 ❷❸④
18 Hillgate St 727 4310 6–2B
"Tucked in behind the take-away", this no-frills but cosy spot,
just off Notting Hill Gate, serves very superior, "good and
cheap" fish and chips. / 10.30 pm; closed Mon & Sun; no credit cards.

Costa's Grill W8 £ 13 ❸❸④
12-14 Hillgate St 229 3794 6–2B
Just off Notting Hill Gate, this "friendly" taverna – half
a century old – is "best if the waiter remembers you";
it offers "cheap, traditional Greek" fare at very fair prices.
/ 10.30 pm; closed Sun; no credit cards.

Côte à Côte SW11 £ 14 ④④④
74-75 Battersea Br Rd 738 0198 5–4C
Prominently located on a Battersea corner, this large, ultra-
budget bistro gets a mixed press, with reports on the cooking
ranging from "surprisingly good" to plain "horrible"; still, for
an affordable group meal it hits a certain spot and can be
"fun" – hint: the best seats are in the boat. / Midnight.

Cottons NW1 £ 25 ⑤⑤❷
55 Chalk Farm Rd   482 1096   8–2B
A visit to this funky Camden Town West Indian can be marred by "slow" service ("more interested in selling cocktails") and by "small portions" of "expensive" food which "do not deliver what they promise"; a shame, as this place's atmosphere "could really make it something special".
/ 11.30 pm; no smoking area.

The Cow W11 £29
89 Westbourne Park Rd   221 0021   6–1B
As we go to press, the dining room above Tom Conran's "designer Suffolk/Derry fishing pub" – mis-located on the fringe of Notting Hill – is being re-launched under the charge of Francesca Melman, a protégée of Alastair Little. / 11 pm;
D only, Mon-Sat & Sun L only; no Amex & no Switch.

Cranks £ 16 ❸⑤⑤
23 Barrett St, W1   495 1340   3–1B
8 Marshall St, W1   437 9431   3–2D
9 Tottenham St, W1   631 3912   2–1B
1 The Market, WC2   379 6508   4–3D
17 Great Newport St, WC2   836 5226   4–3B
Unit 11, 8 Adelaide St, WC2   836 0660   4–4C
"The best selection of vegetarian food" ensures support for what is still London's only veggie chain; service ("slow") and atmosphere ("lacking") could do with a boost though, and portions are "small". / 7 pm - 11 pm; no smoking; no booking.

The Crescent SW3 £ 24 ❸❷❸
99 Fulham Rd   225 2244   5–2C
Fashionably understated new Brompton Cross brasserie-cum-wine bar, offering "above average", but not inexpensive, light modern British fare; the "amazing" wine list has many choices by the glass. / 10.30 pm; no Amex.

THE CRITERION W1 £ 37 ❸④❶
Piccadilly Circus   930 0488   3–3D
Marco Pierre White's new régime at this "absolutely gorgeous" neo-Byzantine chamber has made "improvements all round", the lighting and décor now creating the "special experience" the location demands, and the dishes from the wide-ranging menu sometimes (if by no means always) scaling the heights; perhaps predictably, some feel that "diners are now there for the benefit of the staff". / Midnight, Sun 10.30 pm.

The Cross Keys SW3 £ 29 ④④❸
1 Lawrence St   349 9111   5–3C
A "beautiful" conservatory serves as the dining room of this recently updated Chelsea pub; we enjoyed the simple modern cooking on our visit, but reports are inconsistent, and even some of those who find the fare "relatively good" say it's "a bit too expensive". / 11 pm.

Crown & Goose NW1 £21 ❸④❸
100 Arlington Rd   485 2342   8–3B
*Trendy Camden Town pub, offering a "short menu of modern
bar staples", which are "well-presented" and "filling". / 10 pm;
no food Fri D; no credit cards.*

Cuba Libre N1 £29 ❸❸❷
72 Upper St   354 9998   8–3D
*Large, vibrant Islington Cuban with eye-catching muralled
décor; tasty cooking and good live music add to its popularity
as a 'night out' venue, though prices give nothing away.
/ 11.30 pm, Fri & Sat 12.30 am.*

Cucina NW3 £28 ❷❷❸
45a South End Rd   435 7814   8–2A
*The "one decent restaurant in Hampstead" is a common view
of this modern British yearling (though in Gresslin's it may
now have a competitor); in more favoured parts of town, the
combination of "interesting" (but "sometimes variable")
cooking in agreeable (but "noisy") surroundings might seem
unremarkable – here, they make it "nearly always necessary
to book". / 10.30 pm, Fri & Sat 11 pm; closed Sun D; smart casual.*

Czech Club NW6 £19 ❸❸④
74 West End Ln   372 5251   1–1B
*The dining room at this atmospheric West Hampstead
émigrés club offers solid middle European cooking in a setting
which evokes another age. / 10 pm; closed Mon (ex bank hols) Sat D
& Sun D; no credit cards.*

Da Mario SW7 £20 ❷❷❸
15 Gloucester Rd   584 9078   5–1B
*This PizzaExpress in disguise is one of the few budget places
convenient for the Albert Hall; for a large group, the cellar
provides one of the only modestly priced, dine-and disco
venues in town. / Midnight; no Switch; book for disco.*

Da Pierino SW7 £19 ❸❸④
37 Thurloe Pl   581 3770   5–2C
*"Good, quick, value" Italian, with no pretensions and low
prices, just by South Ken tube. / 11.15 pm; closed Mon; no Amex.*

Dan's SW3 £30 ④❷❶
119 Sydney St   352 2718   5–3C
*"Romantic" atmosphere (particularly in the "beautiful
conservatory extension") and "friendly" service, win this
Chelsea spot much praise (as does the lovely garden); some
people like the English cooking too – quite unaccountably, in
our view. / 10.30 pm; closed Sat L & Sun D.*

Daphne NW1 £20 ❷❷❸
83 Bayham St   267 7322   8–3C
*This "cosy" and "fun" Camden Town taverna is a "good, solid
Greek", upon whose roof you can dine in summer. / 11.30 pm;
closed Sun; no Amex & no Switch.*

Daphne's SW3   £37   ④④❷
110-112 Draycott Ave   589 4257   5–2C
*Is fashion becoming more fickle?, or is it just that people
have quickly got sick of the 'if you're not famous, you can eff
off' approach? – either way, the speed with which this briefly
celebrated, three year old Brompton Cross Italian is falling
from fame (7th most-mentioned last year, 17th this) is really
quite impressive. / 11.30 pm.*

Daquise SW7   £14   ❸❷❸
20 Thurloe St   589 6117   5–2C
*Many love the "special" atmosphere of this time-warped Pole,
particularly conveniently placed for those visiting the South
Kensington museums – tea is a speciality; one reporter's
"Eastern European, 90 year-old aunt approved of the food"
here, hinting at the level of culinary advancement, but prices
are pre-revolutionary. / 11 pm; no credit cards; no smoking area.*

De Cecco SW6   £26   ❷❸❷
189 New King's Rd   736 1145   10–1B
*Since this ultra-popular Parson's Green Italian was taken over
in early 1996 by Antony Worrall Thompson et al, opinion has
been somewhat divided; the majority still feel you get top
value cooking in a "fun" setting with a "great buzz", but to
others it has "lost that special charm". / 11 pm; closed Sun.*

Deals   £27   ④⑤④
14-16 Foubert's Pl, W1   287 1001   3–2C
Chelsea Harbour, SW10   795 1001   5–4B
Broadway Centre, W6   0181-563 1001   7–2C
*De luxe diner chain, praised by some for their "quite good
food" and as being "excellent for family outings"; "service
needs sorting out", however, and too many find them
"rather predictable" and "overpriced". / 11 pm, W1 & W6 – Sat &
Sun 11.30 pm; W1 closed Sun.*

Del Buongustaio SW15   £29   ❶❸❷
283 Putney Br Rd   0181-780 9361   10–2B
*That it's "one of the few genuine, unpretentious Italian
restaurants in London" goes some way to explaining the
disproportionate level of interest in this out-of-the-way Putney
spot; the "consistently innovative" and "authentic" cooking,
and the "wonderful" wine list also play their part. / 11.30 pm;
closed Sat L, Jun-Aug closed Sun L; no Switch.*

Delicious Blue W1   £33   ④❸❷
75 Beak St   287 1840   3–2D
*"Fun and funky", "small" Soho Australian whose "seductive
and private" booths come particularly recommended for
romance; many praise the "interesting" Pacific-rim cooking,
but standards are variable, which, at these prices, is hardly
good enough. / 11.30 pm; closed Sat L & Sun D.*

La Delizia £ 19 ②④②

63-65 Chelsea Manor St, SW3 376 4111 5–3C
Farmers Mkt, Sydney St, SW3 351 6701 5–3C
246 Old Brompton Rd, SW5 373 6085 5–2A
*An "excellent range of well made pizzas" and tasteful,
minimalist décor ensure the popularity of this hip, small
Chelsea chain; to feel like a foreigner in your own country, try
the crowded, largely open-air branch in the Farmers Market.*
/ *Midnight; no credit cards; no booking.*

dell'Ugo W1 £ 32 ④⑤❸

56 Frith St 734 8300 4–2A
*Three-floor Soho landmark whose "modern designer styling,
matched by the food" and "noisy" atmosphere attract praise
from some; however, over-contrivance of the Mediterranean-
inspired dishes and "absolutely unacceptable waits between
courses" lead many to an overall conclusion of
"generally rubbish".* / *Midnight; closed Sun.*

The Depot SW14 £ 26 ④④❷

Mortlake High St 0181-878 9462 10–1A
*A "lovely setting, if you can get a table overlooking the river",
this "lively and friendly" Barnes spot is particularly popular
with families at the weekend; the unambitious menu is
indifferently realised but "reasonably priced".* / *11 pm;
no smoking area.*

Detroit WC2 £ 29 ❸⑤❸

35 Earlham St 240 2662 4–2C
*For a place focused on the bar, this slightly bizarre Covent
Garden newcomer offers surprisingly ambitious modern British
food; as a diner in this "Blake's Seven" cave (previously called
Jones), however, you can find yourself feeling rather beside
the point.* / *Midnight, Sun 10.30 pm; closed Sat L & Sun.*

Diverso W1 £ 40 ④❷❸

85 Piccadilly 491 2222 3–4C
*Not a single report have we received about this swanky new
Italian near the Ritz, rather confirming our view that it's
difficult to see why a local would want to seek out a place this
pricey where the cooking is no more than so-so and which,
while perfectly comfortable, steers well clear of true chic.*
/ *11.30 pm; closed Sun L*

Diwana Bhel-Poori House NW1 £ 14 ❷❸④

121 Drummond St 387 5556 8–4C
*"Still the best value Indian vegetarian", say fans of this
canteen hangover from the '60s, near Euston; the starters for
which the place is named are the top attraction; BYO.*
/ *11.30 pm; no Switch; no smoking.*

Dixie's Bar & Grill SW11 £19 ④④❷

25 Battersea Rs 228 7984 10–2C

"Cheap and cheerful" Battersea Tex-Mex usually "busy" with a "young", local crowd; it has a "good bar", but "mediocre food" and "slow service". / 11.30 pm.

Dôme £20 ④⑤④

57-59 Old Compton St, W1 287 0770 4–3A
32 Long Acre, WC2 379 8650 4–2C
354 King's Rd, SW3 352 2828 5–3B
194-196 Earl's Court Rd, SW5 835 2200 5–2A
Kensington Ct, W8 937 6655 5–1A
341 Upper St, N1 226 3414 8–3D
18 Chalk Farm Rd, NW1 428 0998 8–2B
58-62 Heath St, NW3 431 0399 8–1A
57-59 Charterhouse St, EC1 336 6484 9–1A

Smartly decked out, cod-French hang-outs, which – like their siblings, the Cafés Rouges – attract limited support from reporters; they're "good places to wait if you have to meet someone", though, and the set meal for a fiver is "surprisingly reasonable". / 10.30 pm-11 pm; EC1 closed Sat & Sun; some no Amex.

Don Pepe NW8 £20 ❸①❷

99 Frampton St 262 3834 8–4A

"A bit of Spain" – London's oldest tapas bar, just around the corner from Lord's, benefits from particularly "efficient" and "welcoming" staff; there is a more expensive restaurant which, as ever, is a lesser attraction. / 12.15 am; closed Sun.

Dorchester Grill
Dorchester Hotel W1 £46 ❷①❷

53 Park Ln 317 6336 3–3A

"Old world dining par excellence" – the splendid Spanish Baronial style room at this grand Mayfair hotel has finally re-established itself after the refurbishment of a few years ago; the "warm", "attentive but discreet" service gets the most praise, but the traditional British fare and the "relaxing" atmosphere are also highly applauded. / 11 pm; smart casual.

Dorchester, Oriental
Dorchester Hotel W1 £59 ❷❷❸

53 Park Ln 317 6328 3–3A

"Magnificent" Chinese cooking and "impeccable" service combine to make this Mayfair dining room a "wonderful place to impress, because it's so good"; the rather plain setting generates little emotion one way or the other. / 11 pm; closed Sat L & Sun; smart casual.

La Dordogne W4   £35   ❷①❷

5 Devonshire Rd   0181-747 1836   7–2A
*"Everything you would expect of a long-established, traditional
French restaurant"* – this Chiswick stalwart put in
a particularly strong performance this year, and was
commended for its standards across the board. / 11 pm;
closed Sat L & Sun L.

Dove W6   £14   ❸❸❸

19 Upper Mall   0181-748 5405   7–2B
"If you can sit outside, it's great", at this famous
Hammersmith riverside pub (whose interior is also very
characterful); Thai one-plate specials and more standard grub
are available. / 10 pm; no booking.

Dover St Wine Bar W1   £37   ⑤⑤④

8-9 Dover St   629 9813   3–3C
"No one is there for the food" – and a good job too – at this
dine-and-bop cellar near the Ritz; it's *"a costly night out"*, but
then there are amazingly few places of its type in town. / 2 am;
closed Sat L & Sun; no Switch; no jeans.

Down Mexico Way W1   £24   ⑤④❷

25 Swallow St   437 9895   3–3D
With its *"buzzing"* bar, *"whirling Latin dancers"* and
"beautiful" tiled interior, this large Mayfair Mexican offers
a *"great party night out, in spite of the so-so food"* (if you're
just looking for nourishment, it may seem *"very bad value for
money"*); a new floor is currently being added to house
a resident band. / 11.45 pm, Sun 10.30 pm.

Downstairs at 190 SW7   £36   ❸④❸

190 Queen's Gt   581 5666   5–1B
A *"wide selection of seafood"*, sometimes prepared to
"delicious" effect, wins a number of plaudits for this *"elegant"*
South Kensington basement; service can be
somewhat amateur. / 11.30 pm; D only; closed Sun.

Dragon Inn W1   £16   ❷❸④

12 Gerrard St   494 0870   4–3A
Archetypal crowded Chinatown canteen offering a long menu
and reasonable dim-sum – better value, overall, than
the norm. / 11.45 pm, Fri & Sat midnight.

Drones SW1   £35   ④❷❸

1 Pont St   259 6166   2–4A
Take a classic Belgravia restaurant site, and spice with a good
measure of famous executive chef (Antony Worrall
Thompson), and what do you get? – well, a bit of a damp
squib, it seems; perhaps it was just bad luck to ape the style
of Daphne's (*"Tuscan colours"*, blah ...) at the very point
where the latter is going out of fashion, or perhaps it's just, as
so often with AWT-places, that the menu gives no impression
of coherency or direction. / 11.30 pm.

The Eagle EC1   £ 20   ②④❸
159 Farringdon Rd   837 1353   9–1A
"Go early to get a seat", at this seminal super-pub, on the western fringe of the City; "if you manage to attract the staff's attention", the "robust" Mediterranean cooking can be "sensational", and "the beer and wine are very good too". / 10.30 pm; closed Sun; no credit cards; no booking.

East One EC1   £ 23   ④⑤❸
175-179 St John St   566 0088   9–1A
"Stylish" newcomer north of Smithfield – part of the fad for DIY orientals where "wok-jocks" fry up ingredients chosen by the customer; what service there is is terribly slow, however, and our vote goes with those who find the place overpriced and "tiresome". / 11 pm; closed Sat L & Sun D.

Ebury Street Wine Bar SW1   £ 32   ❸④❸
139 Ebury St   730 5447   2–4A
"Cosy" and "fun" Belgravia fixture, which has something of a reputation for "intrepid, imaginative" modern British fare (if at restaurant prices); service "seems to be getting worse" though, and smoke can be a problem. / 10.30 pm.

Eco SW4   £ 20   ❶❸❷
162 Clapham High St   978 1108   10–2D
"Cool", "in yer face" Clapham "hang out" whose "quality pizza" is reckoned by many to be London's best; "if you're not wearing black" it can seem a "bit over-trendy". / 11 pm, Sat & Sun 11.30 pm; Mon-Fri only, no smoking area.

Ed's Easy Diner   £ 16   ④❷❸
12 Moor St, W1   439 1955   4–2A
362 King's Rd, SW3   352 1956   5–3C
16 Hampstead High St, NW3   431 1958   8–1A
"Good places to satisfy hunger fast", these "always-busy", "'50s-style" burger-bars benefit from generally "quick" and "cheerful" service. / Midnight, Fri & Sat 1 am, W1 Sun 11 pm; no Amex; no booking.

Efes Kebab House   £ 19   ❸④❷
1) 80 Great Titchfield St, W1   636 1953   2–1B
2) 175-177 Gt Portland St, W1   436 0600   2–1B
"Full of Turks, which must say something", these characterful institutions north of Oxford Street continue to offer "excellent value", meaty cooking to a wide-ranging clientele; service is "slipping", though – it is sometimes "over-stretched" and "rude"; go to Efes II for the belly-dancing. / 11.30 pm, Fri & Sat 3 am; Efes I closed Sun; no smoking area.

81 SW1 £36 ④④⑤
81 Jermyn St 839 6379 3–3D
Variable (but sometimes interesting) Spanish-influenced fare is served cheerfully, if slowly, in this re-launched St James's dining room; despite their best efforts, a "dull and faceless" hotel ambience is pervasive. / 10.30 pm, Thu-Fri 11 pm, Sat 11.30 pm.

Elena's L'Etoile W1 £38 ❸②②
30 Charlotte St 636 7189 2–1C
A famous septuagenarian greeter now presides over this resurrected nonagenarian Fitzrovia institution; Elena Salvoni's groupies (who are many) find it "excellent" all round, but our vote is with those who think it "dull" or "good, though not good enough for the price". / 11.30 pm; closed Sat L & Sun; smart casual.

Elistano SW3 £25 ❷②❸
25-27 Elystan St 584 5248 5–2C
Chelsea Green Italian yearling, which has emerged as "a nice, family-run restaurant"; its only real problems are that it gets "too noisy", and that, "as it is great value, it is always booked". / 11 pm; closed Sat L & Sun.

Emile's £21 ❸②❸
144 Wandsworth Br Rd, SW6 736 2418 10–1B
96-98 Felsham Rd, SW15 0181-789 3323 10–2B
Horrifically "suburban" the ambience may be, but the food at these Fulham and Putney "neighbourhood spots" is "very good, actually", and the set menus offer solid fare (such as "the best beef wellie in town") at "a very affordable price". / 11 pm; D only; closed Sun; no Amex.

The Engineer NW1 £26 ❸⑤②
65 Gloucester Ave 722 0950 8–3B
"Trendy" Primrose Hill pub-conversion, which risks becoming a victim of its own success; at its best it offers "good value", simple modern British cooking in a "fun", relaxed setting (with a "lovely garden in the back"); but "when it's full", which is most of the time, "they can't cope", leading to food which is "brilliant/dodgy, alternately". / 11 pm; closed Tue L; no Amex.

English Garden SW3 £40 ④❸❸
10 Lincoln St 584 7272 5–2D
Comfortable Chelsea townhouse restaurant, which offers pricey, "OK"-to-good 'modernish' British cooking; the "great private rooms" are some of the nicest in town. / 11.15 pm; no Switch.

English House SW3 £ 40 ⑤❸❸
3 Milner St   584 3002   5–2D
*"What on earth has happened" at this "cosy", if rather
pretty-pretty and very squashed, Chelsea townhouse?;
reports of "dire, outdated" food have become even more
strident, and the prices here leave little margin for error.*
/ 11.15 pm; no Switch.

Enoteca Turi SW15 £ 28 ❷❷④
28 Putney High St   0181-785 4449   10–2B
*"Excellent", "interesting" food and a "better wine list than
most Italians" is building something of a reputation for this
small establishment, just south of Putney Bridge. / 11 pm;
closed Sat L & Sun; smart casual.*

The Enterprise SW3 £ 28 ❸❷❶
Walton St   584 3148   5–2C
*"Eurotrashy but fun", "converted pub" which offers a solid
package of "decent grub" and "friendly" service; especially
given its ultra-chichi location – between Harrods and
Brompton Cross – prices are very "reasonable". / 11 pm;
smart casual; book Mon-Fri L only.*

Epicuria W1 £ 20 ❷④❸
14 Charlotte St   916 1999   2–1C
*Bright new Fitzrovia corner bistro, which offers Greek and
other fare in pleasant, if rather tightly packed, surroundings;
amiable but slow service. / 10 pm; closed Sun; no Amex.*

Esarn Kheaw W12 £ 22 ❷❸④
314 Uxbridge Rd   0181-743 8930   7–1B
*"Great Thai cooking" to "very spicy traditional recipes" puts
this quite smart but rather stilted Shepherd's Bush oriental
on the culinary map. / 11 pm; closed Sat L & Sun L; no Switch.*

L'Escargot W1 £ 35 ❸❷❸
48 Greek St   437 2679   4–2A
*"Why can they never get it quite right here?" – this
"bright, cheerful" Soho fixture still – for a place with such
a famous past – attracts remarkably little interest, and rather
ambivalent support; chef Garry Hollihead left in the summer
of '96 to set up on his own – perhaps the new team can help
the old slug re-discover its magical past. / 11.30 pm; closed Sat L
& Sun.*

L'Escargot Doré W8 £ 32 ❸❷⑤
2 Thackeray St   937 8508   5–1A
*Though it can seem "a bit morgue-like", this comfortable
Gallic basement, a short walk from Kensington High Street,
pleases its regulars with a warm welcome and dependable
cooking; now perhaps if more people went... / 11.30 pm;
closed Sat L & Sun; smart casual.*

The Establishment SW7 £ 34 ⑤❸④
1 Gloucester Rd   589 7969   5–1B
*"Airy", low-lit South Kensington brasserie; we cannot square
our September 1996 visit with some reports of "much
improved" cooking – we thought the modern British menu
risibly pretentious, poorly realised and horrifically overpriced.*
/ 11 pm; closed Mon L.

L'Estaminet WC2 £ 32 ❸❷④
14 Garrick St   379 1432   4–3C
*Comfortable, very middle-aged Covent Garden restaurant
approved by some (ourselves not included) for its "classic"
French food and "friendly service". / 11 pm; closed Sun.*

Euphorium N1 £ 30 ❷❶❷
203 Upper St   704 6909   8–2D
*"Good", "imaginative" food (which is "not too expensive"),
"a fun atmosphere", and "discreet but very efficient service"
have come together to make this tiny, very artsy Islington
"goldfish bowl" yearling a runaway hit; let's hope that the
major expansion, under way as we go to press, doesn't spoil
it all. / 10.30 pm; closed Sat L & Sun; no smoking area.*

Euten's WC2 £ 28 ❸❷④
4-5 Neal's Yd   379 6877   4–2B
*Black British (ie Caribbean-inspired) newcomer, which
occupies a difficult Neal's Yard site (previously the Brixtonian
Backayard, RIP) that is too often "empty"; a shame, as the
unusual, spicy food and the "great staff" make for an
"interesting experience", and one that's "not pricey". / 10 pm;
winter, closed Sun.*

Exxo W1 £ 26 ④④⑤
33-34 Rathbone Pl   255 1120   2–1C
*"Billed as New York-style – I think not!"; reporters seem to
share our underwhelming impression of this "bizarre,
unforgiving" basement newcomer; the bar, which seems to
have become something of a resort for the local media types,
is the best feature. / 11 pm; closed Sat L & Sun.*

Fables SW6 £ 29 ❷❷❸
839 Fulham Rd   371 5445   10–1B
*Wittily tasteful decoration, a celeb' chef, and "solicitous"
Gallic service combined to launch this summer '96 newcomer
as Fulham's top restaurant; executive chef Richard Neat is
soon to move on, and it remains to be seen whether the
"exquisitely presented", "perfectly cooked", modern French
cooking, "at wonderfully palatable prices", will survive
his departure. / 10.45 pm; closed Sun.*

Fakhreldine W1 £ 35 ❸❸❸
85 Piccadilly   493 3424   3–4C
"Glamorous", "spacious", and "impressive" (if rather glitzy)
Mayfair Lebanese, which, on the food front, generally delivers;
most customers come late, thereby missing the "lovely view"
over Green Park. / Midnight; smart casual.

Il Falconiere SW7 £ 26 ❸❶④
84 Old Brompton Rd   589 2401   5–2B
Long-standing South Kensington trattoria, offering a "very
good value set menu" and a "great welcome"; not an exciting
place, perhaps, but comforting for those unwilling to essay the
wilder slopes of metropolitan dining. / 11.45 pm; closed Sun.

La Famiglia SW10 £ 35 ❸④❷
7 Langton St   351 0761   5–3B
Smart but "traditional" World's End Italian, whose many
admirers find a visit here a "very joyous" experience –
and no one would dispute that in summer the garden is
wonderful; "sometimes, you need a sense of humour to cope
with the service", though, and there are those who think the
cooking "average" and "overpriced". / 11.45 pm.

Fashion Café W1 £ 28 ④❷❸
5-6 Coventry St   287 5888   4–4A
Only one of the four supermodel 'backers' of this latest 'been-
there-done-that-got-the-T-shirt' checkpoint could be bothered
to show at its August '96 launch – perhaps wisely, as most of
the Rialto Cinema, on Leicester Square, has yet to be
converted, making this still rather a micro theme-park;
initially at least, food was OK if unsurprisingly pricey, but
service seemed a touch better than you might expect.
/ 11 pm; no Switch; no smoking area.

Fat Boy's W4 £ 21 ❷❸❸
10a Edensor Rd   0181-994 8089   10–1A
"Hectic", "fun" Chiswick Thai which is positively smart by
the standards of caffs which moonlight as restaurants; it
offers very "good value" for "excellent", "tasty" food (though
some complain of "portions inconsistent with the name");
licensed, but you can BYO. / 11 pm; D only; no credit cards.

Fats W9 £ 18 ❸④④
178 Shirland Rd   289 3884   1–2B
"Fresh, imaginative, flavourful food", from a menu mixing
Caribbean, Creole and Cajun styles, is the special attraction
of this "small", cramped Maida Vale café; it's not especially
cheap, however. / 11 pm; no credit cards.

The Fence EC1 £ 30 ④④❸
67-69 Cowcross St   250 3414   9–1A
*"There's not much competition around here", is as ringing an
endorsement as this "reasonable value" Smithfield brasserie
attracts; that there are "too many investment bankers" may
not be a huge surprise, on the fringe of the City, but it does
keep the prices up. / 10 pm; closed Sat & Sun.*

Feng Shang NW1 £ 32 ❸❷❸
Opp 15 Prince Albert Rd   485 8137   8–3B
*Floating on the canal at the tip of Regent's Park, this jolly
Chinese theme-barge is tailor-made for a night out; it's not,
in fact, quite as naff as it sounds, and the cooking is fairly
good, considering. / 11 pm; no Switch.*

La Fenice W11 £ 25 ❸❷❷
148 Holland Pk Ave   221 6090   6–2A
*"Good natured, reliable Italian local", offering an above-
average level of comfort; the food is nothing special, but the
whole package is good value, especially for Holland Park.
/ 10.45 pm; closed Mon & Sat L; no Switch.*

Ffiona's W8 £ 21 ❷❷❷
51 Kensington Ch St   937 4152   5–1A
*Kensington regulars are fulsome this year in their praise for
this "excellent front-room restaurant" – both for Ffiona as
a "delightfully informal and welcoming hostess", and for her
"unfussy, honest home-cooking". / Midnight.*

The Fifth Floor at
Harvey Nichols SW1 £ 43 ④❸❷
Knightsbridge   235 5250   5–1D
*"Buzzing" and "fashionable", this modernistic dining room
has many admirers; however, even they admit to "variable
standards" of cooking, and some punters decry "indifferent
food at inflated prices" from a selection that verges on
"outlandish" – the shorter lunch menu is tipped as a better
bet than dinner; the adjoining pheromone-charged cocktail
bar remains as popular as ever. / 11.30 pm; closed Sun D.*

Fifth Floor at
Harvey Nichols (Café) SW1 £ 29 ❸❷❸
Knightsbridge   823 1839   5–1D
*The stark, glass and metal styling is stronger in the café than
it is in the neighbouring restaurant at this foodie complex;
most are satisfied with the light international cooking,
especially those who avail themselves of the "cheap, fixed
price menu" (evenings only). / 10.30 pm; closed Sun D; eve only.*

Fileric £ 8 ❸❸④
57 Old Brompton Rd, SW7   584 2967   5–2C
12 Queenstown Rd, SW8   720 4844   10–1C
*Unpretentious, very French pâtisseries, ideal for a snack and
a coffee. / 8 pm; no booking.*

Fina Estampa SE1 £ 24 ❷❷❸

150 Tooley St   403 1342   9–4D

A short step from Tower Bridge, this friendly, family-run Southwark Peruvian offers "a highly enjoyable introduction to some very unusual food", albeit from a "limited" menu. / 10 pm; closed Mon & Sun D; no Switch.

La Finca £ 19 ❸④❸

96-98 Pentonville Rd, N1   837 5387   8–3D
185 Kennington Ln, SE11   735 1061   10–1D

A "good range of tapas", "excellent music" and a "lively atmosphere" make these "packed" and "noisy" bars worth knowing about in their respective, thinly-provided areas. / 11.15 pm; Fri & Sat N1 1.30 am, SE11 11.30 pm.

La Finezza SW1 £ 33 ④❸❸

62-64 Lower Sloane St   730 8639   5–2D

Supporters of this swanky Sloane Square trattoria think it a "friendly", "very professional Italian with good atmosphere"; to detractors, it's just rather too expensive, and "living in the past" – perhaps this will all change after the late-1996 refurb. / 11 pm.

First Floor W11 £ 39 ❸④❶

186 Portobello Rd   243 0072   6–1B

The "comfortable", "light and airy", groovily decorated setting continues to win favour for this "relaxed" Notting Hill dining room (above a hip bar); the modern British cooking is thought "innovative" by some, but even supporters say it's "expensive for what you get"; service can be "really bad". / 11.30 pm.

Florians N8 £ 26 ❷❷❸

4 Topsfield Parade   0181-348 8348   1–1C

"You could be in Milan, but you're in Hornsey", rave fans of this "lively" neighbourhood Italian, which serves "tasty, light" food; the happening wine bar at the front is arguably a greater attraction than the restaurant at the back. / 10.45 pm; no Amex.

La Fontana SW1 £ 37 ❸❸❸

101 Pimlico Rd   730 6630   5–2D

Fungiphiles should sniff out this Pimlico trattoria, whose fare is generally "standard", but which makes much use of truffles in season; the place is "overpriced" and "stuck in a time-warp", but service is "friendly", and some think the setting "romantic". / 11.30 pm; no Switch; smart casual.

Food for Thought WC2 £ 9 ❷❸④

31 Neal St   836 0239   4–2C

"Cheap", "tasty" veggie food tempts shoppers and local workers to play sardines in this "very crowded" Covent Garden basement. / 8.45 pm, Sun 3.45 pm; closed Sun D; no credit cards; no smoking; no booking.

Football Football SW1   £ 23   ⑤❸④
57/60 Haymarket   930 9970   2–2C
*A "fan's dream come true", this new theme-circus may be –
anyone with fully-functioning taste buds, however, may well
resent all ninety nightmarish minutes.* / Midnight; smart casual;
no smoking area; to book need 8+.

Footstool SW1   £ 27   ④④❸
St John's, Smith Sq   222 2779   2–4C
*With the benefit of zero local competition, this characterful
crypt continues to churn out "relatively expensive, dinner
party-standard" cooking to MPs and, on musical
evenings, concert-goers.* / L only but buffet concert eves; closed Sat
& Sun except when eve concerts; no smoking area.

Formula Veneta SW10   £ 29   ④❷❷
14 Hollywood Rd   352 7612   5–3B
*"Popular and fun", remains the general view of this stylish
Chelsea side-street Italian; sadly, though, we find more than
a grain of truth in the growing volume of complaints about it
being "overpriced" or "average all round".* / 11.30 pm; closed Sun.

The Foundation SW1   £ 33   ❸❸⑤
Knightsbridge   201 8000   5–1D
*Harvey Nichols's new basement bar-restaurant makes
a "poor relation of the Fifth Floor"; improbably enough, the
problem is style not substance, and, though the modern
British food is often thought "good quality", the "hard edged"
setting is found "cold, dark, and sterile" ("the waterfall just
makes you want to go the gents'").* / 11 pm; closed Sun D;
no smoking area.

The Four Seasons W2   £ 19   ❸④⑤
84 Queensway   229 4320   6–2C
*Even those deriding this Bayswater Chinese as a "grubby sort
of place" recommend it for its "consistently good cooking".*
/ 11.30 pm.

Four Seasons
Four Seasons Hotel W1   £ 54   ❷❸④
Park Ln   499 0888   3–4A
*Since the summer 1996 departure of Monsieur Novelli,
Mr Shaun Whatling is the new home-grown standard-bearer
at this grand Mayfair hotel dining room, which has always
made a virtue of relatively modest pricing; sadly no change
seems to be afoot regarding the ghastly décor.* / 10.30 pm;
no Switch; smart.

Fox & Anchor EC1   £ 11   ❷❷❷
115 Charterhouse St   253 4838   9–1B
*"A great fry-up and a pint" is the early-morning proposition at
this famous Smithfield institution – one of the few pubs with
a license for 7am opening; "the best hangover cure
in London".* / Bkfast & L only; closed Sat L (but open Sat bkfast) & Sun.

The Fox Reformed N16   £22   ❸❷❷
176 Stoke Newington Ch St   254 5975   1–1C
*"Relaxed", civilised Stoke Newington wine bar, whose
regulars play backgammon and join the wine-club;
the cooking is enjoyable, if not memorable, and there is
a small garden at the back.* / 10.30 pm.

Foxtrot Oscar SW3   £27   ④④④
79 Royal Hospital Rd   352 7179   5–3D
*Clubby, dated Chelsea aristos' diner, where no one is too
fussed about the cooking (though the burgers have their
supporters); a new City branch is set to open as we go to
press – more Bollie anyone?* / 11.30 pm.

Francofill SW7   £19   ❷④❸
1 Old Brompton Rd   584 0087   5–2C
*"Fast, hearty, clean and quick", this "attractive" South
Kensington spot serves inexpensive Gallic dishes that are
"great, and not just to fill a gap" (they can make an "ideal
brunch"); some find "the waiters more interested in one
another than in the customers".* / 11 pm; no smoking area.

Frederick's N1   £33   ❸❷❷
106 Camden Pas   359 2888   8–3D
*Popular and characterful Islington institution, which was
given a bold revamp in late 1995; a year on, "the food,
service and atmosphere are all improved", with the charming,
large conservatory setting remaining the star attraction.*
/ 11.30 pm; closed Sun; smart casual; no smoking area.

French House W1   £29   ❷❷❷
49 Dean St   437 2477   4–3A
*The "very cosy" dining room over this famous Soho pub
continues to provide all-round satisfaction; the short menu
mixing modern and traditional British dishes is well done,
and reasonably priced, the service is "attentive", but the
greatest attraction is the special, "Bohemian" atmosphere.*
/ 11.30 pm; closed Sun.

Frocks E9   £24   ❸④❷
95 Lauriston Rd   0181-986 3161   1–2D
*In the culinary desert north of Victoria Park, this atmospheric
English bistro provides a good degree of charm and not at
all bad simple cooking (with the weekend all-day breakfast
a particular hit); speedy service is not the point.* / 11 pm;
closed Sun D; no booking Sun.

Front Page SW3   £19   ❷④❷
35 Old Church St   352 2908   5–3C
*"Good pub food and a nice casual atmosphere" make this
clubby, discreetly located, Chelsea hostelry, for our money,
one of the nicest places of its type in town.* / 10 pm; no Amex;
no booking.

Fuego EC3   £20   ④④❸
1a Pudding Ln   929 3366   9–3C
*Lively Spaniard, near Monument, which is quite atmospheric
by City standards, and open unusually late for the Square
Mile; the tapas are passable (and there is a more
expensive restaurant).* / 10 pm; closed Sat & Sun; smart casual.

Fulham Road SW3   £41   ❸❸④
257-259 Fulham Rd   351 7823   5–2C
*Stylish, if rather bleak, modern British restaurant in Chelsea,
which a number feel has "lost its way" since the departure of
star chef Richard Corrigan a year ago; "utterly stunning"
results are still reported, but quite a lot of disappointments
too.* / 11 pm; D only; smart casual.

The Fulham Tup SW10   £14   ❸❸④
268 Fulham Rd   352 1859   5–3B
*Spacious – perhaps too much so to generate much
atmosphere – new Chelsea-fringe pub-conversion, offering
high quality, simple modern British dishes; "very good
Sunday roasts".* / 10 pm, Sat 9 pm; book Sun only.

Fung Shing WC2   £31   ❶④⑤
15 Lisle St   437 1539   4–3A
*"Consistently high standards" have made this Chinatown's top
gastronomic choice for years now (with seafood the top
attraction); the staff can be a bit "distant", though, and few
reporters seem to have noticed last summer's refurbishment
– perhaps the new rear conservatory will impress
people more.* / 11.30 pm.

Futures   £22   ❸❷❷
2 Exchange Sq, EC2   638 6341   9–1D
8 Botolph Alley, EC3   623 4529   9–3C
*"Veggie – but it doesn't feel veggie", the "bright" and
"modern" Broadgate branch of this micro-chain has become
a popular City lunch place ("when you don't want to
sleep afterwards"); the cheaper, original take-away, near
the Monument – even if "expensive for every day lunch" –
still offers some of the best value no-meat cooking in town.*
/ EC2 9 pm, EC3 L only; closed Sat & Sun; EC3 no credit cards;
EC2 eves no smoking area; EC3 no booking.

Galicia W10   £23   ❸④❸
323 Portobello Rd   0181-969 3539   6–1A
*"Homely" Portobello tapas bar, popular with the local
Hispanic community; you have to regard the "grumpy
waiters" as a challenge.* / 11 pm; closed Mon; smart casual.

Garbo's W1 £29 ④❸❸
42 Crawford St   262 6582   2–1A
*Greta's old London home is now one of the few Scandinavian
restaurants in town (with a menu majoring in fish and
meatballs), and it's an agreeable if cramped place; the
cooking avoids fireworks, but for the hungry, the basement
£8.95 all-you-can-eat buffet lunch is still one of the capital's
top bargains. / 11 pm; closed Sat L & Sun D; no Switch.*

Garlic & Shots W1 £26 ❸❸❸
14 Frith St   734 9505   4–2A
*"Eccentric", seedy Soho 'shooters bar' where all food
(puds included) and drink comes spiked with the pungent
root; if you are in the mood, it's not nearly as disgusting as it
sounds – some even use the word "fun". / Midnight; D only;
no Amex; no booking.*

Gastro SW4 £21 ❸④❸
67 Venn St   627 0222   10–2D
*"Delightfully French cubby-hole in deepest Clapham"
(opposite the Picture House), equally suited to a lazy
breakfast or a post-movie bite; in the evening, you can either
have a snack at the front or dine at the (literal) table d'hôte
at the rear. / Midnight; no credit cards; no smoking area.*

The Gasworks SW6 £26 ④❸❷
87 Waterford Rd   736 3830   5–4A
*'Hammer House of Horror' Parson's Green experience;
the grub is beside the point and it's the decadent (to some
unnerving) atmosphere which really excites; make sure you
can sit in the main room, which is especially popular
for groups. / 11 pm; D only; closed Mon & Sun; no credit cards.*

The Gate W6 £20 ❶❷❸
51 Queen Caroline St   0181-748 6932   7–2C
*This "consistent, friendly" Hammersmith spot is arguably the
"best vegetarian in London" – certainly of the non-ethnic kind
– and serves "wonderful, cheap" and "interesting" grub,
enjoyed by carnivores and veggies alike. / 11 pm; closed Mon L,
Sat L & Sun.*

El Gaucho SW3 £21 ❷④❶
Chelsea Farmers' Mkt, 125 Sydney St   376 8514   5–3C
*A "very vibrant South American atmosphere" and some of
the best value steaks in town (plus "yummy spit-roast
chicken") create quite a following for this "young and fun"
Argentinian shack; the outside tables waft you as close to the
pampas as you will get in SW3. / 11 pm; closed Mon; no credit cards.*

The Gaucho Grill W1 £31 ④④❷
19-25 Swallow St   734 4040   3–3D
*Standards are "uneven" at this Mayfair South American steak
house, whose exotic modern décor is its most reliable
selling point. / Midnight, Sun 10.30 pm.*

LE GAVROCHE W1   **£79**   ❷❷❷
43 Upper Brook St   408 0881   3–2A
*Mayfair's once pre-eminent temple of gastronomy is fighting
its way back into the top rank; our own experience, frankly,
supported the view that this is "not Premier League stuff",
but the volume of 'best meal of the year' nominations puts
beyond doubt that some special cooking is going on here;
perhaps – with its "warm" service and its "dated" but
comfortable atmosphere – the place is benefiting from
a backlash against the arctic spirit of so many of its
Michelin star-hungry competitors.* / 11 pm;
closed Sat & Sun; jacket & tie.

Gay Hussar W1   **£32**   ④❸❸
2 Greek St   437 0973   4–2A
*For some, this aged and "romantic" Soho trooper remains
a "dependable" choice; we agree, though, with those who say
it's "gone terribly downhill" over the last few years, and that
a "heavy" hand is now applied to the once magically light
Hungarian cooking.* / 10.45 pm; closed Sun; smart casual.

Geale's W8   **£18**   ❷④⑤
2 Farmer St   727 7969   6–2B
*"Great fish and chips, but little else" – even so, you may well
have to queue at this famous west London institution, just off
Notting Hill Gate.* / 11 pm; closed Mon & Sun; no booking.

Geeta NW6   **£14**   ❷④⑤
59 Willesden Ln   624 1713   1–1B
*Décor 'nul points', perhaps, but this Kilburn spot remains
a good bet for inexpensive, south Indian veggie cooking.*
/ 10.45 pm, Fri & Sat 11.45 pm; no Switch.

George & Vulture EC3   **£25**   ④❸❷
3 Castle Ct   626 9710   9–3C
*"Something out of Charles Dickens", this "classic" City chop-
house is "one of a kind"; the cooking is a little more run-of-
the-mill.* / L only; closed Sat & Sun; no Switch; jacket & tie; limited booking.

Ghillies SW6   **£25**   ❸❸❸
271 New King's Rd   371 0434   10–1B
*"Simple and friendly" Parson's Green fish restaurant offering
an unpretentious and reliable environment "ideal for last
minute eating".* / 11.30 pm; closed Sun.

La Giara SW3   **£31**   ❸❷④
6 Yeoman's Rw   591 0210   5–2C
*Small Sicilian yearling, just off Knightsbridge; a "brave attempt
worthy of more support", to some – "too expensive for what
you get", for others.* / 11.30 pm.

Gilbert's SW7 £ 33 ❸❷❸
2 Exhibition Rd   589 8947   5–2C
An "intimate" atmosphere, "helpful, friendly service",
"reliable" modern British cooking, and an "excellent wine list"
all recommend this small South Kensington spot; if there is
a criticism, it is of a general absence of 'fireworks'. / 10 pm;
closed Sat L & Sun.

Gladwins EC3 £ 45 ❸❷❸
Minster Ct, Mark Ln   444 0004   9–3D
"Above-average 'City' food" makes this "bright, colourful
basement" a "welcome addition" to the lunching scene –
"not cheap, but a ray of light"; this is a place "for business",
so it's no surprise that it's "overpriced" and "rather clinical".
/ L only; closed Sat & Sun.

Glaisters £ 22 ④④❸
4 Hollywood Rd, SW10   352 0352   5–3B
8-10 Northcote Rd, SW11   924 6699   10–2C
"There's a good atmosphere" at these attractively decorated
Chelsea and Clapham spots, but too many reporters find
"disappointing" results from the "uninspiring menu", and
service can sometimes be "slow" or "curt". / 11.30 pm.

Golden Dragon W1 £ 21 ❷❸④
28-29 Gerrard St   734 2763   4–3A
Highly praised Chinatown yearling which is "excellent for
dim-sum"; otherwise, for best results, "try the menu written
only in Chinese – even if you don't understand it". / 11.30 pm.

Good Earth SW3 £ 28 ❷❷❸
233 Brompton Rd   584 3658   5–2C
"Delicious", "pricey but worth it" cooking distinguishes this
"friendly" but professional Chinese; its all-round fair value
puts many other ghastly Knightsbridge rip-off joints to shame.
/ 11 pm.

Gopal's of Soho W1 £ 24 ❸④④
12 Bateman St   434 1621   4–2A
As ever, though some vaunt this Soho Indian as a top choice,
many feel that there's nothing that special about it to justify
its premium prices. / 11.15 pm; smart casual; no smoking area.

Gordon's Wine Bar WC2 £ 13 ❸④❷
47 Villiers St   930 1408   4–4D
"No good since they cleaned it up", complains one die-hard
fan of this notoriously decrepit wine bar, by Embankment
tube; most will never notice the change, however, and for
a cheap central rendezvous this hugely atmospheric cellar is
tough to beat; it can get very smoky, but in summer there is
a nice, quiet area outside. / 9.30 pm; closed Sat & Sun; no Amex;
no booking.

Le Gothique SW18   £30   ④④❷
The Royal Victoria Patriotic Bldg, Fitzhugh Gr, Trinity Rd
0181-870 6567   10–2C
*The name speaks the truth about the amazingly overblown
Victorian building in which this bourgeois Wandsworth Gaul is
located; the charming cloister in particular is a "great setting
for al fresco eating", but for too many, the place is "let down"
by poor standards.* / 10.30 pm; closed Sat L & Sun; smart casual.

Gourmet Pizza Company   £19   ❸④❸
7-8 Swallow St, W1   734 5182   3–3C
Gabriels Whf, Upper Ground, SE1   928 3188   9–3A
18 Mackenzie Walk, E14   345 9192   1–3D
*"Consistent", "child-friendly" chain, where "some of the
pizzas are plain daft, but others are worthwhile variations
on old themes"; the SE1 branch "has the bonus of
a Thames view".* / 10.45 pm; W1 & E14 no smoking area;
need 8+ to book.

Gow's EC2   £35   ❸❸④
81/82 Old Broad St   920 9645   9–2C
*"Reliable but very overpriced" fish parlour; a "great lunchtime
venue for City executives", even if "tables are too close
together".* / L only; closed Sat & Sun; smart casual.

The Grafton SW4   £22   ❷❸❸
45 Old Town   627 1048   10–2D
*Useful, all-day Clapham Town establishment, serving above-
average Gallic bistro fare in unpretentious surroundings;
in the evenings, there is the option of the smarter
restaurant upstairs (£28).* / 11.30 pm; closed Mon;
no smoking area.

Granita N1   £29   ❷❸④
127 Upper St   226 3222   8–2D
*"Cool" haunt of Islington intellectuals and apparatchiks,
lauded for its "consistently imaginative", "first rate" modern
British cooking – though "small portions" are a perennial
complaint; the "stark" décor inspires helpful advice such as
"bring your own atmosphere".* / 10.30 pm; closed Mon & Tue L;
no Amex & no Switch.

Great Nepalese NW1   £21   ❷❸④
48 Eversholt St   388 6737   8–3C
*Cognoscenti know not to be put off by the plain façade and
dated interior of this friendly Nepalese, facing the charming
eastern wall of Euston Station; there are standard Indian
dishes, but the specials are best.* / 11.30 pm.

Greek Valley NW8   £19   ❷❸❸
130 Boundary Rd   624 3217   8–3A
*Cheerful St John's Wood taverna with a formidable reputation
for value, in particular the mixed meze; not all can see it,
though, with the odd report saying "OK – no more".* / Midnight;
D only; closed Sun; no Amex.

The Green Olive W9 £ 30 ❸❸❸
5 Warwick Pl   289 2469   8–4A
Behind Little Venice's leafy Clifton Nurseries, this rather superior local (from the same seed-tray as the nearby Red Pepper) offers "vibrant, modern Provençal" cooking in "relaxed" comfort (the "lovely" upstairs, though, being preferable to the "dull" basement); it's a "good all-round package", but they could do with "shaving 15% off the prices", particularly those of the "risible" wine list.
/ 10.45 pm; D only Mon-Fri, Sat & Sun open L & D.

Green's SW1 £ 45 ④❸④
36 Duke St   930 4566   3–3D
"Clubby", "expensive" St James's bastion, much favoured by "stuffy pinstripes"; standards continue to drift, however – too many dishes are found "a trifle dull", and the ambience is not what it was. / 11 pm; closed Sun D, but May-Sep closed Sun; smart casual.

Greenhouse W1 £ 41 ❷❷❸
27a Hays Mews   499 3331   3–3B
As TV chef Gary Rhodes had in recent times had a number of commitments away from his Mayfair stove, there is reason to hope that the "well interpreted British food" – particularly the famous "school puddings" – will survive his now-complete departure; the atmosphere here is cosy and romantic to some, a little lacking to others. / 11 pm; closed Sat L; smart casual.

Grenadier SW1 £ 5 ⑤❷❶
18 Wilton Rw   235 3074   2–3A
Cutesy Belgravia pub that "takes you back 200 years" – and so makes something of an impression on our transatlantic cousins; locals prefer a sausage and a Bloody Mary (for both of which the place is famous) in the bar to the pricey sit-down fare. / 10 pm; no Switch.

Gresslin's NW3 £ 29 ❷❷❸
13 Heath St   794 8386   8–2A
Already arguably the best place in Hampstead, this "light, airy and informal", modern British newcomer offers the cooking of "an ex-Mosimann chef at run-of-the-mill prices"; it's conveniently located near the tube, and the only real drawback is its surprisingly "ageing clientele". / 10.45 pm; closed Sun D & Mon L; no Amex; no smoking area.

Grill St Quentin SW3 £ 31 ❸❸④
3 Yeoman's Rw   581 8377   5–2C
"Reliable, standard", Gallic fare and "charming" service make this "spacious" Knightsbridge eatery a "very good all-rounder" for some; others, like us, are rather put off by the "cavernous underground location". / 11.30 pm; smart casual.

Grumbles SW1 £27 ❸❸❸
35 Churton St   834 0149   2–4B
We find it amazing the way this rather "dingy" ("nice olde worlde") English bistro in Pimlico retains its grip on some reporters' affections – "the cooking can be variable" and "extras bump up the bill". / 11.45 pm.

The Guinea W1 £42 ❸④④
30 Bruton Pl   499 1210   3–2B
Exuding a certain middle-aged charm, this old-fashioned dining room (behind a quiet Mayfair pub) is one of the better steak-houses in town; a good place to take visitors, though it is no bargain. / 11 pm; closed Sat L & Sun.

Gung-Ho NW6 £25 ❸❷❸
330-332 West End Ln   794 1444   1–1B
"The best Chinese in north west London", just off the Finchley Road, is "very popular" – local reporters unanimously extol its "lively" and "slightly 'different'" atmosphere and its reliable cooking. / 11 pm.

Häagen-Dazs £6 ❸④❸
14 Leicester Sq, WC2   287 9577   4–3B
Unit 6, Covent Gdn, WC2   240 0436   4–3D
228-230 Fulham Rd, SW10   351 7706   5–3B
83 Gloucester Rd, SW7   373 9988   5–2B
88 Queensway, W2   229 0668   6–1C
They may be "overpriced", but many reporters lack the will-power necessary to resist these bright, modern ice-cream parlours. / 11 pm, Leic Sq & NW3 later weekends; no credit cards at many branches; all but SW10 no smoking; no booking.

Haandi NW1 £16 ❸❸④
161 Drummond St   383 4557   8–4C
The "very cheap buffet" at lunchtime remains this 'Little India' establishment's top attraction; at other times, though you may find "good, unpretentious food", some note a degree of "complacency". / 11.30 pm, Sat & Sun midnight; closed Sat L; no Switch.

Halcyon Hotel W11 £46 ❶❷❷
129 Holland Pk Ave   221 5411   6–2B
This "informal, chic" Holland Park "hideaway" – popular with stars of the silver screen who 'want to be alone' – rarely disappoints, with "splendid", "accurate" modern British cooking, "attentive" service and an "intimacy" that recommends it for romance. / 10.30 pm, Fri & Sat 11 pm; closed Sat L; smart casual.

Halepi W2 £25 ❸❷④
18 Leinster Ter   262 1070   6–2C
Kitsch, dated Bayswater taverna where the slightly "overpriced" cooking varies from "very good to fair". / 12.30 am; no Switch.

The Halkin SW1 £53 ④④❸
5 Halkin St   333 1234   2–3A
*This chic, marbled hotel dining room, a stone's throw from
Belgrave Square, continues to provoke rather mixed reactions
– even those who approve the Italian fare can find it "VERY
expensive", and though the setting is "stylish" to some, others
say it's "stark" and somewhat "corporate".* / 11 pm; closed Sat L
& Sun L; smart casual.

Hamine W1 £14 ❸④④
84 Brewer St   439 0785   3–2D
*"Open very late", this well worn Soho noodle bar –
encouragingly full of Nipponese customers – offers simple
Japanese cooking "at very reasonable prices".* / 2.30 am, Sat
1.30 am, Sun midnight; no credit cards; no smoking area; no booking.

Hanover Square W1 £28 ❸❸④
25 Hanover Sq   408 0935   3–2C
*Mayfair's sibling to Theatreland's venerable Cork & Bottle is
not as long established nor yet as well known; it's "trying
hard", however, and – having the benefit of more spacious,
if less characterful, accommodation – already developing
a following for its "good selection of food and wine".* / 10.45 pm;
closed Sat & Sun; smart casual; no smoking area.

Harbour City W1 £25 ❷④⑤
46 Gerrard St   439 7859   4–3B
*"For the hard-core lover of Chinese food", this Chinatown
fixture is tipped by many to offer the "best dim-sum" in
town – the "great selection" being a particular strength; the
evening menu is much less of an attraction.* / 11.15 pm, Fri & Sat
11.45 pm.

Hard Rock Café W1 £25 ❸④❸
150 Old Park Ln   629 0382   3–4B
*If size of queue is anything to go by, this "dated" superstar
holds its own with the newer mega theme-diners, and many
still tip the burgers here as the capital's best; if you don't like
crushingly loud 'background' music, don't go.* / 12.30 am, Fri & Sat
1 am; no smoking area.

Hardy's W1 £26 ❸❸❷
53 Dorset St   935 5929   2–1A
*Though primarily a watering hole, this atmospheric wine bar,
just off Baker Street, serves some "pretty good" food
alongside the "first class" vino.* / 10.30 pm; closed Sat & Sun.

The Havelock Tavern W14 £19 ❸④❸
57 Masbro Rd   603 5374   7–1C
*Olympia boozer, understatedly revamped to provide an
airy and relaxed home-from-home for the local young
professionals; the blackboard menu offers solid – we thought
rather unexciting – modern British fare.* / 10 pm, Sun 9.30 pm;
no credit cards.

Haweli SW13 £ 20 ❷❸④
7 White Hart Ln   0181-876 4441   10–1A
"Reliably good" cooking distinguishes this superior, if slightly oppressively decorated, Barnes curry house. / Midnight.

The Heights W1 £ 44 ❷❶④
St George's Hotel, Langham Place   636 1939   2–1B
Many recommending this fifteenth floor dining room caution that it is often "disappointingly empty", despite being practically the only venue in town with a "fabulous view" over the inner core of central London; "if they dropped the prices this could be an excellent place", as the "superb", modern British cooking gets a strong thumbs-up. / 10 pm; closed Sat L & Sun; smart casual.

Henry J Beans SW3 £ 19 ④④❸
195 King's Rd   352 9255   5–3C
This long-serving Chelsea theme-diner is not without its fans, especially for the burgers, although the surprisingly large rear garden remains its only indisputable attraction. / 10.30 pm; no booking.

Hilaire SW7 £ 45 ❸❷❸
68 Old Brompton Rd   584 8993   5–2B
"Traditional" South Kensington restaurant offering "reliable" modern French cooking; some find the setting a touch "dull", and a regular warns that it's "vital to sit on the ground floor, not downstairs". / 11.30 pm; closed Sat L & Sun.

Hodgson's WC2 £ 29 ④❸❸
115 Chancery Ln   242 2836   2–2D
"Cool and quiet", and with a most unusual pillared setting, this attractive legal-land restaurant makes a reasonable choice in a thin area, though the cooking can be rather "erratic"; the basement wine bar is a useful informal rendezvous. / 10.30 pm; closed Sat & Sun.

Hollihead W1 £ 27
76 Wigmore St   224 2992   3–1A
An opening scheduled for around the launch-date of this book – Michelin-starred chef Garry Hollihead (who recently quit L'Escargot) seems likely to draw attention to this graveyard site near St Christopher's Place, lately occupied by Baboon (RIP). / 11.15 pm; closed Sun.

Hope & Sir Loin EC1 £ 30 ❷❸❷
94 Cowcross St   253 8525   9–1B
The "amazing offal-laden mixed grills" at this characterful pub dining room (overlooking Smithfield Market) would have done Gargantua proud – "who says size doesn't matter?" / L only; closed Sat & Sun; smart casual.

Hothouse Bar & Grill E1 £ 29 ❸❸❷
78/80 Wapping Ln   488 4797   1–3D
*Like much of the rest of Docklands, this converted Wapping
warehouse offers a striking, rather 'different' space which few
people from outside the area seem to make the effort to
visit; a pity, as the affordable, modern British cooking and
"relaxed" ambience usually find favour. / 11 pm; closed Sat L
& Sun D.*

Hoults SW17 £ 26 ④④❷
20 Bellevue Rd   0181-767 1858   10–2C
*With its "great location", this wine bar overlooking
Wandsworth Common provides a lively hang-out and benefits
from a particularly good atmosphere; the basic English fare is
variable, though, and "far too expensive". / 10.45 pm;
no smoking area.*

House on Rosslyn Hill NW3 £ 29 ④④❷
34a Rosslyn Hl   435 8037   8–2A
*The "food's a bit pricey for what it is" ("though vegetarian
options are quite good") at this "buzzy" and atmospheric
"brasserie hang-out, perennially popular with the Hampstead
younger set". / Midnight; no Amex.*

Hujo's W1 £ 24 ❸⑤❸
11 Berwick St   734 5144   3–2D
*Sleezily located Soho bistro; its principal merit is that it is
cheap, but the "simple, rustic Mediterranean dishes" are
better than you might expect and the twentysomething crowd
provides a good buzz; over-stretched staff, however, can be
brusque to the point of rudeness. / Midnight; closed Sun.*

Hyde Park Hotel
Park Room SW1 £ 17 ❸❷❷
Knightsbridge   235 2000   2–3A
*Recommended for those in search of a "proper English
breakfast", this "beautiful" dining room, overlooking Hyde
Park, provides a relaxing start to the day; (as a place for
dinner, it attracts little comment). / 11 pm; eve, jacket & tie.*

I Thai W2 £ 80
31-35 Craven Hill Gdns   298 9000   6–2C
*Anouska Hempel – of Blakes fame – is scheduled finally to
open her new hotel, 'The Hempel', at about the time this
book hits the streets; some credit her South Kensington
establishment as the start of the 'townhouse hotel'
phenomenon world-wide and if this Bayswater outpost can
half match its success, this should become quite a place;
a spectacular Italian/Thai restaurant is promised. / 11.30 pm.*

Ikeda W1   £ 50   ❸❷④

30 Brook St   629 2730   3–2B
*A little "overpriced", possibly, but this Mayfair Japanese serves
some good sushi; a visit at lunch rather than dinner
aids economy. / 10.30 pm, Sat 10 pm; closed Sat L & Sun; no Switch;
smart casual.*

Ikkyu   £ 25   ❶❸❷

67 Tottenham Ct Rd, W1   636 9280   2–1C
7 Newport Pl, WC2   439 3554   4–3B
*The many fans hail "the most interesting Japanese food in
London, and some of the cheapest" at Ikkyu's original,
obscure Fitzrovia basement (to which the ratings relate); the
WC2 sibling, though a perfectly useful place, "lacks the menu
and atmosphere of the W1 branch". / 10.30 pm, WC2 Fri & Sat
11.30 pm; W1, closed Sat & Sun L; W1 no Switch, WC2 no Amex;
WC2 no smoking area.*

The Imperial Arms SW6   £ 22   ❶④④

577 King's Rd   736 9179   5–4A
*The "best Guinness and oysters in town", claim admirers of
this Fulham hostelry; our vote is with the reporter who finds
"great food, but a dreadful pub", surprisingly lacking
in atmosphere. / 11 pm.*

Imperial City EC3   £ 27   ❷❷❸

Cornhill   626 3437   9–2C
*"Always consistent and reliable" Chinese, intriguingly located
in a stylish cellar beneath the Royal Exchange; though it's
a very popular City lunching venue, some scent the first hints
of complacency setting in. / 8.30 pm; closed Sat & Sun; smart casual.*

Inaho W2   £ 24   ❶❷④

4 Hereford Rd   221 8495   6–1B
*"Amazing sushi" and other "excellent, good value" cooking
win strong support for this "cramped but pleasant" Bayswater
Japanese; the "polite and attentive" service also wins high
praise, but it "can be slow". / 11 pm; closed Sat L & Sun; no Amex
& no Switch.*

L'Incontro SW1   £ 52   ④⑤⑤

87 Pimlico Rd   730 6327   5–2D
*"Chic", very "'80s" Pimlico Italian, whose supporters admit
that it is "enjoyable – so long as you are not the one paying";
for far too many, though, the experience is "a real let down"
– the food is "no great shakes" (but "unbelievably
expensive"), and service is "patronising", "supercilious",
and "couldn't-care-less". / 11.30 pm; closed Sat L & Sun L;
smart casual.*

India Club WC2   £15   ②③④
143 Strand   836 0650   2–2D
"Décor as plain as you can get" only adds to the experience
at this quirky dining room, on the first floor of the Aldwych's
Strand Continental Hotel; some find it "variable", but most
praise "simple dishes, very well prepared"; BYO (or bring over
a pint from the hotel bar). / 10 pm, Sun 8 pm; no credit cards; need 6
to book.

Indian Ocean SW17   £19   ②②④
216 Trinity Rd   0181-672 7740   10–2C
Smart Wandsworth curry house, which dispenses much
above-average fare – "you can taste the individual ingredients
in the sauces". / 11.30 pm; no Switch.

Inmala EC2   £29   ③④④
9 Liverpool Arc   623 5750   9–2D
"Not too expensive for the City", this tacky Malaysian, just by
Liverpool Street station, offers "reliable but unspectacular"
cooking. / 9.30 pm; closed Sat & Sun.

Interlude de Chavot W1   £53   ②③③
5 Charlotte St   637 0222   2–1C
Dependable Gallic cuisine "exactly as one might hope for"
is the particular strength of this "intimate" Fitzrovia yearling,
also praised for its "friendly, discreet" staff; given the evidently
high level of aspiration, however, there are those who detect
"something missing" – perhaps the overall package is just
too "understated". / 11 pm; closed Sat L & Sun.

Italian Kitchen WC1   £26   ③③④
43 New Oxford St   836 1011   2–1C
Our repeated experience of this aptly named spot, near the
British Museum, is of "freshly cooked, authentic and original
Italian food" at reasonable prices; one cannot ignore the fact,
though, that there are those who have emerged thoroughly
underwhelmed. / 11 pm.

THE IVY WC2   £41   ②②①
1 West St   836 4751   4–3B
"The formula's just perfect" – people positively glow about
this restored Theatreland classic; no one pretends that the
"good but not fantastic" British cooking is the key to its
attraction, but – thanks to its "electrifying", "star-studded"
atmosphere and staff who remain "attentive, even when
busy" – it's now snatched the crown as reporters'
No 1 favourite. / Midnight.

Iznik N5   £19   ②③②
19 Highbury Pk   354 5697   8–2D
Highbury Turk, whose good, "low cost" cooking and cheerful,
unusual and attractive décor make it a very superior local.
/ 11 pm; no credit cards.

Jade Garden W1 £ 23 ❸❸❸

15 Wardour St 437 5065 4–3A

*Unusually dependable and "good value" Chinatown spot,
offering "well cooked food" in a comfortable if
standard setting. / 11.30 pm; smart casual.*

The Jam SW3 £ 23 ④❸❸

289a King's Rd 352 8827 5–3C

*Known for its odd but cosy double-decker booths, this Chelsea
Italian serves somewhat variable pizza and pasta – it has yet
to begin to match its Clapham cousin, Buona Sera. / 1 am;
closed Sun; no Amex.*

James R SW6 £ 25 ❸④④

175 New King's Rd 731 6404 10–1B

*"Potentially good" Parson's Green "neighbourhood restaurant"
– a year or so on, the potential does not, however, appear to
have been realised. / 11 pm; closed Sun D; no smoking area.*

Japanese Canteen EC1 £ 19 ④④④

394 St John St 833 3222 8–3D

*Though some like this "fun", "affordable" Japanese, with its
"stripped down" décor, others feel it serves "crummy,
unimaginative food" in surroundings for which the term "staff
canteen" would be more apt. / 11 pm; no credit cards;
no smoking area; no booking.*

Jason's W9 £ 30 ❶❷❸

Opposite 60 Blomfield Rd 286 6752 8–4A

*"Heaven for fish-lovers" – Sylvain Ho Wing Cheong is widely
praised for his "unusual", "fresh and delicious" dishes,
including a number of Mauritian specialities; the "friendly"
welcome is also appreciated, and helps to make the
atmosphere at this "unpretentious, café-like" venue, whose
outside tables, by the canal in Little Venice, are a particular
summer attraction. / 10.30 pm; closed Sun D.*

Jigsaw W12 £ 15 ❸❸❸

74 Askew Rd 0181-743 8002 7–1B

*"Cheap and cheerful" Shepherd's Bush bistro; its prix-fixe,
three course menu provides "not great food, but
excellent value". / 11 pm; closed Mon, D only Tue-Sat, open all day Sun.*

Jim Thompson's SW6 £ 24 ④⑤❷

617 King's Rd 731 0999 5–4A

*The "very fashionable, animated ambience" draws bar-flies
and diners thick and fast around this "buzzy", "fun" bar-
restaurant, in a converted Fulham pub; comments on the pan-
Eastern cooking are mixed, and "appalling service" is
a common complaint. / 11 pm.*

Jimmy Beez W10 £29 ❷④❷
303 Portobello Rd   0181-964 9100   6–1A
*"Laid back, mellow and chilled" joint which is especially
popular (above all at the outside tables) as a brunch mecca
for W10 groovers; the eclectic cooking is "creatively
put together". / 11 pm.*

Jin W1 £24 ❷❷④
16 Bateman St   734 0908   4–2A
*Soho Korean offering a worthy but dull combination of quality
cooking and hospitable service in smart but slightly
stilted surroundings. / 11 pm; closed Sun; no Switch.*

Jin Kichi NW3 £21 ❷❷④
73 Heath St   794 6158   8–1A
*"Local, wacky, jolly" Hampstead Japanese, serving "excellent
value" food (particularly the yakitori – Nipponese kebabs);
it's "a little cramped" and basic, though. / 11.30 pm; Mon, Wed,
Thu & Fri D only, open L & D Sat & Sun.*

Joe Allen WC2 £28 ④④❷
13 Exeter St   836 0651   4–3D
*Subterranean Theatreland stalwart, which continues to
attract complaints that it is "outmoded", and that its
"consistent American food" is "unimaginative" – no one
doubts, though, that it's "still good for a late bite".
/ 12.45 am; no smoking area.*

Joe's Brasserie SW6 £27 ❸❸❸
130 Wandsworth Br Rd   731 7835   10–1B
*They've considerably bucked up the cooking at this packed
and raucous Fulham hang-out, which now offers "tasty,
adventurous" modern British food alongside more standard
brasserie fare. / 10.45 pm.*

Joe's Café SW3 £37 ❸❸❸
126 Draycott Ave   225 2217   5–2C
*Just off ultra-fashionable Brompton Cross, this predictably
"stylish", predictably "pricey" restaurant serves "safe but
unexciting" modern British food to a predictably
"glamorous" clientele. / 11 pm; closed Sun D; no Switch.*

Julie's W11 £39 ④❸❶
135 Portland Rd   229 8331   6–2A
*This "magical", subterranean Holland Park labyrinth has –
since the '70s – been the ultimate romantic choice for many;
"ugh!" is not an uncommon reaction to the dated culinary
standards however – though prices have certainly moved with
the times – and service can be "slow". / 11.15 pm; closed Sat L;
no Switch.*

Julie's Bar W11 £28 ④④❶

137 Portland Rd 727 7985 6–2A

"The bill comes as a shock every time" at this long-established Holland Park bar, which offers rather a dated international menu, indifferently realised; the "delightful time-warp" of "drawing rooms full of hidden corners and fireplaces" remains upstairs, but the ground floor has just had a bold refit. / 10.45 pm; no Switch.

Kalamaras, Mega W2 £23 ❸❸❸

76-78 Inverness Mews 727 9122 6–2C

"A regular for years" notes a "decided lowering in standards" under the new ownership of this aged taverna (hidden away in a mews off Queensway), which was for a long time west London's best Greek; "OK, but not exceptional" cooking now seems the norm, but a "relaxing atmosphere remains". / Midnight; closed Sat L & Sun; no Switch; smart casual.

Kalamaras, Micro W2 £17 ❸❸④

66 Inverness Mews 727 5082 6–2C

This rather tatty, "tiny" restaurant – the cheaper, BYO (wine only) sibling of Mega – retains a "good buzz"; as at the grander establishment, however, ratings suggest that standards are not as they once were. / 11 pm; D only; closed Sun; no credit cards.

Karahi NW6 £17 ❷❸④

212 West End Ln 431 3074 1–1B

"Unusual flavours" justify a detour to this West Hampstead Afro-Indian, housed in an unpretentious basement; "not your standard curry", at all. / 11.30 pm; D only.

Kartouche SW10 £34 ④④❷

329-331 Fulham Rd 823 3515 5–3B

"Very loud and buzzy", modern British spot, prominently situated in the heart of Chelsea's younger-scene trendsville; the cooking divides opinion – its many fans say it offers "the best grazing food in town", but the rating is held back by those who find the dishes "either all off, or disappointing"; a sibling, Kassoulet, is due to open at 127 Ledbury Road W11 (tel 792 9191) in October 1996. / Midnight; no Amex; book L only.

Kaspia W1 £44 ❷❸④

18-18a Bruton Pl 493 2612 3–2B

"Good food – and I don't even like caviar", says a representative report of this discreet Mayfair mews dining room, whose menu concentrates almost solely on fish; "smart but dull" is the general view of the décor, however, and it's "expensive (but caviar is, isn't it?)". / 11.30 pm; closed Sun; no Switch; smart casual.

Kastoori SW17 £14 **①①③**
188 Upper Tooting Rd   0181-767 7027   10–2C
"Exceptionally good value, and terrifically tasty into the
bargain" – the "fabulous" cooking at this Indian/East African
vegetarian justifies the journey even to distant Tooting;
it's a family-run place, and service is "pleasant, eager and
very knowledgeable". / 10.30 pm; closed Mon & Tue L; no Amex
& no Switch.

Kavanagh's N1 £27 **③③④**
26 Penton St   833 1380   8–3D
Very "pleasant", if "cramped" and "café-like", Islingtonian
whose "well-presented", carefully prepared modern British
cooking make it a useful neighbourhood spot; reporters note
"charming" but scatty service. / 10.30 pm; closed Mon; no Amex.

Ken Lo's Memories SW1 £38 **②②④**
67-69 Ebury St   730 7734   2–4B
Well established, "smart" Victoria Chinese whose admirers
find it "worth every penny" for sound cooking in civilised
comfort; others think the whole experience a little "dull".
/ 10.15 pm; closed Sun L; no Switch; smart casual.

KENSINGTON PLACE W8 £36 **③③②**
201-205 Kensington Ch St   727 3184   6–2B
Many fans vociferously hail the "great buzz" and
"interesting food" at this large, striking and "noisy" "fishbowl",
near Notting Hill Gate, which almost a decade ago helped
revolutionise the modern British dining experience;
"disimproved service" and sometimes "average" cooking now
contribute to an undercurrent of dissatisfaction, but "bags of
atmosphere" generally save the day. / 11.45 pm, Sun 10.15 pm.

Kettners W1 £20 **⑤⑤③**
29 Romilly St   437 6437   4–2A
It's a shame that this once-excellent central rendezvous
now seems to rely for custom solely on the attractions of its
"fantastic", rambling Edwardian building in the heart of Soho,
whose "great atmosphere" (especially in the champagne bar)
keeps the place buzzing; realisation of the pizza-and-more
menu is "mediocre", and service "unimpressive". / Midnight;
smart casual; no booking.

Khan's W2 £13 **③⑤②**
13-15 Westbourne Gr   727 5420   6–1C
Reassuringly, "the waiters are as rude as ever" at this "hectic,
packed but fun" Bayswater Indian; the sheer scale of the
place makes it "ideal to take kids and adults on a treat", but
the fact that it offers "good food at an extremely reasonable
price" has much to do with its continuing appeal. / 11.45 pm.

Khan's of Kensington SW7 £20 ❷❶❷
3 Harrington Rd   581 2900   5–2B
"Nothing beats this place", say advocates of the "fresh-tasting" cooking at this "nicely decorated" (if oddly proportioned) Indian restaurant, just by South Ken station; our recent visit found an impressive display of eye-avoidance-as-an-art-form, but reporters' experiences seem to have been quite the opposite. / 11.30 pm.

Khun Akorn SW3 £35 ④⑤④
136 Brompton Rd   225 2688   5–1C
This swanky oriental near Harrods pleases some ("more pricey than usual Thai, but execution is in a different league") and disappoints others ("average to poor food"); the service is even more variable. / 10.30 pm.

Khyber Pass SW7 £19 ❷❸④
21 Bute St   589 7311   5–2B
This long-standing South Ken Indian may look "slightly dingy", but it is frequented by a well-heeled local crowd drawn by superior cuzzas at reasonable prices. / 11.30 pm; no Switch.

King's Road Café SW3 £17 ❸❸❸
206 King's Rd   351 1211   5–3C
"A cheap, cheerful place to hang out with friends for lunch", the Mediterranean café on the first floor of Chelsea's Habitat shop offers "efficient service, good food (with better desserts) and OK atmosphere"; "you have to share tables". / open shop hours only, with L till 3 pm; no credit cards; no smoking area.

Kolossi Grill EC1 £16 ❷❷❸
56-60 Roseberry Ave   278 5758   8–4D
Wonderfully unimproved '50s taverna, world-famous in Clerkenwell for the value of its set lunches. / 11 pm; closed Sat L & Sun; no Switch.

Krungtap SW10 £14 ❸❸❸
227 Old Brompton Rd   259 2314   5–2A
"Cheap, good Thai food" makes this "tatty", "steamy" and "squashed" Earl's Court spot a "great little standby". / 10.30 pm; D only; no Amex.

Kundan SW1 £23 ❸❸④
3 Horseferry Rd   834 3211   2–4C
The cooking is "different from usual Indian" – it's Pakistani, for a start – at this large, subterranean spot in Westminster, whose extraordinary, deeply '70s décor is very 'different' indeed. / 10.30 pm; closed Sun.

The Ladbroke Arms W11 £20 ❷❸❷
54 Ladbroke Rd   727 6648   6–2B
"Excellent" pub-grub makes it often "difficult to get a seat" at this quietly located Notting Hill Gate local, whose Anglo-French menu "changes daily"; "tables outside are a bonus". / 9.45 pm; no Amex & no Switch; no booking.

Lahore Kebab House E1   £ 14   ❶④④
2 Umberston St   488 2551   1–2D
*"Rough", "ready", "basic" and "scruffy", this ultra-no-frills
Indian East Ender may be, but its "superb cheap food"
ensures a sizeable fan-club; BYO.* / Midnight; no credit cards.

The Lancers W1   £ 28   ❷❸④
34 Brook St   629 6555   3–2B
*You won't find Indian cooking much better than at this
comfortable, if expensive, Mayfair basement newcomer,
near Claridges; curiously, an 'international' menu is also
available, but – given the quality of the subcontinental fare on
offer – there seems little reason to try it.* / Midnight; closed Sun;
smart casual; no smoking area.

The Lanesborough W1   £ 50   ⑤❸❷
Hyde Pk Corner   259 5599   2–3A
*The "very expensive" modern British cooking served in
the "fabulous Brighton Pavilion-style dining room" of this
ultra-swanky Knightsbridge hotel continues to wallow in
mediocrity – "plain awful", says one who applauds the
setting itself; some claim the place offers "the best afternoon
tea experience", however, and an even better bet is a drink
in the splendidly OTT Library Bar.* / Midnight; no Switch;
dinner, jacket & tie.

Langan's Bistro W1   £ 29   ④❷④
26 Devonshire St   935 4531   2–1A
*"Quaint", parasol-lined Anglo-French standby in Marylebone;
"comfortable", "but not special".* / 11.30 pm; closed Sat L & Sun;
no Switch.

Langan's Brasserie W1   £ 36   ④❸❷
Stratton St   493 6437   3–3C
*"Poor quality food" continues to let down this once-glamorous
and still very atmospheric Mayfair brasserie, which "should
be such a fun and pleasant restaurant"; "how come, if it's so
bad, the place is always fully booked?" – "presumably tourists
and out-of-towners".* / 11.45 pm, Sat 12.45 am; closed Sat L & Sun;
no Switch.

Lansdowne NW1   £ 21   ❷④❷
90 Gloucester Ave   483 0409   8–3B
*"TV and media types" chill out time and again at this very
popular Primrose Hill 'super-pub' – one of the first to make
a name for its "interesting" and "imaginative" cooking.* / 10 pm;
closed Mon L; no credit cards; book Sun L only.

Latymers W6   £ 16   ❷❸⑤
157 Hammersmith Rd   0181-741 2507   7–2C
*Do not abandon hope, all ye who enter here – "the back
room of a miserable pub" (not far from the Hammersmith
roundabout) it may be, but it's a "friendly" place offering
"fast, cheap and tasty" Thai food, which is "excellent for
what it is".* / 10 pm; closed Sun; no Switch; no booking at lunch.

Launceston Place W8 £39 ❷❷❷
1a Launceston Pl   937 6912   5–1B
"Discreet" Kensington townhouse, whose "cosy", "drawing room" ambience makes it a "romantic" favourite; the "charming service" wins particular praise, and while the modern British cooking can be a touch "erratic", most find it "delicious". / 11.30 pm; closed Sat L & Sun D.

Laurent NW2 £21 ❶❸④
428 Finchley Rd   794 3603   1–1B
The "best cous-cous in London" – and "good value" too – ensures a steady stream of visitors to this unpretentious Cricklewood café. / 11 pm; closed Sun; no Switch.

The Lavender SW11 £22 ④⑤❸
171 Lavender Hill   978 5242   10–2C
It started off so well, but this "noisy", modern Battersea yearling – though "still a popular neighbourhood restaurant", "cosy for an evening out with friends" – has magnificently failed to live up to its initial culinary promise; service is "erratic". / 11 pm.

Lazy Jack's W12 £22 ❸❸④
47a Goldhawk Rd   0181-740 6814   7–1C
By night, a rather scruffy Shepherd's Bush BYO bistro, offering competent modern British fare; by day a "rowdy, informal" café whose breakfast is "tops for hangovers". / 11 pm.

Leadenhall Tapas Bar EC3 £18 ❸❸❸
27 Leadenhall Mkt   623 1818   9–2D
"Fine for a relaxed lunch", this agreeable place, looking down into the market, offers "good" (if not particularly Spanish) tapas, and "pleasant" service. / 9 pm; closed Sat & Sun; need 6+ to book.

Leith's W11 £54 ❸❸❸
92 Kensington Pk Rd   229 4481   6–2B
Supporters of this long-established modern British townhouse restaurant in Notting Hill find "everything perfect", and laud both "food to delight all palates" and "incredibly discreet service"; neither Alex Floyd's cooking, nor the staff, nor the ambience commands universal acclaim, however, and, for a number of reporters, the price of a meal here is "just not justified". / 11.30 pm; closed Mon L, Sat L & Sun; closed Sat L & Sun.

Leith's at the Institute EC2 £34 ④❸❸
Moorgate Pl   920 8626   9–2C
"Glossy", if rather chilling, City basement, which – with its "well spaced tables" and "discreet service" – is "good for business"; the food is "interesting but variable". / L only; closed Sat & Sun; no Switch; no smoking area.

Lemonia NW1 £24 ❸❷❷
89 Regent's Pk Rd 586 7454 8–3B
*Primrose Hill's large "local taverna, with an updated feel
about it" continues to draw support from far and wide –
it's "always busy" (and parking nearby is notoriously difficult);
the secret? – "enjoyable, well prepared" food at "very
reasonable prices", together with "warm and friendly service".*
/ 11.30 pm; closed Sat L & Sun D; no Amex & no Switch.

Leonardo's SW10 £26 ❷❷❸
397 King's Rd 352 4146 5–3B
*From the outside, it looks very clichéd, so it's all the more
surprising just how consistent reports are on this "excellent,
established Italian restaurant" at World's End; "great fish
dishes" and the "good value early-evening menu" are among
the particular recommendations.* / 11.45 pm; closed Sun D.

The Lexington W1 £25 ❹❷❹
Lexington St 434 3401 3–2D
*Rather Bohemian, modern British spot in a Soho backwater;
reports are mixed, reflecting the fact that the setting is not
to all tastes and that, although the evening set menu offers
"exceptional value", prices can otherwise seem "outrageous";
service, if amateur, is "always welcoming"; (the restaurant
changed hands in September '96, so things may be different
under the new régime).* / 11 pm; closed Sat L & Sun; no Switch.

Lindsay House W1 £40 ❺❸❶
21 Romilly St 439 0450 4–3A
*This Soho townhouse's OTT, olde worlde style is found
"wonderfully romantic" by many – it's certainly a much
greater attraction than the "not particularly good" and not
inexpensive cooking.* / Midnight, Sun 10 pm; no Switch; smart casual.

Lisboa Patisserie W10 £ 5 ❶❸❸
57 Golborne Rd 0181-968 5242 6–1A
*Popular Portuguese pâtisserie in North Kensington, supplying
the ultimate in custard tarts.* / 8 pm; no credit cards; no booking.

The Little Bay NW6 £12 ❸❸❸
228 Belsize Rd 372 4699 1–2B
*"Amazingly cheap, creative food" maintains the popularity
of this candle-lit, ultra-budget bistro, in a Kilburn side street.*
/ 11.45 pm; no credit cards.

Little Italy W1 £25 ❸❷❶
21 Frith St 734 4737 4–2A
*This "lively" Soho newcomer's formula – "good standards of
traditional food, served in a trendy atmosphere" – "seems
a bit odd, but it works"; indeed, the worst complaint noted
so far is that the plates "are an unattractive shape".*
/ 4 am, Sun midnight.

Livebait SE1   £31   **❶**②④

43 The Cut   928 7211   9–4A

"Fab fresh fish" and "a wide choice of interesting seafood dishes" have instantly propelled this South Bank newcomer to richly deserved gastronomic prominence (a "fabulous plaice!"); the atmospheric tiled dining room, conveniently located for the Old Vic, is "fun" if "cramped", though expansion is under way as we go to press. / 11 pm, Thu-Sat 11.30 pm; closed Sat L & Sun; no Amex.

Lobster Pot SE11   £35   **❷❷❷**

3 Kennington Ln   582 5556   1–3C

This "small, family-run French fish restaurant" is a remarkable oasis in "the culinary desert around the Elephant & Castle", offering "excellent", if not inexpensive, cooking; the décor – complete with goldfish behind the portholes – is a triumph of nautical kitsch. / 11 pm; closed Mon & Sun; smart casual.

The Lobster Trading Co EC2   £33   **❷❸❸**

31 Broadgate Circle   256 5045   9–2D

"Reliable fish dishes" and "friendly and attentive service" make this Broadgate parlour one of the best City lunching spots – "shame you can never get a table". / 8 pm; closed Sat & Sun.

Los Remos W2   £18   **❸❷**④

38a Southwick St   723 5056   6–1D

Some think its basement premises a touch "dingy", but this "good, traditional tapas bar" offers some relief in the grim area near Paddington Station, and boasts a fine selection of Spanish wines; the upstairs restaurant is of less interest. / Midnight; closed Sun; no Switch.

Lou Pescadou SW5   £36   **❸**⑤④

241 Old Brompton Rd   370 1057   5–3A

For a growing number of reporters, Earl's Court's long-established and very popular fish restaurant has "lost its charm"; views such as "it used to be very good, but poor food now matches the arrogant French service" and "service (on three occasions) so bad I won't go again" explain why the place is "losing its clientele". / Midnight; no booking.

Luc's Brasserie EC3   £31   **❸❸**④

17-22 Leadenhall Mkt   621 0666   9–2D

"Bustling" and "efficient" Gallic spot in Leadenhall Market, whose "consistent quality" cooking is widely approved; complaints are almost invariably along the lines that it's "overcrowded and noisy". / L only; closed Sat & Sun; no Switch; smart casual.

Luigi Malones SW7   £22   ❸②②
73 Old Brompton Rd   584 4323   5–2B
*Reporters unanimously sing the praises of this "cheap,
cheerful and great fun" spot not far from South Ken station,
where "excellent" cocktails, "hearty American food" and
"welcoming and friendly" service combine to produce a place
whose "only possible drawback is the massive portions";
we just can't see it. / 11 pm.*

Luigi's WC2   £38   ④④❸
15 Tavistock St   240 1789   4–3D
*"Very overpriced", traditional Covent Garden Italian,
whose cooking and service are in a mould which now seems
anachronistic; its townhouse setting is potentially charming –
especially the panelled upstairs rooms – but in need of
some updating. / 11.30 pm; closed Sun; smart casual.*

Luigi's Delicatessen SW10   £11   ❶④❸
349 Fulham Rd   351 7825   5–3B
*"Sooo... casual", "cheap and chic", "young and fun",
"Eurotrash" venue, in the heart of Chelsea's trendsville;
top-notch risotto, pizza and salads are chaotically self-served.
/ 8 pm, Sat 6 pm; closed Sun; no credit cards; no booking.*

Luna NW1   £23   ❸❸④
48 Chalk Farm Rd   482 4667   8–2B
*Bleakly located, modern Italian bistro in Chalk Farm; some
laud the "unusual menu combinations", but our visit found
the cooking by no means consistent. / 11.30 pm; no Amex.*

Ma Goa SW15   £23   ❸②❸
244 Upper Richmond Rd   0181-780 1767   10–2B
*"Small, intimate and vibrant", "Indian bistro" in Putney which
"packs a punch with flavours"; even supporters note that
"it's expensive, and quantities are small". / 11 pm; D only,
closed Sun.*

Mackintosh's Brasserie W4   £22   ④②②
142 Chiswick High Rd   0181-994 2628   7–2B
*This "reliable" Chiswick spot is "always busy" – "you can't
book, so arrive early" – and is lauded by many locals for its
agreeable buzz, "very friendly staff" and "good range
of dishes". / Midnight; no smoking area; no booking.*

Made in Italy SW3   £22   ❸❸❸
249 King's Rd   352 1880   5–3C
*"Good food on the King's Road", and at a reasonable price,
makes this slightly scruffy pizza-and-pasta stop popular with
Chelsea locals and Saturday shoppers. / 11 pm; no credit cards;
no booking.*

Maggie Jones's W8 £ 33 ❸❸❷
6 Old Court Pl   937 6462   5–1A
*"Like a cosy country cottage inside", this perennially popular
English spot, just off Kensington High Street, provides "huge
portions" from a wide-ranging menu of traditional dishes; the
set lunch is "always good value for money". / 11 pm.*

Magno's Brasserie WC2 £ 31 ④❸④
65a Long Acre   836 6077   4–2D
*Covent Garden bistro/brasserie, whose "main appeal is still
the set menu and the efficient service which should get you to
the theatre on time"; the cooking has never been its
strongest point. / 11.30 pm; closed Sat L & Sun.*

Maison Bertaux W1 £ 5 ❸❸❷
28 Greek St   437 6007   4–2A
*London's oldest pâtisserie, founded in Soho in 1871, is
a mellow spot for a coffee and a cake. / 8.30 pm (Sun, closed
1 pm - 3 pm); no credit cards; no smoking area.*

Maison Novelli EC1 £ 40 ❸④④
29 Clerkenwell Gn   251 6606   9–1A
*J-C Novelli (much fêted when at the Four Seasons) set up on
his own in the summer of '96, in characterful, if slightly tacky,
Clerkenwell premises (formerly Café St Pierre); though it was
early days on our visit (towards the end of a rolling
refurbishment programme), we found a place lacking in
excitement or refinement, but with prices already leaping
ahead; the ground floor brasserie probably offers better value
than the restaurant upstairs. / 10.45 pm; closed Sat & Sun; no Switch.*

Malabar W8 £ 24 ❷❷❸
27 Uxbridge St   727 8800   6–2B
*"Consistently good over many, many years", this "fabulous",
understated Indian (which looks more like an Italian), just off
Notting Hill Gate, continues to please the punters; "avoid the
lower level", though. / 11.15 pm.*

Malabar Junction WC1 £ 27 ❷❷❸
107 Gt Russell St   580 5230   2–1C
*Bloomsbury newcomer "with less trade than it deserves" –
perhaps because its "elegant conservatory" setting is "hidden
from the street"; it offers a "cool, restful haven" in which to
enjoy some "excellent south Indian cooking". / 11.30 pm;
no Switch; no smoking area.*

Mamta SW6 £ 18 ❷❷⑤
692 Fulham Rd   371 5971   10–1B
*"Great" Fulham South Indian vegetarian – "too bad it's
so ugly". / 10.30 pm; closed Mon L & Tue L; no Switch; no smoking area.*

Mandalay W2 £14 ②②④
444 Edgware Rd   258 3696   8–4A
Burmese cooking (Indian with oriental twists) adds culinary interest to this "good, cheap local" – a shop-conversion round the corner from Lord's; charming and solicitous service.
/ 10.45 pm; closed Sun; no Switch.

Mandarin Kitchen W2 £28 ①④④
14-16 Queensway   727 9012   6–2C
"You go for the cooking, and you aren't disappointed" by this dated Bayswater establishment which offers "Chinese seafood at its best"; on the downside, meat dishes are rather undistinguished, the service "surly" and the environment "chaotic". / 11.30 pm.

Mandeer W1 £19 ②③③
21 Hanway Pl   323 0660   4–1A
The "excellent lunchtime buffet" at this basement veggie Indian (in a warren of streets near Tottenham Court Road tube) is one of the top bargains in town; the "tasty food" on the main menu is also "very reasonably priced" and served in an adjoining Aladdin's cave-style dining room. / 10 pm; closed Sun; no smoking.

Mandola W11 £20 ②③③
139 Westbourne Gr   229 4734   6–1B
"Yummy", "fresh", "unusual" food and a "fun" atmosphere ensure that this cheery Sudanese, opposite the Bayswater '7-Eleven', is often too "overcrowded" (even though it's "not that cheap"); BYO. / 11.30 pm; closed Sun L; no credit cards.

Mange 2 EC1 £38 ④④③
2 Cowcross St   250 0035   9–1A
Funkily designed Modern French place in Smithfield, whose cooking gives rise to very mixed opinions – "decent" and "not too expensive" to some, but "too clever" and "over fancy" to others. / 10.30 pm; closed Sat & Sun.

Manna NW3 £19 ③③④
4 Erskine Rd   722 8028   8–3B
It's still re-finding its feet, but "food and service continue to improve" at the UK's oldest vegetarian (Primrose Hill, 1968) – re-launched a year ago, minus characterful pine décor.
/ 11 pm; Mon-Sat, closed L; no Amex & no Switch; no smoking area.

Manzara W11 £16 ②③④
24 Pembridge Rd   727 3062   6–2B
"Cheap and delicious" Turkish café/bistro, just off Notting Hill Gate; "the £3.35 meze is a whole dinner". / 11.30 pm; no smoking area.

Manzi's WC2   **£ 35**   ❷④④

I Leicester St   734 0224   4–3A
*An "unchanging favourite" – traditionalists find this "old
fashioned" fish and seafood parlour near Leicester Square "a
happy place", and with "very friendly" service (even if "it's not
that efficient"); fish is "fresh and well done" but, for best
results, "stick to the simple dishes"; sit downstairs. / 11.30 pm,
Cabin Room 10.30 pm; closed Sun L.*

Mao Tai SW6   **£ 26**   ❷❷❸

58 New King's Rd   731 2520   10–1B
*"The best Chinese food anywhere" – well at least in west
London – continues to make this "attractive" Parson's Green
spot "a consistent favourite"; the "only downside is noise and
uncomfortable seats". / 11.45 pm.*

Marché Mövenpick   **£ 19**   ④④④

Bressenden Place, SW1   630 1733   2–4B
Swiss Centre, Leicester Sq, W1   494 0498   4–4A
*A love-it-or-hate-it experience; some find "the best value in
town" at these "excellent self-service refectories", where "it's
good to see the cooking before your very eyes"; others speak
of a "vile" visit to a place whose "contrived setting is almost
anti-atmosphere"; beware "overpriced" drinks. / Midnight, SW1
Sun 10 pm; no smoking area.*

Marine Ices NW3   **£ 22**   ❸❸❷

8 Haverstock Hl   485 3132   8–2B
*"The best ice cream" (they supply a number of top places)
and not bad pizza and pasta have made this relaxed Chalk
Farm spot a favourite – not just for north London families –
since the '20s. / 11 pm; no Amex; no smoking area.*

Maroush   **£ 30**   ❸❸④

I) 21 Edgware Rd, W2   723 0773   6–1D
II) 38 Beauchamp Pl, SW3   581 5434   5–1C
III) 62 Seymour St, W1   724 5024   2–2A
*If you stick to the excellent snack/take-away sections (I and II
only), you get "excellent value" at these glitzy Lebaneses,
where "great food is served into the early hours"; the
adjoining restaurants are much pricier – at number I there is
music nightly (and a minimum charge of £48), and number II
benefits from an elegant first-floor conservatory. / W2 1 am,
SW3 5 am, W1 1 am.*

Mars WC2   **£ 24**   ❸④❷

59 Endell St   240 8077   4–1C
*"Cool, cool" Covent Garden bar-restaurant whose
twentysomething fans think it a "great hang-out/eat place".
/ 11.30 pm; closed Sat L & Sun; no credit cards.*

Mas Café W11 £ 27 ④⑤④
6-8 All Saints Rd   243 0969   6–1B
*This "typically Notting Hill" spot was once extremely
promising, but shows some signs of having "died" – its ratings
certainly have; quite a number still recommend it for brunch,
however, when its "lazy, relaxed atmosphere" comes into
its own. / 11.30 pm; Winter, Mon-Fri closed L; no Amex.*

Masako W1 £ 54 ❷❷❸
6 St Christopher Pl   935 1579   3–1A
*Comfortable, hospitable Japanese whose solid quality cooking
attracts a band of regulars to this bijou shopping backwater,
just off Oxford Street. / 10 pm; closed Sun.*

The Mason's Arms SW8 £ 19 ❷④❷
169 Battersea Park Rd   622 2007   10–1C
*A "top class effort in an unpromising location", this
fashionably revamped pub (by Battersea Park railway station)
serves an accomplished, small modern British menu, and is
good for brunch; service can be a touch "slow". / 10.10 pm;
no Amex.*

Matsuri SW1 £ 45 ❷❶④
15 Bury St   839 1101   3–3D
*"Delicious, fresh" food from the teppan-yaki and "very
efficient, friendly service" make this St James's basement
"a helpful introduction to Japanese", though the atmosphere
does not exactly set the pulse racing; there is also an
"excellent sushi bar". / 10 pm; closed Sun; no Switch; smart casual.*

Maze W1 £ 32 ④④❸
29 Old Burlington St   437 9933   3–3C
*Our early-days visit to this summer '96 newcomer found the
sort of "tolerable" modern British cooking you might fear in
a "stark, metallic" dining room newly tacked on to an '80s
Mayfair nightclub (Legends); it may improve. / Mon-Thu L only, Fri
& Sat midnight.*

Mekong SW1 £ 18 ④❸④
46 Churton St   834 6896   2–4B
*Long-standing Pimlico Vietnamese/Chinese – a "friendly" and
"inexpensive" place, where "really good food" is sometimes to
be had; that's not always the case, though, and some
scent decline. / 11.30 pm; no Amex & no Switch.*

Melati W1 £ 22 ❷❸④
21 Great Windmill St   437 2745   3–2D
*"Cheap and good food" (with the odd really outstanding dish)
makes this consistent Indo-Malaysian (not far from Piccadilly
Circus) "well worth a visit" for West End value-seekers; the
surroundings are "bland" and cramped. / 11.30 pm, Fri & Sat
12.30 am; no Switch.*

Memories of India SW7   £ 20   ❸❷❸
18 Gloucester Rd   589 6450   5–1B
*"Good value, for the area", is to be found at this South
Kensington Indian, whose reliable cooking and civilised
attitude maintain its following.* / 11.15 pm; no Switch.

Le Mercury N1   £ 18   ④❷❷
140a Upper St   354 4088   8–3D
*"Pleasant atmosphere and décor, but very mediocre food" is
the proposition at this Bohemian budget bistro, in the heart of
Islington's trendy Upper Street.* / 1 am; no Amex & no Switch.

Meson Don Felipe SE1   £ 20   ❸❷❷
53 The Cut   928 3237   9–4A
*To enter this "great" bar near the Old Vic is to be transported
briefly to sunnier climes; the tapas are very reliable, and there
is a nightly flamenco guitarist.* / 11 pm; closed Sun; no Amex; book pre
1 pm only.

Le Mesurier EC1   £ 30   ❷❸④
113 Old St   251 8117   9–1B
*"Tiny" north City-fringe restaurant, whose (necessarily) limited
following only has words of praise for Gillian Enthoven's "good
value", modern French cooking.* / L only; closed Sat & Sun;
smart casual.

Le Metro SW3   £ 26   ❸④❸
28 Basil St   589 6286   5–1D
*Coolly decorated, percussive basement wine bar, just by
Harrods, offering competent and not hugely expensive
modern British cooking; service can be surprisingly distrait.*
/ 11 pm; closed Sun; no booking.

Mezzaluna NW2   £ 34   ❸❸④
424 Finchley Rd   794 0452   1–1B
*"Please don't ignore this deserving restaurant again", say
supporters of this slightly tacky trattoria, on the way to
Golder's Green; the "pasta is particularly good", but some
locals agree with us that the place is on the "expensive" side.*
/ 11 pm; closed Mon & Sat L; no Switch.

Mezzanine SE1   £ 26   ❸❸④
National Theatre, South Bank   928 3531   2–3D
*"A pleasant surprise after the theatre"; the stylish, if rather
undercharged restaurant of the RNT makes "a useful place to
eat on the South Bank".* / 11 pm; closed Sun; no smoking area.

MEZZO W1 £39 ④④❸
100 Wardour St 314 4000 3–2D
"A less fun version of Quaglino's", perhaps best sums up the hundreds of views on Soho's 'mother of all mega-restaurants'; reactions to the modern British cooking scale most possible peaks and troughs, with "overpriced and under-achieved" the overall verdict; the setting gets a similarly mixed press – from "tremendous buzz" to "wannabee glitz"; (see also Mezzonine). / Mon-Wed midnight, Thu-Sat 1 am (crustacea till 3 am), Sun 11 pm; closed Sat L.

MEZZONINE W1 £29 ❸❸❸
100 Wardour St 314 4000 3–2D
"A real bun fight", it may be, but the cramped, noisy, and uncomfortable ground floor refectory of this huge Soho mega-newcomer offers, for our money, a much better 'package' than the pricier Mezzo (in the basement); when they come off, the "oriental-based" concoctions are interesting and enjoyable, and the place has a good buzz. / Mon-Wed 12.30 am, Thu-Sat 2.30 am, Sun 11 pm; book only pre 7 pm.

Mildreds W1 £16 ❸❸❸
58 Greek St 494 1634 4–2A
Cramped, no-frills, veggie café, providing an inexpensive Soho standby. / 11 pm; closed Sun D; no credit cards; no smoking.

Mimmo d'Ischia SW1 £47 ❸❸②
61 Elizabeth St 730 5406 2–4A
"Much improved since the renovations" (including a "brand new conservatory"), this "warm and friendly" Belgravia stalwart offers "generous portions of very fresh, Italian fare"; though the bills are higher than ever, the reworking of the old formula – "good food at top prices, and stars too" – means the place now has more to recommend it. / 11.30 pm; closed Sun D; smart casual.

Mirabelle W1
56 Curzon St 499 4636 3–4B
This once classic Mayfair site was taken over by Marco Pierre White and Jimmy (L'Escargot) Lahoud in the summer of '96; at the time of writing, its large dining room is for function use only, but a major re-launch seems likely in 1997.

Mitsukoshi SW1 £55 ❶❸④
14-16 Regent St 930 0317 3–3D
Suntory is grander, and Tatsuso better known, but this smart, if stark, Nipponese is in the running for offering the "best Japanese food in London" – "fresher sushi would be impossible to find". / 9.30 pm; closed Sun; no Switch.

Miyama W1　　　　　　　£ 50　　②②⑤
38 Clarges St　499 2443　3–4B
*"Sterile" décor is the only drawback at this laudable,
well established Mayfair Japanese, which, though
"very expensive", serves top quality food; there is
a basement teppan-yaki.* / 10.30 pm; closed Sat L & Sun L;
smart casual.

Mon Petit Plaisir W8　　　　£ 33　　②②②
33C Holland St　937 3224　5–1A
*"Sweet", "very small" Kensington bistro with consistently high
culinary standards; for many, it is a romantic favourite, even
though "other people are never very far away".* / 10.30 pm;
closed Sat L & Sun.

Mon Plaisir WC2　　　　　£ 33　　③②②
21 Monmouth St　836 7243　4–2B
*"French at its best, and very consistent", this excellent,
"authentic" Covent Garden bistro celebrated its half-century
with the "courtesy, style and efficiency" which are its
trademarks; the set lunch and pre-theatre (out by 8) menus
are some of the best deals in town.* / 11.15 pm; closed Sat L & Sun.

Mona Lisa SW10　　　　　£ 12　　③②④
417 King's Rd　376 5447　5–3B
*"A World's End workmen's caff" – under the same ownership
as nearby Leonardo's – "that serves delicious breakfasts all
morning and excellent set lunches and dinners"; prices that
look a couple of decades out-of-date draw a diverse crowd for
the rough and ready grub.* / 10 pm; closed Sun D.

Mondo W1　　　　　　　£ 26　　③④①
13 Greek St　734 7157　4–2A
*"Funky" Soho basement newcomer; principally a groovy bar,
it also does "surprisingly innovative food".* / 11 pm,
snacks till 2 am; D only, closed Sun; Fri & Sat no booking.

Mongolian Barbecue　　　　£ 20　　④④③
12 Maiden Ln, WC2　379 7722　4–3D
31 Parson's Gn Ln, SW6　371 0433　10–1B
61 Gloucester Rd, SW7　581 8747　5–2B
1-3 Acton Ln, W4　0181-995 0575　7–2A
88-89 Chalk Farm Rd, NW1　482 6626　8–2B
183 Lavender Hl, SW11　228 2660　10–2C
*Some hail the "great concept" of these all-you-can-eat,
concoct-your-own-dish-and-we-stirfry-it-for-you 'orientals';
for a budget bash, they certainly have their appeal – as
a culinary experience, 'non!'* / 11 pm; D only.

Monkeys SW3   £39   ❷❷❷
1 Cale St   352 4711   5–2C
"Civilised", Gallic spot, quietly located on Chelsea Green,
which exerts a hold on the hearts of well-heeled
traditionalists, who approve the "well spaced" tables,
the "good game" in season, and the "nice wine list";
it is "expensive", though. / 11 pm; closed Sun D; no Amex.

Montana SW6   £33   ❷❷❷
125-129 Dawes Rd   385 9500   10–1B
"Especially in Fulham", this "unusual" establishment makes
an "excellent discovery"; really "zingy" south west USA
cooking (with "pungent spicing") combines with "striking
décor, plus jazz" to create "the perfect local spot to come to
again and again – even if you're not a local"; "very friendly
and efficient" staff complete the package; "ideal for brunch".
/ 11 pm, Fri & Sat 11.30 pm.

Montpeliano SW7   £37   ⑤❸❸
13 Montpelier St   589 0032   5–1C
Sometimes "atrocious", old-style fare seems to do little to
discourage custom at this dated but potentially "attractive"
Knightsbridge trattoria; the "anachronistic, Heffner-esque
Ferraris and bosoms décor is in poor taste, but rather suits
the clientele". / Midnight; no Switch.

Moshi Moshi Sushi   £13   ❶❷❸
Unit 24, Liverpool St Station, EC2   247 3227   9–2D
7-8 Limeburner Ln, EC4   248 1808   9–2A
"Conveyor belt sushi" – you grab a plate as it glides along the
bar and pay per empty – is "lots of fun", and as the fare is
good quality and "affordable", it offers an "unbeatable value"
package in the Square Mile; the new Limeburner Lane
branch is slightly less praised than the hard-to-find original,
overlooking the tracks at Liverpool Street Station. / 9 pm;
closed Sat & Sun; no smoking; no booking.

Motcomb's SW1   £38   ❷❷❷
26 Motcomb St   235 9170   2–4A
"Clubby atmosphere, simple English food and pleasant
service" combine to make this "intimate" Belgravia basement
a continuing success. / 11.15 pm; closed Sun D; smart casual.

Mr Chow SW1   £40   ⑤④④
151 Knightsbridge   589 7347   5–1D
Efforts to re-launch this long-standing "Knightsbridge crowd"
oriental – a time-bubble of '60s style – do not seem to have
been wholly successful; some do find "beautiful presentation,
good food, and nice atmosphere", but too many are
left unmoved. / 11.45 pm.

Mr Frascati W2 £ 32 ❸❸④
34 Spring St   723 0319   6–1D
*"Amongst all the grot of Paddington", this traditional Italian,
by the station, comes as something of a surprise, with its
professional service and properly prepared, sometimes
"excellent" cooking; though a civilised place, it is quite
"boring", and rather "expensive". / 11.30 pm; closed Sat L & Sun L.*

Mr Kong WC2 £ 19 ❸❸④
21 Lisle St   437 7341   4–3A
*"Not the best Chinese, but all round the best value",
applaud the many supporters of this Chinatown "favourite",
which offers "absolutely solid" Cantonese cooking; avoid
the basement. / 1.45 am; no Switch.*

Mr Wing SW5 £ 34 ④❷❶
242-244 Old Brompton Rd   370 4450   5–2A
*West London's leading party-Chinese may be a touch
"expensive", but its jungle-basement setting certainly gives the
punters "an experience", and – as the food is perfectly OK
and the service much improved – a very pleasant experience
too; an atmospheric new cocktail bar was added in the
summer of '96. / Midnight; no smoking area.*

Le Muscadet W1 £ 37 ❸❸❸
25 Paddington St   935 2883   2–1A
*After all these years, M Bessonard has departed from this
small and much-loved bourgeois French restaurant in
Marylebone, and the chef is now also the patron; service
under the new régime is not quite as wonderful as of old,
and the place is still "a bit expensive", but it's early days.
/ 10.45 pm, Sat 10 pm; closed Sat L & Sun; no Amex; smart casual.*

Museum St Café WC1 £ 30 ❷❷④
47 Museum St   405 3211   2–1C
*"Extremely consistent" – sometimes "scintillating" – modern
British cooking and "very friendly and attentive service" win
high praise for this "great value" Bloomsbury spot; the
"limited menu" and the "slightly uncomfortable seating" are
the only drawbacks. / 9.30 pm; closed Sat & Sun; no smoking.*

Mustards Brasserie EC1 £ 28 ④❸❸
60 Long Ln   796 4920   9–1B
*"Pricey but decent" food makes this "very crowded",
"traditional City" wine bar/brasserie (and neighbouring 'bistro-
à-vin') a reasonably satisfactory standby in a thin area. / 11 pm;
closed Sat & Sun; no Switch.*

Nachos £22 ④❸❸

212 Fulham Rd, SW10   351 7531   5–3B
147-149 Notting Hl Gt, W11   221 5250   6–2B
29 Chiswick High Rd, W4   0181-995 0945   7–2B
57 Upper St, N1   354 3340   8–3D
79-81 Heath St, NW3   431 0908   8–1A
Under new ownership, this formerly rather ghastly chain has been re-launched in the summer of 1996 in a more elegant format, in which the Mexican element is much lower key; our initial impression is that these place now make quite a good spot for a light bite – if a slightly pricey one for a full meal. / Midnight, Fri & Sat SW10 1 am, W4 Thu-Sat 2 am.

Naked Turtle SW14 £27 ❸❷❷

505 Upper Richmond Rd   0181-878 1995   10–2A
"Good fun, live jazz and reasonable food" is proving a winning combination for this extremely popular East Sheen wine bar, which some claim to be "the best place for parties". / 11 pm; no smoking area.

Nam Long SW5 £28 ❸❸❶

159 Old Brompton Rd   373 1926   5–2B
Many a west Londoner's night out begins with "sinful cocktails" in this low-lit, atmospheric South Kensington bar-restaurant; though the Vietnamese cooking is hardly inexpensive, it is often "delicious". / 11.30 pm; closed Sat L & Sun; smart casual.

Nanking W6 £25 ❸❸❸

332 King St   0181-748 7604   7–2B
Agreeable Hammersmith Chinese whose "attentive service" and "simple, well presented" cooking make it the top oriental thereabouts. / 11.30 pm; no Switch.

Nautilus NW6 £19 ❷❸④

27 Fortune Gn Rd   435 2532   1–1B
"Always the best fish and chips", proclaim fans, who are prepared to travel some distance for the matzo-meal fry-ups at this pleasantly tacky West Hampstead parlour. / 10.15 pm; closed Sun; no credit cards; no booking.

Nayab SW6 £24 ❷❷④

309 New King's Rd   731 6993   10–1B
"Very reliable", "quite pricey" Parson's Green Indian, of above average culinary ambition; service, similarly, is superior, but the décor is rather oppressive. / 11.45 pm; smart casual; no smoking area.

Neal Street WC2 £53 ④④❸
26 Neal St   836 8368   4–2C

As always, it's the issue of money which divides opinions on Antonio Carluccio's "relaxed", light and attractive Covent Garden Mediterranean; for some, the bills "are high but not over the top for the quality of the produce" (especially mushrooms, the house speciality) – others find the place so "grossly overpriced as to spoil the experience". / 11 pm; closed Sun; smart casual.

Neal's Yard Dining Rooms WC2 £13 ❸❸❸
14 Neal's Yd   379 0298   4–2C

The "nice courtyard to look out over" means that summer is the best time to visit this simple "good value" Covent Garden café, which offers a variety of tasty international dishes; BYO. / generally 7.30 pm, summer Mon & Sat 5 pm, winter often 5 pm; closed Sun; no credit cards; no smoking; no booking.

New Culture Revolution £13 ❸④④
305 King's Rd, SW3   352 9281   5–3C
42 Duncan St, N1   833 9083   8–3D
43 Parkway, NW1   267 2700   8–3B

"Good value", smart but unadorned "dumpling and noodle" bars, ideal for a quick but "healthy" bite. / 10.30 pm; N1 closed Sun; no Amex; no smoking area; to book need 4+ .

New World W1 £20 ④⑤⑤
Gerrard Pl   734 0677   4–3A

"Enormous", grungy Chinatown spot, "only good for lunchtime dim-sum", when the "hectic" criss-crossing of trolleys makes for quite a performance; in the evening, you may well find "off hand service and poor cooking". / 11.45 pm; no Switch.

Newton's SW4 £24 ④❸❷
33 Abbeville Rd   0181-673 0977   10–2D

Clapham local "good for suburban nosh when the kitchen at home is empty", and whose outside tables make it "nice in summer". / 11 pm; no smoking area.

Nico Central W1 £37 ❸④④
35 Great Portland St   436 8846   3–1C

Admirers of Nico Ladenis's upmarket Marylebone bistro find "well cooked" Gallic fare at "sensible prices"; service, though, can be "blasé", and the "stark" setting and "breathe in" seating-plan win little support. / 11 pm; closed Sat L & Sun; smart casual.

Nicole's W1 £39 ❸④④
158 New Bond St   499 8408   3–3C

This "good central rendezvous", in the basement of a Mayfair fashion store, remains "great for a shopping lunch" – "pastries and light dishes are good"; the more serious cooking can be a touch variable, however, and the setting is "noisy"; "the bar menu offers the best value". / 10.45 pm; closed Sat D & Sun; no smoking area.

Nikita's SW10   £32   ④❸❷
65 Ifield Rd   352 6326   5–3B
The "great atmosphere" ("if you like that kind of thing") of this Chelsea-fringe cellar and the "vodkas of several flavours" maintain this Russian stalwart's popularity with those who put ambience above culinary satisfaction. / 11.30 pm; D only; closed Sun; smart casual; no smoking area.

Nineteen SW3   £23   ❸❸❸
19 Mossop St   589 4971   5–2D
A "good choice" of "home-style food" makes this inexpensive, long-standing bistro, a few steps from Brompton Cross, worth knowing about in an expensive area. / 11.45 pm; closed Sat L; no Switch.

Nippon-Tuk SW3   £15   ❸❷④
165 Draycott Ave   589 8464   5–2C
Tiny Chelsea Japanese, decorated in a cheerful, unoriental style; it offers an affordable pit-stop in a pricey part of town. / 10.30 pm; closed Sun.

Nizam SW5   £26   ❸❷④
152 Old Brompton Rd   373 0024   5–2B
Despite its slightly tired appearance, this South Kensington Indian is a pretty consistent performer; indeed, some claim it's "underrated". / 11.45 pm.

Nontas NW1   £17   ❷❸❷
14 Camden High St   387 4579   8–3C
"Good Greek food", a charming atmosphere and "friendly service" continue to make a winning formula at this long-established taverna and ouzerie, near Mornington Crescent tube; the "nice walled garden" is a particular attraction. / 11.30 pm; closed Sun; no Switch.

Noor Jahan SW5   £24   ❷❸④
2a Bina Gdns   373 6522   5–2B
"Utterly consistent" South Kensington favourite, whose "spicy and good" Indian cooking ("all the classics, perfectly done") is enthusiastically endorsed; the setting is "refreshingly traditional" or "gloomy", to taste. / 11.45 pm; no Switch.

C Notarianni & Sons SW11   £18   ❷④❸
142 Battersea High St   228 7133   10–1C
The "best pizzas" get star billing at this "relatively quiet" Battersea spot, which numbers "decent pasta" and a "'50s atmosphere" among its supporting attractions; for a family-run place, service can be surprisingly "grumpy". / 11.30 pm; closed Sat L & Sun; no Amex & no Switch.

F S A

Noto £16 ③②⑤

2/3 Bassishaw Highwalk, EC2   256 9433   9–3B
7 Bread St, EC4   329 8056   9–2C

"Friendly" City Nipponese noodle-parlours, whose "flavourful
broths" are "excellent for a quick lunch". / EC2 10 pm, Sat 9 pm –
EC4 9 pm; EC2 closed Sat & Sun – EC4 closed Sat; EC2 no Amex and
no credit cards at lunch – EC4 no credit cards; EC2 no smoking at L;
no booking.

Noughts 'n' Crosses W5 £30 ④④③

77 The Grove   0181-840 7568   1–3A

Attractive but deeply suburban restaurant, behind Ealing's
Broadway Centre, offering rather overwrought English cooking.
/ 10 pm; closed Mon; D only ex Sun when L only; smart casual;
no smoking area.

O'Conor Don W1 £27 ②①①

88 Marylebone Ln   935 9311   3–1A

An "Irish gem" – the first floor dining room of a characterfully
converted Marylebone boozer – which inspires rave reviews
for its "warm & friendly" service and "charming", "comfy"
setting; the Guinness is "excellent" – to be sure – but we
would praise the "good solid grub" rather less wholeheartedly
than many reporters; the snacks in the downstairs bar are
undoubtedly well above average. / 10 pm; closed Sat L & Sun;
smart casual.

Oak Room
Hotel Meridien W1 £50 ③①②

Piccadilly   465 1640   3–3D

Even if former number two chef Pascal Villain is still "finding
his feet", this "cavernous", chandeliered Piccadilly dining room
– with its "superlative" service and relatively modest pricing
(especially from the evening 'menu vingt-huit') – is still among
London's best value grand dining experiences. / 10.30 pm;
closed Sat L & Sun; no Switch; jacket & tie.

L'ODÉON SW1 £41 ③④④

65 Regent St   287 1400   3–3D

As with all this year's new mega-brasseries, Pierre Condou and
Bruno Loubet's yearling is consistent in its inconsistency;
the Bruno-groupie majority hails "remarkably interesting",
modern French cooking, but this description would not be
recognised by the not insignificant minority which finds
the food "pretentious and poorly executed"; similarly, the
partitioned first-floor premises are "cramped" and "austere"
to some, but "a breath of fresh air in the West End"
to others. / Midnight; no smoking area.

Odette's NW1 £37 ❷❷❶
130 Regent's Pk Rd   586 5486   8–3B
The "delightfully dreamy, cosily seductive", many-mirrored
setting – and the "quiet, intimate" and "friendly" atmosphere
it creates – contributes to the long-running and deserved
success of this Primrose Hill fixture; the cooking – "modern
without being too trendy" – generally proves very reliable.
/ 11 pm; closed Sat L & Sun.

Odin's W1 £33 ❸❶❶
27 Devonshire St   935 7296   2–1A
"Formal and relaxed at the same time", this "beautiful",
"comfortable" Marylebone restaurant (adorned with the late
Peter Langan's art collection) is currently on very good form;
the modern British fare, if not remarkable, is consistent, and
the place wins recommendations both for romance and as the
"best location for business if you don't know your guests well".
/ 11.30 pm; closed Sat & Sun; no Switch; smart casual.

Ognisko Polskie SW7 £27 ❸❸❷
55 Prince's Gt, Exhibition Rd   589 4635   5–1C
Connoisseurs of decaying grandeur will relish the dining room
of South Kensington's Polish club; the hearty cooking is not
remarkable, but it is inexpensive, and there are very pleasant
outside tables in summer. / 10.30 pm; no Switch; no jeans.

Oliver's Island W4 £31 ④❸❷
162 Thames Rd   0181-747 8888   1–3A
Five minutes' walk from Kew Bridge, this cheerful Chiswick
neighbourhood spot makes an agreeable destination (and is
the only 'proper' restaurant thereabouts); dread hints of
suburbia lurk, however, in the indifferent realisation of the
modern British menu (which has a fish emphasis) and the
toppish prices. / 10.30 pm; closed Sat L & Sun.

Oliveto SW1 £29 ❸❸❸
49 Elizabeth St   730 0074   2–4A
Belgravia's new "minimalist younger sibling of Olivo" offers
a "more snacky menu" than at its elder, but one "which is no
less tasty or filling"; "designer pizzas" attract special praise.
/ 11.30 pm.

Olivo SW1 £31 ❷❷❸
21 Eccleston St   730 2505   2–4B
"Reliable, good cooking" and "value for money" are –
after a slightly sticky patch – winning back support for this
"friendly", "cheerful", "little gem" of a modern Mediterranean
restaurant, not far from Victoria Station. / 11 pm;
closed Sat L & Sun.

192 W11 £33 ④④❷
192 Kensington Pk Rd   229 0482   6–1A
*Perennially "trendy" and "easy-going" Portobello spot,
which, as always, generates mixed reviews; to its fans, it's still
"the very example of what a contemporary English restaurant
should be" – to too many, though, it's just "overcrowded"
and "overpriced".* / 11.30 pm; no smoking area.

L'Oranger SW1 £36 ❶❶❷
5 St James's St   839 3774   3–4D
*"State of the art" modern French cooking and "well honed
service" has made this "comfortable" St James's newcomer
(from the same stable as the much-fêted Aubergine) a
huge success; we share the reservation that the kitchen is
"exact rather than exciting", but that is not to question the
exceptional value currently on offer – "watch for the prices
going up soon".* / 11.15 pm; closed Sun L

Oriel SW1 £26 ❸④❷
50-51 Sloane Sq   730 2804   5–2D
*Sloane Square's prominently located, "casual" brasserie
remains a "fun place to meet for drinks or a light dinner",
or, of course, for the weekend breakfasts which are its
natural forte.* / 10.45 pm; no smoking area; no booking.

Orsino W11 £37 ④④❸
119 Portland Rd   221 3299   6–2A
*Chicly furnished and discreetly located Holland Park Italian –
the country-cousin of Orso (below) – which is "still not getting
there"; some culinary successes are reported, but "overpriced
and under-exciting" remains the summary view.* / 11 pm;
no Switch; no smoking area.

Orso WC2 £33 ④④❸
27 Wellington St   240 5269   4–3D
*Thanks to its late-night buzz, this Covent Garden basement
Italian can still make a "good choice after the opera";
but "disappointing" cooking still mars too many visits here,
and the loss is keenly felt by the many who remember what
a great place it used to be; hold the front page – Orso Now
Takes Credit Cards!* / Midnight; no smoking area.

Oslo Court NW8 £34 ❷❶❷
Prince Albert Rd   722 8795   8–3A
*"Perfect in every way", say devoted followers of this supremely
old-fashioned International restaurant – at the foot of an
anonymous apartment block, north of Regent's Park –
which "never varies"; "my mother dotes on this place,
and all her bridge-playing cronies are here – every night!"*
/ 11 pm; closed Sun; smart casual.

Osteria Antica Bologna SW11   £27   ❷❸❷
23 Northcote Rd   978 4771   10–2C
*This "well priced", "rustic" spot near Clapham Junction has
a strong reputation for its fare which is "more traditional and
authentic than your average Italian"; the place is "always
packed", and service, especially in the evenings, can
be "rushed".* / 11 pm, Fri & Sat 11.30 pm.

Osteria Basilico W11   £24   ❷❸❶
29 Kensington Pk Rd   727 9957   6–1A
*This "buzzing, hearty, genuine", "slightly Bohemian" Italian,
in Notting Hill's trendy restaurant strip goes from strength to
strength, with "great bread" and "world class pizzas"
numbered among its culinary attractions; just occasionally,
service can be found "aggressive".* / 11 pm; no Amex;
no booking Sat L.

Osteria Le Fate SW3   £30   ❸⑤❷
5 Draycott Ave   591 0070   5–2D
*"The first Italian nouvelle cuisine?", muses a reporter about
the cooking at Chelsea's discreet new Ligurian restaurant
(it certainly gives rise to similar complaints – "portions so
minute you need a pizza afterwards"); some, ourselves
included, found cooking of very good quality, but others are
unhappy with flavours "which fail to ignite the palate", and
service can be desperately slow.* / 11.30 pm; closed Sun; smart casual.

OXO TOWER SE1   £40   ④④❶
Barge House St   803 3888   9–3A
*Harvey Nichols's stunning, new, eighth-floor South Bank
bar/brasserie/restaurant has a wonderful panoramic view
and the best outside tables in central London; on a day I visit
to the brasserie, we found lacklustre modern British cooking
in a rather predictable mould; at this early stage, criticism of
the kitchen's production speed would be unfair.* / 11.30 pm;
no smoking area.

LE PALAIS DU JARDIN WC2   £30   ❷❷❷
136 Long Acre   379 5353   4–3C
*An "outstanding all-rounder", this "slick, buzzing" Covent
Garden brasserie scores highly for its "delicious" – and "good
value" – Gallic dishes (including a "fantastic range of
seafood"); even allowing for occasionally "lax" service, it is the
consistent standards across the board – on such a scale and
at very reasonable prices – which is so impressive.* / Midnight.

Palio W11   £29   ④❸❸
175 Westbourne Gr   221 6624   6–1B
*Some find a "terrific atmosphere" at this "loud" Notting
Hill/Bayswater bar/restaurant; the eclectic cooking gets mixed
reactions – "cheap for a snacky meal, but not good enough
for anything more" is representative.* / 11.30 pm.

Palms-on-the-Hill W8   £ 21   ④④❸
3 Campden HI Rd   938 1830   5–1A
"OK, but not inspiring in any sense" – this airy corner-site
pasta and salad stop near Kensington Town Hall may be
"cheap for W8", but is now a pale shadow of its former self.
/ 11.30 pm; no Amex; need 8+ to book.

Paparazzi Café SW3   £ 24   ④④❸
58 Fulham Rd   589 0876   5–2C
Raucous Chelsea Euroscene pizzeria, where "the food is very
average, and the staff are under the misapprehension that
they are personalities". / 1 am; no Switch; smart casual.

Park Inn W2   £ 20   ❷❸④
6 Wellington Ter, Bayswater Rd   229 3553   6–2B
This affordable Chinese (opposite the entrance to Kensington
Gardens) serves some interesting "mainland" cooking, with
seafood the speciality; its appeal is limited, though, by the
terribly bland décor. / 11.30 pm; no Amex.

Parks N5   £ 20   ④❷❸
104 Highbury Pk   359 9042   8–1D
No one would make great culinary claims for this agreeable
Highbury wine bar, but it is a cosily atmospheric local. / 11 pm;
closed Mon L, Sat L & Sun; no Amex.

Parsons SW10   £ 20   ❸❷❸
311 Fulham Rd   352 0651   5–3B
"Still the best burger/pasta place for lunch with children, or
a hangover", this atmospheric Chelsea institution, – also the
classic "pre-cinema venue" – is now back on its old form.
/ 12.30 am; no smoking area; no booking 8 pm - 10 pm.

Pasha N1   £ 21   ❸❷❸
301 Upper St   226 1454   8–3D
Though it avoids excitement in all departments, this large,
"reliable" Islington Turk is recommended by a fair number of
reporters; "choose the feast for a lot of choice". / 11.30 pm,
Fri & Sat midnight; no Switch.

Il Passetto WC2   £ 31   ❷❷❸
230 Shaftesbury Ave   836 9391   4–1C
Unencumbered by the baggage of a foodie reputation, this
"cosy", if cramped, archetypal Theatreland trattoria churns
out much better than acceptable, solid Italian cooking,
year in year out. / 11.30 pm; closed Sat L & Sun; smart casual.

Pâtisserie Valerie £19 ❷❷❷

105 Marylebone High St, W1   935 6240   2–1A
44 Old Compton St, W1   437 3466   4–2A
79-81 Regent St, W1   439 0090   3–3D
RIBA Centre, 66 Portland Pl, W1   631 0467   2–1B
8 Russell St, WC2   240 0064   4–3D
215 Brompton Rd, SW3   823 9971   5–2C
256 Brompton Rd, SW3   225 1664   5–2C
*The "best pâtisseries in town" (at least of the multiples) are
still drawing enthusiastic reports – and for many, the cramped
Soho original remains "the only place for breakfast"; the other
branches offer a greater range of dishes and are all worth
considering for light meals – the one near Harrods is a useful
shopping lunch spot; the group continues to expand, so let's
hope the quality holds up. / 6 pm-8 pm, Sun earlier; Portland Pl,
closed Sun; no smoking area; no booking.*

Paulo's W6 £23 ❸❸❸

30 Greyhound Rd   385 9264   7–2C
*First-timers are often wowed by the excellent value eat-all-
you-can buffet offered by the jovial Paulo and his wife at their
cheerful Brazilian (and veggies are particularly well provided
for); second time around, it can all seem a little 'samey'; it's
located next to Charing Cross Hospital – to enter, use the
door on the left and ring the lower bell. / 10.30 pm; D only;
no credit cards.*

The Peasant EC1 £29 ❸④④

240 St John St   336 7726   8–3D
*Some are "amazed by the high standards" of the "very
original" Mediterranean cooking at this roughly made-over
Clerkenwell pub; others come away much less impressed,
however, and service is "disjointed". / 10.45 pm; closed Sat L & Sun.*

Pélican £27 ❸❸❷

45 St Martin's Ln, WC2   379 0309   4–4C
2nd Floor, Cabot Place East, E14   513 0513   1–3D
*Enormous Theatreland brasserie, in art deco-ish style,
which is a sort of better Café Rouge (it is owned by the
same people); the atmosphere – especially the "lovely late
night feeling" – has its own attraction, but it's often as
a "convenient" spot (pre/post-Coliseum, for example) that
the place wins support; (we haven't yet visited the new
Canary Wharf offshoot). / WC2 12.30 am, Sun 10.30 pm; E14 9 pm;
E14 closed Sat & Sun.*

The Pen SW6 £27 ❸❸❷

51 Parson's Green Ln   371 8517   10–1B
*An atmospheric dining room, over a modishly converted pub
(close to Parson's Green tube), where quite a serious
modern British menu is "well prepared and presented" by
"professional young staff". / 11 pm; closed Sat L & Sun D.*

The People's Palace SE1 £29 ❸❸④
South Bank Centre   928 9999   2–3D
*Generally "interesting", modern British food and a convenient
location make this "cold" "barn" of a place "useful" before
or after a South Bank concert – though it's "not as good as
when it first opened"; on a fine day – especially at lunch –
the view over the river is magnificent. / 11 pm.*

The Pepper Tree SW4 £16 ❸❸④
Clapham Common Southside   622 1758   10–2D
*"Reasonably priced", "good Thai curries" whose quality
"never varies" have rightly made this unpretentious but
welcoming occidental-style refectory (by Clapham Common
tube) a "favourite local restaurant". / 11 pm, Mon 10.30 pm;
no Amex; no smoking area.*

Le P'tit Normand SW18 £26 ❷❷⑤
185 Merton Rd   0181-871 0233   10–2B
*Despite this family-run establishment's "unlikely" Southfields
location, its "excellent", "heavy", Norman fare attracts
a surprisingly broad following; service is "reminiscent of being
in France", and décor authentically tacky. / 10 pm, Sat 11 pm;
closed Sat L; smart casual.*

Phoenicia W8 £29 ❸❶④
11-13 Abingdon Rd   937 0120   5–1A
*"Good quality Lebanese" – just off Kensington High Street –
which has been run by the same family for many years; those
in the know tend to go for the "superb lunchtime buffet" –
diners don't get quite such good value. / 11.45 pm; smart casual.*

Phoenix Bar & Grill SW15 £26 ❸❷❸
Pentlow St   0181-780 3131   10–1A
*Putney's slightly stark son of Sonny's has a lot to live up to;
a "good start" is the general view, but there is some way to
go before the "inventive but not outlandish" modern British
cooking achieves the same consistent acclaim as at its
Barnes parent. / 11.30 pm, Sun 10 pm; closed Sat L.*

Phuket SW11 £19 ❸❷④
246 Battersea Pk Rd   223 5924   10–1C
*"Decent", "reliable" Battersea Thai; it "lacks ambience" and
perhaps does not get the following it deserves. / 10.50 pm; D only.*

Picasso SW3 £18 ❸❸❸
127 King's Rd   352 4921   5–3C
*The long-time rôle of this '60s-survivor coffee-shop
as a prime, sunny-day Chelsea posing spot has now been
enhanced by the opening of the Harley-Davidson shop
next door. / 11.15 pm.*

Pied à Terre W1 £62 ❸④ –

34 Charlotte St   636 1178   2–1C

Chef Richard Neat recently bowed out from this much-lauded
Fitzrovia foodie hot-spot, leaving his ex-partner David Moore
to team up with former sous-chef Tom Aikens; our
experience, in July '96, raised some questions as to whether
the quality of the inventive modern French cooking will be
maintained; a long-overdue complete refurb is in hand as
we go to press. / 11 pm; closed Sat L & Sun; smart casual.

Pierre Victoire £19 ⑤④④

6 Panton St, SW1   930 6463   4–4A
9 William St, SW1   823 2070   2–3A
11 Charlotte St, W1   608 0248   2–1C
29-31 Foubert's Pl, W1   439 2557   3–2C
5 Dean St, W1   287 4582   3–1D
42 New Oxford St, WC1   436 0707   4–1B
404 North End Rd, SW6   381 3810   10–1B
19-21 Notting Hill Gate, W11   460 4455   6–2B
88 Upper St, N1   704 2997   8–3D
31 Kentish Town Rd, NW1   482 5050   8–2A
136 Upper R'mond Rd, SW15   0181-789 7043   10–2B
38 Charterhouse St, EC1   608 0234   9–1B

Burgeoning budget Gallic bistro chain which divides opinion –
we think the reporter who says "OK for the £5 set lunchtime
menu but overpriced and stingy portions otherwise" has it
about right. / 11 pm; some branches closed Sun; no Amex.

La Piragua N1 £17 ❸❷❷

176 Upper St   354 2843   8–2D

"Great value", "cheap and cheerful" Islington South
American which is a fun, cramped destination mainly for
a twentysomething crowd; no stinting on the portions here.
/ Midnight; no credit cards.

Pitcher & Piano £19 ④❸❷

69-70 Dean St, W1   434 3585   4–2A
40-42 King William IV St, WC2   240 6180   4–4C
214 Fulham Rd, SW10   352 9234   5–3B
871-873 Fulham Rd, SW6   736 3910   10–1B
18-20 Chiswick High Rd, W4   0181-742 7731   7–2B
8 Balham Hill, SW12   0181-673 1107   10–2C

"Good atmosphere" and "great tottie" (whatever that means)
seem to be at the root of the success of these "loud" and
very popular twentysomething bars; the food, if incidental,
is "not bad". / 10 pm - 11 pm; W1 closed Sun.

Pizza Chelsea SW3 £21 ❸④④

93 Pelham St   584 4788   5–2C

"Good food, reasonably cheap" is not that easy to find in the
environs of Brompton Cross, making it all the more surprising
that this "reliable" place can seem "under-inhabited". / 11 pm;
no smoking area.

Pizza Metro SW11 £18 ❷❷④
64 Battersea Rise 228 3812 10–2C
*Cramped Battersea pizzeria, currently attracting a vogue
following for its "great, metre-long pizzas, just like Naples";
some, ourselves included, remain impervious to its
alleged charm. / 11 pm; D only; closed Sun; no Amex.*

Pizza On The Park SW1 £19 ❸④❷
11 Knightsbridge 235 5273 2–3A
*The "pizzas are always excellent", say the many fans of
this airy Hyde Park Corner spot – which is, of course,
a PizzaExpress in disguise; there's "good jazz" too, in the
basement (where a substantial music charge applies).
/ Midnight; no smoking area; no booking.*

Pizza Pomodoro SW3 £20 ❸④❶
51 Beauchamp Pl 589 1278 5–1C
*Some think the grub no more than satisfactory at this
celebrated, "scruffy dive", off Knightsbridge; however, the
"live music every night makes a great evening" and it's
"always packed" – "sometimes wild" – making this still one
of the best late night bets in town. / 1 am; no booking.*

Pizza Pomodoro £24 ❸④❸
7 Steward St, E1 377 6186 9–1D
110 Old St, EC1 250 0544 9–1B
*"Good pizzas in the City", with "a good price" to match,
make the non-Knightsbridge Pomodoros useful standbys in
thin areas. / 11 pm-midnight; City closed Sat & Sun; no Amex.*

Pizza the Action SW6 £17 ❸❷❸
678 Fulham Rd 736 2716 10–1B
*"Always busy", this "cheap and cheerful" deepest Fulham
hang-out provides a "decent" pizza, pasta and more menu.
/ Midnight.*

PIZZAEXPRESS £18 ❸❷❸

154 Victoria St, SW1   828 1477   2–4B
10 Dean St, W1   437 9595   3–1D
133 Baker St, W1   486 0888   2–1A
20 Greek St, W1   734 7430   4–2A
21-22 Barrett St, W1   629 1001   3–1A
23 Bruton Pl, W1   495 1411   3–2B
29 Wardour St, W1   437 7215   4–3A
7-9 Charlotte St, W1   580 1110   2–1C
30 Coptic St, WC1   636 3232   2–1C
9-12 Bow St, WC2   240 3443   4–2D
363 Fulham Rd, SW10   352 5300   5–3B
6-7 Beauchamp Pl, SW3   589 2355   5–1C
895 Fulham Rd, SW6   731 3117   10–1B
7 Rockley Rd, W14   0181-749 8582   7–1C
26 Porchester Rd, W2   229 7784   6–1C
252 Chiswick High Rd, W4   0181-747 0193   7–2A
35 Earl's Ct Rd, W8   937 0761   5–1A
335 Upper St, N1   226 9542   8–3D
194 Haverstock Hill, NW3   794 6777   8–2A
70 Heath St, NW3   433 1600   8–1A
Chapter Ho, Montague Cl, SE1   378 6446   9–3C
230 Lavender Hl, SW11   223 5677   10–2C
46 Battersea Br Rd, SW11   924 2774   5–4C
305 Up R'mond Rd W, SW14   0181-878 6833   10–2A
144 Up R'mond Rd, SW15   0181-789 1948   10–2B
539 Old York Rd, SW18   0181-877 9812   10–2B
43 Abbeville Rd, SW4   0181-673 8878   10–2D
125 London Wall, EC2   600 8880   9–2B

"Reliable, and slick as ever", "the nicest of the chains by far" continues to demonstrate that even fast-growing multiples can do it right – it's not just the "first-class pizza" that wins support, but the utter consistency across the group; good new additions include Baker Street, Beauchamp Place, Bruton Place and Greek Street. / 11 pm-midnight, Greek St Wed-Sat 1 am, Chapter Hs 4.30 pm, London Wall Sat 8 pm; Chapter Hs & Bruton Pl closed Sat & Sun; not all branches take bookings.

Pizzeria Castello SE1 £16 ❶④❸

20 Walworth Rd   703 2556   1–3C
"It's good, it's cheap", and supporters claim that "the best pizzas in town" can be had at this "terrible location", by the Elephant & Castle; the "unfailingly cheerful atmosphere" can be "raucous in the extreme". / 11 pm; closed Sat L & Sun; smart casual.

Pizzeria Condotti W1 £19 ❸❶❸

4 Mill St   499 1308   3–2C
Some claim this Mayfair "haven" as the "smartest, most stylish pizza restaurant in London"; they must be talking about the evening – at lunch, 'haven' is probably the last word which would come to mind. / Midnight.

PJ's SW3 £30 ⑤④❸
52 Fulham Rd   581 0025   5–2C
The "buzzing" atmosphere of this "relaxed" Chelsea
bar-grill is its principal – some would say only – attraction;
the American menu "sounds good, but isn't", and the service
is "hit and miss". / 11 pm; smart casual.

The Place Below EC2 £13 ❷❷❸
St Mary-le-Bow, Cheapside   329 0789   9–2C
"Imaginative food in an interesting setting" explains why
there are "often long queues" at this "superb" self-service
vegetarian restaurant below St Mary-le-Bow; it's priced for the
City market, however. / L only; closed Sat & Sun; no Amex; no smoking;
no booking.

Planet Hollywood W1 £29 ④❸❷
13 Coventry St   287 1000   4–4A
After its promising start, there is a growing feeling that this
impressive Tinseltown-themed joint has "lost its shine",
and is now "strictly for tourists and children's
birthday parties". / 1 am; no smoking area; no booking.

Plummers WC2 £24 ❸❷④
33 King St   240 2534   4–3C
Rather oddly provincial-feeling English establishment, right
in the heart of Covent Garden; it occasionally misfires
disastrously, but "pleasant and efficient service and
reasonable prices" are among the virtues which often
commend it. / 11.30 pm.

Poissonnerie de l'Avenue SW3 £42 ❶❸❸
82 Sloane Av   589 2457   5–2C
Last year's chic face-lift has breathed new life into this
"frightfully Chelsea" dowager of a restaurant; it has always
been "rather expensive", but for "fresh fish with few frills"
many of a traditional bent tip it as the best place in town;
it can get "crowded". / 11.30 pm; closed Sun; smart casual.

Pollo W1 £14 ❸❸④
20 Old Compton St   734 5917   4–2A
"Down to earth budget meals" mean that there are often
"big queues" for this "cheap, cheerful" and "reliable" Soho
"student place". / Midnight; no credit cards.

Pomegranates SW1 £35 ❸❷❸
94 Grosvenor Rd   828 6560   2–4C
You would never know that this Pimlico basement was a
great culinary ground-breaker in the '70s, and its eclectic
menu survives pretty much unaltered – now seeming "nothing
special, but quite pleasant"; the atmosphere is curiously illicit
– "where MPs spend their undisclosed earnings?" / 11.15 pm;
closed Sat L & Sun; no Switch.

La Pomme d'Amour W11 £29 ③①②
128 Holland Pk Av 229 8532 6–2A
This romantic Holland Park restaurant has been revitalised by its recent remodelling; the competent cooking provides "good value", and "on first greeting, they make you feel like a friend". / 10.45 pm; closed Sat L & Sun; no Switch; smart casual.

LE PONT DE LA TOUR SE1 £52 ③④②
36d Shad Thames 403 8403 9–4D
The grandest of the Conran river-siders may be only half a decade old, but it already seems like "an old stalwart" to many advocates of its "outstanding location", "superb outside tables" (with views of Tower Bridge) and "sometimes excellent" modern French cuisine; the chorus which finds the place "overpriced" or "conceited, with no reason to be" gets ever louder, however, leaving the current food rating within a whisker of down-grading. / 11.30 pm; closed Sat L

Le Pont de la Tour Bar & Grill SE1 £34 ③③②
36d Shad Thames 403 8403 9–4D
Especially if you can nab an outside table, the "fresh seafood" or the "late night steaks" here offer probably the best value option among Conran's riverside restaurants. / 11.30 pm; no booking.

Poons WC2 £18 ②④④
4 Leicester St 437 1528 4–3A
This very conveniently located and inexpensive spot, just by Leicester Square, remains many reporters' default selection for a West End Chinese; some find "very rude service". / 11.30 pm.

Poons at Whiteleys W2 £27 ③④④
Queensway 792 2884 6–1C
Bayswater shopping mall Chinese, "perfect for pre movie dim-sum"; it "lacks atmosphere", though, and it's difficult to see why anyone would seek it out on other occasions. / 11.45 pm.

Poons in the City EC3 £29 ④④④
2 Minster Pavement 626 0126 9–3D
"Good food" (if at Square Mile prices) in an "unexciting atmosphere" makes the main restaurant here rather "average" overall; the "fast food" oriental canteen at the back, however, offers "superb value", at least by City standards. / 10.30 pm; closed Sat & Sun.

Poons, Lisle Street WC2 £18 ①③④
27 Lisle St 437 4549 4–3B
It's "hard to find better Chinese" – certainly at the price – than at the 'original' Poons on the border of Chinatown; to say that its "unpretentious" interior "would discredit the back streets of Shanghai" is something of an exaggeration. / 11.30 pm; no credit cards.

Popeseye W14   £ 25   ❷④④
108 Blythe Rd   610 4578   7–1C
"Brilliant steaks and claret" make a "very simple but
effective" formula at this "extremely good quality and value"
Brook Green restaurant. / 10.30 pm; D only; closed Sun; no credit cards.

La Porte des Indes W1   £ 42   ④④❷
32 Bryanston St   224 0055   2–2A
"Lavish", Indian mega-newcomer, near Marble Arch, which is
almost "as pretty as its sibling, the Blue Elephant"; some have
found "beautifully presented", "interesting" food, but we were
amongst those who experienced "terribly ordinary" cooking at
"absurd" prices – the restaurant had initial difficulties getting
visas and work-permits for its chefs, so perhaps things are set
to improve. / Midnight, Sun 10.30 pm; smart casual; no smoking area.

Porters WC2   £ 19   ④④④
17 Henrietta St   836 6466   4–3D
Views vary on the traditional cooking (with pies the speciality)
at this large, well known English-theme restaurant in Covent
Garden; successes are reported, but "very average" is too
often the sentiment. / 11.30 pm; no Switch.

La Poule au Pot SW1   £ 37   ④❸❶
231 Ebury St   730 7763   5–2D
Those who find the Gallic fare here "like a provincial hotel
thirty years ago", or who have encountered "snotty" service
may be utterly mystified by this rustic Pimlico Green survivor's
continued popularity; they miss the point – once again this
year, reporters proclaim its candle-lit, "quiet corners" as
London's most "romantic" dining environment. / 11.15 pm.

Prego TW9   £ 29   ④④❸
100 Kew Rd   0181-948 8508   1–4A
Brightly decorated Richmond Mediterranean, with an
"extensive menu"; some claim it is "consistently good" –
compared to other options locally this may well be true,
but our vote is with those who say find the place "fussy"
and "dreary". / 11 pm, Fri & Sat 11.30 pm; no smoking area.

Pret A Manger £ 9 ❸①❸

12 Kingsgate Pd, Victoria St, SW1 828 1559 2–4B
75b Victoria St, SW1 222 1020 2–4C
120 Baker St, W1 486 2264 2–1A
163 Piccadilly, W1 629 5044 3–3C
173 Wardour St, W1 434 0373 3–1D
18 Hanover St, W1 491 7701 3–2C
298 Regents St, W1 637 3836 4–1A
54-56 Oxford St, W1 636 5750 3–1C
63 Tottenham Court Rd, W1 636 6904 2–1C
7 Marylebone High St, W1 935 0474 2–1A
122 High Holborn, WC1 430 2090 2–1D
240-241 High Holborn, WC1 404 2055 2–1D
77/78 St Martins Ln, WC2 379 5335 4–3B
80 King's Rd, SW3 225 0770 5–2D
8-10 King St, W6 0181-563 1985 7–2C
Kensington Arcade, W8 938 1110 5–1A
27 Islington High St, N1 713 1371 8–3D
157 Camden High St, NW1 284 2240 8–3B
10 Leather Ln, EC1 831 7219 9–2A
140 Bishopsgate, EC2 377 9595 9–2D
17 Eldon St, EC2 628 9011 9–2C
28 Fleet St, EC4 353 2332 9–2A
*Are these ultra-smart sandwiches, salads and sushi spots
becoming "almost too successful?" – they may offer
"brilliant" quality and "cheery" service, but "some items are
very overpriced", and "their range can get very boring after
a few visits".* / 4 pm-11 pm; closed Sun except some more central branches;
no credit cards; no smoking area; no booking.

The Prince Bonaparte W2 £ 19 ❸④❷

80 Chepstow Rd 229 5912 6–1B
*"A quirky touch to traditional dishes" makes this trendy
Bayswater boozer a "really great pub" for its "young, hip and
fairly studenty" crowd; "eat early before it's too busy".*
/ 10.20 pm; no credit cards; no booking.

Princess Garden W1 £ 45 ④❸④

8 North Audley St 493 3223 3–2A
*Grand but characterless Mayfair Chinese which is
thoroughly "overpriced".* / 11.45 pm; smart casual.

Princess of Wales SW3 £ 23 ❸❸❸

145 Dovehouse St 351 1155 5–2C
*Former pub, revamped and re-launched in the summer of
1996 as a brasserie, and serving "good, snack-like food";
with its "great terrace" – overlooking a quiet Chelsea
back street – it's probably more a sunny day place.*
/ 11 pm; no Amex & no Switch.

Prost W11 £26 ❸❷⑤
35 Pembridge Rd   727 9620   6–2B
You get "good food, but no atmosphere" at this "friendly, bistro-type" central European, just off Notting Hill Gate – all in all, a "fair-to-mitteling experience". / 11 pm; D only, ex Sat & Sun open L & D; no Switch.

Pucci Pizza SW3 £18 ❸④❷
205 King's Rd   352 2134   5–3C
Perennially popular with a young, trashy crowd, this "trendy" Chelsea pizzeria offers "good music, friendly staff and quite good food". / 11.30 pm; closed Sun; no credit cards.

QUAGLINO'S W1 £41 ④④❷
16 Bury St   930 6767   3–3D
It's "still an experience" to visit this vast St James's brasserie, which, four years on, "manages to retain its glitz and glamour"; results from the modern British menu (with lots of seafood) are often proclaimed "good", and the indifferent food rating reflects the fact that the menu-pricing is fierce; service can be "perfunctory". / Midnight, Fri & Sat 1 am, Sun 11 pm.

Le Quai EC4 £43 ④④④
1 Broken Whf   236 6480   9–3B
"Expensive", very business-orientated restaurant, which has little competition in the south west quarter of the City, presumably explaining why it continues to get away with indifferent cooking and "poor" service. / 8 pm; closed Sat & Sun; smart casual.

The Quality Chop House EC1 £29 ❷❷❸
94 Farringdon Rd   837 5093   9–1A
"Predictably good food" maintains enthusiastic support for this lovingly restored 'progressive working class caterer' on the unlovely northern fringe of the City; few reports fail to mention the "uncomfortable benches", but attractions such as the "great brunch" and "lovely staff" more than compensate. / 11.30 pm; closed Sat L; no credit cards.

Quincy's NW2 £32 ❸❷④
675 Finchley Rd   794 8499   1–1B
As ever, the only real reservation about this small and "friendly" English restaurant in Finchley – where they are "always genuinely pleased to see you" – is that it is rather "cramped" (a condition some find "romantic"). / 10.30 pm; D only; closed Mon & Sun.

Quo Vadis W1
26-29 Dean St   437 4809   4–2A
The gossip columns will no doubt have a field day when backers including Marco Pierre White and Damien Hirst re-launch this classic Soho site (which is scheduled for November 1996); whether offal is to be prominent on the menu is not known.

Ragam W1   £18   ❸④⑤
57 Cleveland St   636 9098   2–1B
*"Authentic south Indian food" – with vegetarian cooking the
speciality – maintains a following for this modest and
cramped restaurant, near the Telecom Tower.
/ 11.30 pm; no Switch.*

Randall & Aubin W1   £22   ❷⑤❸
16 Brewer St   287 4447   3–2D
*High quality, simple fare – seafood, soup, rôtisserie – is eaten
at the counter of this classy, new Soho delicatessen-conversion
diner; it makes an ideal vantage-point from which to spectate
on the comings and goings at the neighbouring sex shops,
perhaps explaining the distracted service. / 11 pm; closed Sun.*

Rani   £22   ❸④④
7 Long Ln, N3   0181-349 4386   1–1B
3 Hill St, TW9   0181-332 2322   1–4A
*The original Finchley branch has been joined by a spartan,
modern sibling – one of the only half-decent places in
Richmond; though generally they offer good quality
vegetarian Indian cooking, prices are too high given the
"variable" standards. / 11 pm; N3 D only – TW9 closed Mon L,
Tue L & Sun L; no smoking areas.*

Ranoush W1   £14   ❶④④
43 Edgware Rd   723 5929   6–1D
*"Excellent Lebanese fast fare" makes this "freshly decorated"
café near Marble Arch especially popular as a late-night
pit-stop; remember to stop at the cash-dispenser first.
/ 3 am; no credit cards.*

Ransome's Dock SW11   £33   ❸❷❷
35 Parkgate Rd   223 1611   5–4C
*"Reliable and enjoyable", modern British brasserie, situated
just over Battersea (or Albert) Bridge, which wins support for
its "good, original food" – with fish recommended – and its
"superb wine list"; the "understated", "easy-modern"
surroundings are found romantic by some. / 11 pm;
closed Sun D; smart casual.*

Raoul's Café W9   £23   ❸❸❸
13 Clifton Rd   289 7313   8–4A
*Though most reputed as a brunch venue, this pleasant
Maida Vale bistro cum pâtisserie also offers good, simple
international fare all day. / 10 pm; closed Sun D;
no smoking area; book eve only.*

Rasa N16   £19   ❶❷❸
55 Stoke Newington Ch St   249 0344   1–1C
*Outstanding value and an intriguing menu make this Stoke
Newington South Indian worth the pilgrimage, even for
non-veggies, and service makes a real effort. / 11 pm, Fri-Sat
midnight; closed Mon; no smoking.*

Rebato's SW8 £22 ❷❷❶

169 South Lambeth Rd   735 6388   10–1D
*"Step into another world" (Spain that is, not Vauxhall) –
this "lovely", "unfussy" bar is "full of atmosphere" and dishes
out very "good value tapas"; the adjoining restaurant is not
bad but less of an attraction.* / 10.30 pm; closed Sat L & Sun;
no Switch; smart casual.

Red SW3 £28 ❸❸④

8 Egerton Garden Mews   584 7007   5–2C
*Louche-feeling mews-basement oriental, near Knightsbridge,
whose small but devoted following proclaim the virtues of its
"decent, healthy Chinese cooking".* / 11.15 pm; smart casual.

Red Fort W1 £33 ❷❸④

77 Dean St   437 2525   4–2A
*The "food has improved a lot this year" at this well known,
culinarily ambitious Soho Indian; objectively its performance is
quite reasonable, but we side with those who think it's "a nice
place, but a bit boring and expensive".* / 11.30 pm.

The Red Pepper W9 £26 ❷④❸

8 Formosa St   266 2708   8–4A
*"Thin crust Italian pizza swarming with fresh mozzarella and
tomato, spiced with basil" is the sort of simple dish done to
a turn which continues to win a more than local following for
this obscurely located Mediterranean bistro in Maida Vale;
the rather hard-edged accommodation, especially in the
basement, is not to all tastes.* / 10.45 pm; closed Mon; no Amex.

RESTAURANT MARCO PIERRE WHITE
HYDE PARK HOTEL SW1 £98 ❸④⑤

Knightsbridge   259 5380   2–3A
*Are Mr White's "heart-stopping" prices justified?; for some,
"sublime" and "fantastic" dishes from the "star chef of the
'90s" make the premium worthwhile – "be prepared to sell
your house"; most reports, however, express some shade of
disappointment, be it about the atmosphere ("oppressive"),
the service ("in need of improvement") or, most importantly,
the cooking – too often it "completely fails to live up
to expectations".* / 11 pm; closed Sat L & Sun.

Reynier Wine Library EC3 £14 ❸④❸

43 Trinity Sq   481 0415   9–3D
*An atmospheric City cellar, where a simple buffet is provided
to accompany the wine, which you buy in the adjoining arch
at merchant's prices; book ahead.* / L only; closed Sat & Sun.

Rib Room
Hyatt Carlton Tower Hotel SW1   £48   ❷❷❸
2 Cadogan Pl   235 1234   2–4A
"If you're determined to get BSE, this is the place to get it",
says an enthusiast for the "really very good" grills at this
"impeccable" Knightsbridge dining room; some find the
"hotely" ambience rather "boring". / 11.15 pm; no Switch;
smart casual.

Riccardo's SW3   £23   ❸④❷
126 Fulham Rd   370 6656   5–3B
"A menu full of starter-size portions" might sound
a nightmare formula, but has re-affirmed this well established
address as a "cheap" (by Chelsea standards) and "cheerful",
"local favourite"; "nice on a sunny day, if you sit outside";
service is capable of much improvement. / Midnight.

Ristorante Italiano W1   £27   ❷❷❸
54 Curzon St   629 2742   3–3B
Very "traditional" Italian, by Shepherd Market; the particular
attraction is the old-style service, but the food is not bad, and
quite reasonably priced. / 11.15 pm; closed Sat L & Sun;
no smoking area.

The Ritz W1   £60   ④❷❶
150 Piccadilly   493 8181   3–4C
This "wonderful" Louis XVI-style restaurant looks even
more ravishing after its recent refurbishment – "how
could you avoid falling in love, dancing in that room on
a Saturday night?"; the modern French cooking, however,
is significantly below par; breakfast, à l'anglaise, comes
highly recommended. / 11 pm; jacket & tie.

Riva SW13   £33   ❶❷④
169 Church Rd, Barnes   0181-748 0434   10–1A
"Good, sometimes sublime" cooking has created a deserved
reputation for this "unlikely" Barnes Italian; some approve the
atmosphere, but the more general view is that the place is
a touch "crowded" and "uncomfortable". / 11 pm, Fri & Sat
11.30 pm, Sun 9.30 pm; closed Sat L; smart casual.

THE RIVER CAFÉ W6   £43   ❶❸❷
Thames Whf, Rainville Rd   381 8824   7–2C
"Outstandingly good", "interesting and creative" cooking,
involving "simple treatment" of "top ingredients" makes this
"chic", modern dining room indubitably London's leading
Italian; though it is "the perfect place on a summer evening",
it has a "difficult" Hammersmith location, and some feel that
prices are pushed to the limit. / 9.30 pm; closed Sun D.

Rock Island Diner W1   £23   ❸❸❸
2nd Fl London Pavilion   287 5500   3–3D
"Lively", '50s-theme burger-restaurant, by Piccadilly Circus –
"great for kids" and "a good evening out for groups".
/ 11.30 pm; no booking.

Rodos WC2 £ 23 ③③⑤
59 St Giles High St   836 3177   4–1B
Scruffy family-run Greek, in the shadow of Centre Point,
which serves decent, cheap nosh and which – especially in
a group – can be fun. / 11.15 pm; closed Sat L & Sun; no Switch.

Rôtisserie £ 25 ③③④
56 Uxbridge Rd, W12   0181-743 3028   7–1C
134 Upper St, N1   226 0122   8–3D
"Fresh, no-nonsense cooking", principally from the grill
or rôtisserie, makes these "good local restaurants" in
Shepherd's Bush and Islington worth knowing about; the
best value is from the fixed price menu. / 11 pm, Fri &
Sat 11.30 pm; W12 closed Sat L & Sun.

Rôtisserie Jules £ 18 ③③④
338 King's Rd, SW3   351 0041   5–3C
6-8 Bute St, SW7   584 0600   5–2B
133 Notting Hill Gate, W11   221 3331   6–2B
The "competently cooked rôtisserie" – any flavour so long
as it's chicken (or, to advance order, lamb) – wins a steady
following for these chic, but rather bare, Chelsea and South
Kensington canteens; a new Notting Hill branch opens in the
autumn of 1996. / 11 pm, SW3 midnight.

Rowley's SW1 £ 34 ⑤③④
113 Jermyn St   930 2707   3–3D
Some proclaim this unusual tiled restaurant (the original
home of Wall's sausages) as a "reliable" St James's spot,
"good for steak and chips after the theatre"; that it has
"gone downhill" and is "no longer cheap" are sentiments on
too many lips, however, but the introduction of a new menu –
expanding the previously limited choice – may be
a positive sign. / 11.30 pm; smart casual.

Royal China W2 £ 26 ②④③
13 Queensway   221 2535   6–2C
"Fabulous dim-sum, as good as Hong Kong" is the special
attraction at this "spacious" Bayswater oriental – be prepared
for "long waits" for tables at weekends; at other times, this is
still one of the better Chineses in town. / 10.30 pm; no booking
Sun L.

Royal China SW15 £ 28 ②③③
3 Chelverton Rd   0181-788 0907   10–2B
Putney's Royal China (no longer related to Bayswater's)
retains, so far at least, its characterful, deeply '70s décor;
staff are "friendly" and it consistently serves food that is
"great" – if "pricey", by Chineses standards; dim-sum are
a speciality here too. / 10.30 pm.

RSJ SE1 £27 ❷❷❸

13a Coin St 928 4554 9–4A

*"Well priced" and "relaxing" modern British South Banker
(convenient for the Festival Hall) whose ratings are on the up;
it's "not a gourmet restaurant, and it doesn't pretend to be",
but it does "makes your feel at home", and a particular
attraction is a huge list of "wonderful Loire wines at very
fair prices".* / 11 pm; closed Sat L & Sun.

Ruby in the Dust £21 ④❸❷

70 Upper St, N1 359 1710 8–3D
102 Camden High St, NW1 485 2744 8–3C

*"Friendly, good value" small chain, popular with a younger
crowd, which offers sometimes "interesting" international fare
and a "lively" atmosphere.* / 11.15 pm; no Amex.

Rudland & Stubbs EC1 £30 ❸❸④

35 Cowcross St 253 0148 9–1A

*There are some (ourselves included) who think that the joke –
"a fish place in Smithfield, ha, ha, ha" – is on the customer;
others, however, proclaim the virtues of this "hidden gem",
which offers a "good choice" of "well-cooked fish dishes to
suit every pocket".* / 11.45 pm; closed Sat L & Sun.

La Rueda SW4 £21 ④❸❶

66-68 Clapham High St 627 2173 10–2D

*Famous Clapham institution, which – atmospherically if not
gastronomically speaking – is "as close to a real Spanish
tapas bar as one could wish".* / 11.30 pm; book only in restaurant.

RULES WC2 £34 ❸❷❷

35 Maiden Ln 836 5314 4–3D

*London's oldest restaurant (1798) could easily rely on the
charms of its "impressive" and "clubby" Covent Garden
premises to become a fully paid-up tourist trap; the food is,
in fact, "surprisingly good" (especially, of course, the "great
puddings"), helping to make this one of the best all-round
performers in the West End.* / 11.30 pm; smart casual.

Rupee Room EC2 £23 ❸❸④

10 Copthall Ave 628 1555 9–2C

*"Good food, if a little expensive" (well, it is the City) makes
this gaudy but somewhat "uninspiring" basement a "useful
addition" to the local lunching scene, opposite the Chartered
Accountants' HQ.* / 10 pm; closed Sat & Sun; no smoking area.

S&P £24 ❷❶④

Beauchamp Pl, SW3 581 8820 5–1C
181 Fulham Rd, SW3 351 5692 5–2C

*"The same quality every time" ensures a strong following
for these "great, reasonably priced" Chelsea and
Knightsbridge Thais.* / 10.30 pm; no-smoking area at Beauchamp Pl.

Sabai Sabai W6 £ 23 ❷❸⑤
270-272 King St   0181-748 7363   7–2B
*"Good food", especially the "mixed Thai starters" commend
this Hammersmith spot to some; others share our feeling that
the "total lack of atmosphere" takes the edge off
the experience. / 11.30 pm; closed Sun L.*

Le Sacré-Coeur N1 £ 18 ❸❸④
18 Theberton St   354 2618   8–3D
*Cramped, no-nonsense Gallic bistro newcomer, just off
Islington's Upper Street, offering real food at
reasonable prices. / 11.30 pm, Fri & Sat midnight.*

Saga W1 £ 46 ❸❸④
43-44 South Molton St   408 2236   3–2B
*"The sushi bar is as close as you can get to real Japan", and
the "noodles are outstanding", claim fans of this rather dated
basement, just by Oxford Street; our vote goes with those who
think the food is "not good – not bad". / 10 pm; closed Sun.*

Saigon W1 £ 24 ❸❸❸
45 Frith St   437 7109   4–2A
*Soho Vietnamese which deserves to be better known and
is too often "empty"; perhaps they are just no good at PR,
because, even though service can be "slow", the "consistent"
oriental fare is "good" and quite interesting. / 11.30 pm;
closed Sun.*

Saint WC2 £ 32 ④④❶
8 Great Newport St   240 1551   4–3B
*"Very funky", new West End hang-out – complete with velvet
rope, cool design, groovy staff and very large bar – whose
"clientele might melt under the lights, they are so plastic";
the ambitious and expensive modern British food can take an
age in coming and, though some do rate it highly, consistency
is not its key strength. / 11.30 pm; closed Sat L & Sun.*

St John EC1 £ 29 ④❸④
26 St John St   251 0848   9–1B
*"I liked it – my three companions didn't" and "a love/hate
relationship" are two characteristic comments on this
"impressive" and "interesting" former Smithfield smokehouse;
it's the number of people who feel that the "imaginative"
menu is "turning into a caricature of itself – only food
critics like this much offal" – that significantly depresses
the ratings, but if you visit a restaurant whose motto is
'nose-to-tail-eating', what do you expect? / 11.30 pm; closed Sun D.*

St Moritz W1 £ 26 ❸❷❸
161 Wardour St   734 3324   3–1D
*Small, sweet, Swiss Soho survivor from another age that still
does its fondues, steaks and schnitzels rather better than you
might expect – especially as its following seems to consist
largely of foreign visitors. / 11.30 pm; closed Sat L & Sun.*

Sale e Pepe SW1 £36 ❸❸❶
9-15 Pavilion Rd   235 0098   2–3A
"The deliberate noise" – the waiters are prone to bursting into song – "can detract from the fine food" at this "friendly" and agreeably tacky Knightsbridge trattoria; it's "always great fun", though. / 11.30 pm; closed Sun.

Salloos SW1 £45 ❸⑤⑤
62-64 Kinnerton St   235 4444   2–3A
It may be "excruciatingly expensive", but supporters claim its worth it for the "superb"-tasting "authentic Pakistani cooking" at this discreet Belgravia mews restaurant; "not an inspired ambience", though, and service is not up to snuff. / 11.15 pm; closed Sun; smart casual.

Sambuca SW3 £32 ❸❶④
6 Symons St   730 6571   5–2D
"Time-warp Italian", behind Peter Jones, which "never disappoints"; service is the particular strength, and the cramped setting the weakness. / 11.30 pm; closed Sun.

San Carlo N6 £35 ④❸④
2 Highgate High St   0181-340 5823   8–1B
Lack of much in the way of local mid-range competition means this grand and airy, rather old-fashioned Highgate trattoria continues to get away with being "overpriced and complacent". / 11 pm; closed Mon; no smoking area.

San Frediano SW3 £42 ⑤④④
62 Fulham Rd   584 8375   5–2C
Chelsea's dear old 'San Fred' – the former trattoria on this site – was at least cheap; new owners have shifted its aspirations up a gear, and it's now "grossly overpriced". / 11.45 pm.

San Lorenzo SW3 £50 ⑤⑤④
22 Beauchamp Pl   584 1074   5–1C
Knightsbridge trattoria, famous as "a great place – in the 1970s"; nowadays, some kinder souls say the food's "not bad, until you get the bill", but for many the experience is just a "rip-off" – "appalling", "pretentious", "overrated" and "hugely disappointing" – and, to add insult to injury, the "very bad service" labours under the misapprehension that "it is doing you a favour". / 11.30 pm; closed Sun; no credit cards; smart casual.

San Martino SW3 £32 ❸❸❸
103 Walton St   589 3833   5–2C
"Reliable, well-cooked" Italian fare and "pleasant" service make this "comfortable" Knightsbridge fixture a "fair value", low-risk choice in that pricey part of town. / 11.30 pm, Sun pm; smart casual; no smoking area.

FSA

Sandrini SW3 £34 ④④❸
260 Brompton Rd 584 1724 5–2C
An attractive, "jovial" Brompton Cross trattoria of long-standing; once it was chic, and it is sad now to read reports of a "rather touristy" place, where "not great" food comes at "high prices", and service is "up and down". / 11.30 pm.

Santini SW1 £50 ④④④
29 Ebury St 730 4094 2–4B
Very high prices and "too minimal" décor continue to limit enthusiasm for this smart, smug Belgravia Italian; expansion is in progress as we go to press, however, and – who knows? – in an establishment which has always seemed pushed for space, this might just make all the difference. / 11.30 pm; closed Sat L & Sun L; smart casual.

Sarastro WC2 £26 ④⑤❸
126 Drury Ln 836 0101 2–2D
Whimsical Theatreland newcomer, which bills itself as 'the show after the show'; the Byzantine/Baroque setting is certainly impressive, but it's tourist fodder which is dished up, and some of the staff, though quite charming, seem to be straight off the boat. / 11.30 pm.

Sarcan N1 £18 ❷❷❸
4 Theberton St 226 5489 8–3D
"Great value, freshly grilled Turkish food in huge quantities" and "delicious mixed starters" win unanimous praise for this no-frills but comfortable spot, just off Islington's Upper Street. / Midnight; no Switch.

Sash SW6 £19 ❸❸❸
825 Fulham Rd 736 9429 10–1B
"Always fun, busy and friendly", this popular Fulham 'oriental tapas bar' continues to fill a useful niche; "quality can vary". / 11 pm.

Les Saveurs W1 £56 ④❷❸
37a Curzon St 491 8919 3–4B
Ex-chef, Joël Antunès, cooked up some of the best value haute cuisine in London at this "formal" and "well spaced" Mayfair basement; since its annexation by the Marco Pierre White empire, and the installation of Richard Stuart as chef, "things are not as they were", however – our August '96 visit found prices up and cooking standards down (though service was as good as ever). / 10.30 pm; closed Sat L & Sun; jacket & tie.

SAVOY GRILL WC2 £59 ❸❷❸
Strand 836 4343 4–3D
If you want "to feel part of the fabric of industry and politics" there's still no substitute for power-lunching in this elegantly understated room; the food is precisely as the punters demand – "always consistent", "reliable, not exciting", and, of course, very expensive. / 11.15 pm; closed Sat L & Sun; jacket & tie.

SAVOY RIVER ROOM WC2 £ 65 ❸❸❷
Strand 836 4343 4–3D
"Genteel", "elegant", "orderly" and "comforting", this vast
dining room, with its very special atmosphere, continues to
win high praise – "get a table by the window, and the world
is yours"; the grand Anglo-French cooking is not, of course,
the main attraction. / 11.30 pm; jacket & tie.

Scalini SW3 £ 38 ④❸❷
1-3 Walton St 225 2301 5–2C
Foodwise it may be somewhere between "unpredictable" and
"ghastly", but this tightly packed Knightsbridge trattoria "still
has a buzz which cannot be beaten" – "no good for a cosy
chat", but "ideal for a large party". / 11.45 pm; smart casual.

The Scandinavian Restaurant SW1 £ 28 ❸④④
14-15 Little Chester St 245 1224 2–4A
This stilted (to some "cold") upstairs dining room
(formerly called Schillerströms) above a Belgravia boozer
offers competent, mainly Swedish fare. / 10.30 pm;
closed Sat L & Sun.

The Scarsdale W8 £ 19 ④❸❷
23a Edwardes Sq 937 1811 7–1D
The "pretty" but tiny summer garden is the key attraction at
this charmingly situated, eighteenth century Kensington pub;
the English fare is now very ordinary. / 9.45 pm; no Amex
& no Switch; smart casual.

Scoffers SW11 £ 22 ④④❷
6 Battersea Rs 978 5542 10–2C
"Complacent but popular" younger-scene Battersea bistro,
with an unusually "spacious", sky-lit rear room; it's a relaxed
place, with a good atmosphere, best for "casual suppers"
or breakfast. / 11 pm.

Scott's W1 £ 38
20 Mount St 629 5248 3–3A
A major refit of this famous Mayfair fish and seafood
establishment had still not been completed at the time of our
September 1996 'early-days' visit; initial impressions were of
a place with some potential, but lacking the singular style of
former days. / 11 pm; Sat L only oyster bar open, closed Sun.

Seafresh SW1 £ 18 ❷❸④
80-81 Wilton Rd 828 0747 2–4B
"Good fish and chips", served in "huge portions" maintain
a devoted following for this "charming, dated" Pimlico chippie.
/ 10 pm; closed Sun.

Seashell NW1 £21 **❶❸**⑤
49 Lisson Gr   723 8703   8–4A
This famous (but characterless) chippie, behind Marylebone Station "continues to pull in the crowds", thanks to the "excellent value" of its staple – the other offerings may be found less reliable. / 10.30 pm; closed Sun D; no smoking area; no booking.

755 SW6 £31 **❷❸**④
755 Fulham Rd   371 0755   10–1B
"Fulham foodie place", recently opened by protégés of Knightsbridge restaurateur, Brian Turner; a "pleasant, Frenchish restaurant", it gets general praise for its "clever" menu and its "very good" cooking; the ambience, though, is a let-down – "depending on your mood, it's either very soothing, or too dull to last". / 11 pm, Sun 9 pm; closed Mon L.

Shampers W1 £27 **❷❸❸**
4 Kingly St   437 1692   3–2D
"Old favourite" Soho wine bar offering a "friendly, welcoming" environment; contradicting its evident '70s heritage, it provides "simple food, well done". / 11 pm; closed Sun.

Shaw's SW7 £48 **❸❷❸**
119 Old Brompton Rd   373 7774   5–2B
"Intimate", "calm" modern British restaurant in South Kensington which splits opinion – those who proclaim "excellent" food and "polite" service win by a narrow margin over younger-at-heart souls who think it a "dreadful, overpriced, pretentious" place, "staid enough for your maiden aunt". / 11 pm; closed Sat L & Sun D; smart casual.

Sheekey's EC4 £37 ⑤④**❸**
11 Queen Victoria St   489 8067   9–3C
"What are they trying to achieve?", in this "hushed" basement, where "overpriced" and sometimes "unimaginative and sloppy" lunching fodder is served; presumably – as so often at places "handy in the City" – the answer is maximum revenue from minimum effort. / L only; closed Sat & Sun; smart casual.

Sheekey's WC2 £47 ④**❷**④
28-32 St Martins Ct   240 2565   4–3B
Even those vaunting the "excellent", simple fish dishes at this venerable, cramped Theatreland fish parlour often note that they are "overpriced" (and the sums demanded for vegetables are just "extortionate"). / 11.30 pm; closed Sun.

Shepherd's SW1 £32 ❸❶❸
Marsham Ct, Marsham St 834 9552 2–4C
*"Many a cabinet minister's postprandial slump is thanks to
the sticky toffee pudding" served in these congenial,
clubby premises, not far from the House; all in all, this son-of-
Langan's makes a very "dependable" place, the more notable
for being in an area with few competing attractions. / 11.30 pm;
closed Sat & Sun; no Switch.*

The Ship SW18 £24 ❸④❷
41 Jews Row 0181-870 9667 10–2B
*"Good bar food" from a "varied menu" makes this riverside
pub by Wandsworth Bridge popular all year round; it's in
the summer, though, that – thanks to the famous barbecue –
it becomes everyone's "favourite haunt" (especially for
singles), attracting "simply too many people". / 10.30 pm.*

Shoeless Joe's SW6 £28 ④④❷
555 King's Rd 384 2333 5–4B
*"The best atmosphere in London for a big sporting event",
say fans of this far-King's Road sports bar; the American fare
served in the smoothly decorated dining room is certainly not
the attraction. / 11 pm.*

Shogun W1 £46 ❷❷❸
Adam's Rw 493 1255 3–3A
*"Good ambience – a commodity rare enough in Japanese
restaurants" – is the Unique Selling Proposition of this Mayfair
basement, which offers a wide selection of dishes, including
"good sushi". / 10.30 pm; D only; closed Mon; no Switch.*

Le Shop SW3 £19 ❸❸❸
329 King's Rd 352 3891 5–3C
*Though no special bargain, this classic Chelsea crêperie
hits a spot for locals and visitors in search of a light bite;
loud classical music enhances the superior atmosphere.
/ Midnight; no Switch.*

Shree Krishna SW17 £17 ❶⑤⑤
192-194 Tooting High St 0181-672 4250 10–2D
*"Delicious southern Indian food" (much of it vegetarian) at
"good value prices" earns this Tooting local numerous tips
as "top south London Indian"; service, however, is
"legendarily bad". / Mon-Thu 10.45 pm, Fri & Sat 11.45 pm; no Switch.*

Signor Sassi SW1 £41 ❸④❷
14 Knightsbridge Gn 584 2277 5–1D
*Though there's "nothing exceptional about the food",
"the atmosphere is great" say supporters of this "loud but
fun" Knightsbridge trattoria; those averse to "tables on top of
each other" can find it all a touch too much. / 11.30 pm;
closed Sun; smart casual.*

Silks & Spice W1   £21   ❷❸❸

23 Foley St   636 2718   2–1B
*"Always reliable", "friendly" Thai/Malay which draws
a younger crowd to these cheerfully cramped premises,
north of Oxford Street.* / 11 pm.

Simply Nico SW1   £35   ❷❷④

48a Rochester Rw   630 8061   2–4C
*The "best all-in deal", claim proponents of star chef Nico
Ladenis's quietly located bistro-offshoot in Victoria; even those
who find it "delightful", however, may feel it's "cramped", and
to others it's just "harshly lit and uncomfortable" – "a bleak
little room".* / 11 pm; closed Sat L & Sun; smart casual.

Simpson's of Cornhill EC3   £19   ❸❸❶

38 1/2 Cornhill   626 9985   9–2C
*"Dickensian steak house" pronounced "incapable of
improvement" by its devoted City following; "good school
food" is served by "friendly Cockney matrons" in an olde
English setting which could have come straight from
Central Castings.* / L only; closed Sat & Sun; no booking.

Simpsons-in-the-Strand WC2   £38   ④❸❸

100 Strand   836 9112   4–3D
*We have no truck with all this BSE nonsense, but this
"time-warp homage" to traditional roasts shows worrying
signs of succumbing to mad restaurant disease – "currently
a tourist-trap", "quite disgusting" and "a disgrace" may be
minority sentiments, but they are still not the sort which
a Savoy Group property should ever attract; the cooked
breakfast here, served on weekdays only and until noon,
is, however, "simply the best".* / 11 pm, Sun 9 pm; no Switch;
smart casual.

Singapore Garden NW6   £26   ❷❸❸

83-83a Fairfax Rd   328 5314   8–2A
*"Friendly, no hassle" Swiss Cottage oriental – offering
a medley of South East Asian cuisines – which attracts
a wider than local following; "it can vary", notes one
supporter – it certainly did on our most recent visit.* / 10.45 pm.

Singapura   £24   ❸❸❸

78/79 Leadenhall St, EC3   929 0089   9–2D
1-2 Limeburner Ln, EC4   329 1133   9–2A
*"Interesting, varied pan-South East Asian cuisine" makes
these smart, slightly stark City spots a reliable choice,
though the "friendly" service can be "slow"; coming soon –
not one but two offshoots in the basement of Covent Garden's
Thomas Neal shopping mall.* / EC3 L only, EC4 10 pm ; closed Sat
& Sun; smart casual.

606 Club SW10 £29 ④❷❷
90 Lots Rd   352 5953   5–4B

For a night out with a difference, you might try Chelsea's only jazz-club-in-a-basement-opposite-a-power-station; it's an atmospheric place, going on till late, and the music is often good – on the food front, stick to the cheaper 'filler' items; non-members must eat to drink. / Mon-Thu 1.30 am, Fri & Sat 2 am, Sun 11.30 pm; D only; no Amex.

Smollensky's Balloon W1 £26 ❸❸❷
1 Dover St   491 1199   3–3C

Reliable, if "ordinary", American food is on offer at this Mayfair establishment; it's quite a characterful place (with a good bar), and even if it's "not as smooth as the Strand branch" (see below), it has "better atmosphere". / Midnight, Sun 10.30 pm.

Smollensky's on the Strand WC2 £26 ④❸❸
105 The Strand   497 2101   4–3D

The grander sibling of the Balloon (above) isn't quite as consistent a performer; later in the week, though, it benefits from a "very lively atmosphere" (with dancing), making it "a great place for office parties"; at weekends, it's "super for kids". / Midnight, Thu - Sat 12.30 am, Sun 10.30 pm.

Snows on the Green W6 £31 ④❸④
166 Shepherd's Bush Rd   603 2142   7–1C

"Very tasty" Mediterranean fare has made something of a reputation for this Shepherd's Bush neighbourhood restaurant; quality, though, is "variable" and the atmosphere can seem a fraction "uptight". / 11 pm; closed Sat L & Sun D.

Sofra W1 £24 ❷❸❸
18 Shepherd St   493 3320   3–4B

The original Shepherd Market Sofra still offers "terrific value" Turkish fare; it's "always crowded, but it has charm", and there are some nice outside tables; see next and also Café Sofra. / Midnight.

Sofra £24 ④④④
1 St Christopher's Pl, W1   224 4080   3–1A
(Bistro Sofra) 18 Shepherd Mkt, W1   499 4099   3–4B
17 Charing Cross Rd, WC2   240 3972   4–4B
36 Tavistock St, WC2   240 3773   4–3D

The 'other' Sofras are a mixed bag; Bistro Sofra is quite chic and welcoming, but the Covent Garden branch is short on charm and has proved less impressive in every department; an early visit to the new Theatreland branch, found competent cooking in a rather characterless setting; St Christopher's Place is a summer 1996 newcomer. / Midnight.

Soho Soho W1   £32   ❸④❷
11-13 Frith St   494 3491   4–2A
*Popular, "easy-going", central institution whose "vibrant",
"no-nonsense", no-booking downstairs rôtisserie makes
"a lively place for lunch or dinner"; the more ambitious
upstairs restaurant is more expensive and can
"lack atmosphere".* / rôtisserie 12.45 am, restaurant 11.45 pm;
restaurant closed Sat L & Sun; no smoking area; no booking in rôtisserie.

Sol e Luna WC2   £29   ④❷❸
22 Short's Gdns   379 3336   4–2C
*"A lovely place – apart from the food"; this Covent Garden
Italian has a "great location" in the stylish basement of
a trendy shopping mall, but even those who vaunt the pizza
from the wood-burning oven admit that the cooking can be
"very good or a little flat".* / Midnight, Sun 10.30 pm; smart casual;
no smoking area.

Sol e Stella W1   £24   ④❷❸
43 Blandford St   487 3336   2–1A
*Like its sibling, Sol e Luna, this carefully decked-out
Marylebone restaurant elevates style over substance and,
despite boasting a wood-burning pizza oven, turns out food of
uniform mediocrity; willing staff try hard.* / 11.30 pm; closed Sun D;
smart casual; no smoking area.

Solly's NW11   £28   ❷④❸
148 Golders Green Rd   0181-455 0004   1–1B
*"The most incredible pitta bread" and the "best falafel
in town" justify the schlep to Golder's Green, home
of London's leading Kosher restaurant; service is
"100% chaotic" ("with Solly acting as ringmaster") and
the décor is 100% kitsch – all in all, a real experience.*
/ 11.30 pm; closed Fri D & Sat; no smoking area.

Sonny's SW13   £31   ❸❷❷
94 Church Rd   0181-748 0393   10–1A
*This "unique" Barnes "jewel" continues to sparkle, "never
failing to please" its many fans with its "unfussy" English food;
an excellent, buzzing all-rounder, it suits "a romantic dinner
just as well as lunch with your mother-in-law".* / 11 pm;
closed Sun D; smart casual.

Sotheby's Café W1   £26   ❸❸❸
34 New Bond St   408 5077   3–2C
*The auctioneers who play at being gentlemen are now having
a go at being chefs too, and making quite a success of it;
"a limited but good light menu" is served in this "artful" room
(off the main foyer), whose "ingenious use of space" manages
to disguise its "corridor" origins.* / L only; closed Sat & Sun, but May-
Jul and Sep-Dec open Sun L.

Le Soufflé
Inter-Continental Hotel W1   **£56**   ❷❷④
1 Hamilton Pl   409 3131   3–4A
*As the streamlined dining room itself is actually quite
inoffensive, it must be the "terrible", '70s décor of the hotel
foyer which puts people off coming here – as ever, reports
are incredibly thin on the ground; such feedback as there
is, however, confirms that Peter Kromberg's ambitious
modern French fare continues to satisfy, and that service
is commendable. / 10.30 pm, Sat 11.15 pm; closed Mon,
Sat L & Sun D; jacket.*

Soulard N1   **£24**   ❸❷❸
113 Mortimer Rd   254 1314   1–1C
*"A patron like a character from a Pink Panther film" lends
added spice to this "cheerful", cramped and unpretentious
Gallic bistro, on the Islington/Hackney fringe. / 10.30 pm; D only,
closed Sun & Mon; no Switch.*

South Bank Brasserie SE1   **£25**   ④❸❷
Gabriel's Wharf, 56 Upper Ground   620 0596   9–3A
*The point of visiting this self-descriptive spot is a "picture
postcard view of the Thames and of the City skyline";
reports barely mention the food – a sort of compliment,
really. / 11 pm.*

Spago SW7   **£19**   ❸④❸
6 Glendower Pl   225 2407   5–2B
*"Especially for South Kensington", this basic Italian is "a value
for money venue" with "good pizza and pasta"; some find the
"busy" environment "cheerful". / Midnight; no credit cards.*

Sporting Page SW10   **£18**   ❷❸❷
6 Camera Pl   376 3694   5–3B
*Superior modern pub in Chelsea whose "tasty and not
expensive", simple dishes and "casual atmosphere" attract
a fashionable crowd. / 10 pm; no Amex & no Switch; no booking.*

Springbok Café W4   **£29**   ❷❷❸
42 Devonshire Rd   0181-742 3149   7–2A
*South African newcomer which offers some excellent,
unusual cooking (with much for fish lovers) in a tranquil
Chiswick backwater; the IKEA-style setting is cheerful but not
especially comfortable. / 10.30 pm; closed Sat L & Sun; no Amex.*

Lo Spuntino SW3   **£26**   ❷❸④
330 King's Rd   351 3634   5–3C
*"Cheap and very cheerful" Italian, which is surprisingly little
known, given its quality cooking (pizza a speciality) and its
useful location, near the kink in the King's Road. / Midnight;
closed Mon; no Amex.*

The Square W1 £ 56 ❷❸ –

6-10 Bruton St   495 7100   3–2C
*"A really good overall experience" is the general view on this
"very professional" modern British restaurant, which, as we
go to press, is leaving St James's for larger new premises in
Mayfair; perhaps the impending move has been a distraction,
as the food rating, though still commendable, has declined
since last year. / 11.45 pm; closed Sat L & Sun L; smart casual.*

Sri Siam W1 £ 26 ❷❷❸

16 Old Compton St   434 3544   4–2A
*"Very popular", "consistently good" Soho spot whose
"excellent Thai food" "never fails to please" – "a thousand
visits, and never disappointed", claims one reporter who is
doubtless exaggerating only slightly. / 11.15 pm; closed Sun L.*

Sri Siam City EC2 £ 29 ❷❷❸

85 London Wall   628 5772   9–2C
*"Excellent" Thai food and "efficient service" makes this
"large and elegant" basement, "a lunchtime favourite in
the City"; it's "ideal for business meetings – they don't rush
you through". / 7.45 pm; closed Sat & Sun.*

Sri Thai EC4 £ 28 ❷❸❸

3 Queen Victoria St   827 0202   9–3C
*Though service has some way to go at the latest addition to
the excellent Sri Siam group, the cooking is well up to speed,
and the City basement setting – with its "mirrors, glitz and
style" – really is impressive. / 8.30 pm; closed Sat & Sun.*

The Stamford W6 £ 25 ④❷❷

320 Goldhawk Rd   0181-741 1994   7–1B
*"Good setting, good bar, good mood and – usually –
good food", say supporters of this "light and airy" new
pub-conversion, near Queen Charlotte's Hospital; we have
some sympathy for those who baulk at "restaurant prices"
for "sound, not superior" modern British grub. / 10.30 pm;
closed Sat L & Sun D.*

Standard Tandoori W2 £ 19 ❷❷④

21-23 Westbourne Gro   229 0600   6–1C
*Large, inexpensive Bayswater Indian, whose cooking is
"always delicious", and "efficiently" served; atmosphere-wise
the place deserves its name, but it's a much more
comfortable bet than its notorious neighbour, Khan's.
/ 11.45 pm; no smoking area.*

Star Café W1 £ 12 ❸④❸

22 Gt Chapel St   437 8778   3–1D
*For a good, cheap brekkie, the fry-ups at this Soho
café (a short step south of Oxford Street) have a loyal
local following. / 4 pm; closed Sat & Sun; no credit cards; no smoking area.*

Star of India SW5   £34   ❷④❷
154 Old Brompton Rd   373 2901   5–2B
"Extraordinarily consistent" cooking continues to pack crowds of fashionable Londoners into this long-running subcontinental success story – reporters' favourite Indian; the "electric" atmosphere of its "camp" muralled South Kensington premises is a special plus – its sometimes "unprofessional" service is not. / 11.45 pm.

Stephen Bull W1   £38   ❷❶❸
5-7 Blandford St   486 9696   2–1A
"Maintaining good standards without pretensions", this well established Marylebone modern Britisher continues to please its punters who find it "pricey, but worth it for the food"; the year-old softening of the stark décor has improved the atmosphere, but it's still "for business" that the place wins most votes, thanks, in part, to its excellent service. / 10.45 pm; closed Sat L & Sun.

Stephen Bull Bistro EC1   £30   ❸❸④
71 St John St   490 1750   9–1A
"Now back to the form of two or three years ago", this rather stark modern British spot in Smithfield is re-establishing itself as a top City lunching venue; fish and seafood get a particular thumbs-up. / 10.30 pm; closed Sat L & Sun.

The Stepping Stone SW8   £28   ❶❶❷
123 Queenstown Rd   622 0555   10–1C
'Sympathique' Battersea spot, where acclaim for the "excellent" modern British cooking continues to grow; though the setting is "a little stark", the staff are "welcoming and genuinely concerned about the satisfaction of the customer". / 11 pm, Mon 10.30 pm; closed Sat L; no smoking area.

Stick & Bowl W8   £11   ❸❸④
31 Kensington High St   937 2778   5–1A
"Very authentic", stuff-yourself-for-a-tenner, oriental diner/take-away, long beloved of Kensington shoppers and residents – Chinese and otherwise; rush-hour dining at Waterloo would be about as relaxing. / 11 pm; no credit cards; no smoking area.

Sticky Fingers W8   £20   ④❸❸
1a Phillimore Gdns   938 5338   5–1A
Stick to the burgers at Bill Wyman's Kensington diner and you'll be OK; with its "friendly" staff, 'Stones memorabilia décor and reliably buzzy atmosphere, it's ideal for kids of all ages. / 11.30 pm; book L only.

Stock Pot £11 ④❷④

40 Panton St, SW1   839 5142   4–4A
18 Old Compton St, W1   287 1066   4–2B
50 James St, W1   486 1086   3–1A
273 King's Rd, SW3   823 3175   5–3C
6 Basil St, SW3   589 8627   5–1D

"Don't be put off by dowdy 'décor'", this super-budget chain has many fans – even they admit "the food is hardly exciting", but there are few places where "you can get such a great range of dishes for the price". / 11 pm-midnight; no credit cards.

Stratford's W8 £36 ❷❷④

7 Stratford Rd   937 6388   5–2A

We can't quite see it ourselves, but reporters sing the praises of the "brilliant selection of fish and shellfish" served in this Kensington backwater; some claim it's "light and summery" too – but to us, it's just rather crowded and over-lit. / 11 pm; closed Sun.

The Sugar Club W11 £34 ❷❷❸

33 All Saints Rd   221 3844   6–1B

"First class food with a 'Front Line' frisson" make a winning combination at this widely praised, "trendy" Pacific Rim spot, on the unlovely fringes of North Kensington; "what's all the fuss about?", says a small minority. / 11 pm; Mon-Fri closed L; no smoking area.

Sumos W6 £21 ❷❸④

169 King St   0181-741 7916   7–2C

"Cheap and cheerful" Hammersmith Nipponese serving superior food in rather grim, cafeteria-like premises. / 10.45 pm; closed Sat L & Sun; no credit cards.

Suntory SW1 £72 ❸❷④

72 St James's St   409 0201   3–4D

"Not one for the 'personal' account" – London's grandest Japanese is (unsurprisingly enough) "far too expensive", and has a "very formal", "soulless and starchy" atmosphere; the food, however (from teppan-yaki to the sushi and other dishes) is "superb", and the kimonoed service charm itself. / 10 pm; closed Sun; smart casual.

Le Suquet SW3 £36 ❸⑤❸

104 Draycott Av   581 1785   5–2C

The "atmosphere of a fun French eatery" and seafood that is "always fresh, well cooked and presented" still make a winning formula at this long-standing Cannes-comes-to-Chelsea fish-parlour; that's "just as well given the prices", however, and "appalling", "surly" service does the place absolutely no favours. / 11.30 pm.

Sushi Bar Gen SW6 £23 ❷④④
585 Fulham Rd 610 2120 5–4A
Bright Fulham Broadway café whose "excellent value sushi"
is the main – indeed the only – attraction. / 10.45 pm;
no smoking area.

Sweetings EC4 £30 ❸❸❷
39 Queen Victoria St 248 3062 9–3B
"A good spot for a glass of champagne with a pal", perhaps,
but lacklustre cooking and meals "costing far too much"
are beginning to dent the popularity of this unique and still
wonderful Victorian City fish parlour; simple dishes can be
"excellent", but sentiments of the "gone downhill" variety
are expressed worryingly often. / L only; closed Sat & Sun;
no credit cards; no booking.

Tabac W10 £29 ❶❷❸
46 Golborne Rd 0181-960 2433 6–1A
"Fresh, relaxed and cool" North Kensington restaurant, whose
"always interesting" and "unusual" modern British cooking
provides ample incentive to brave its recherché location.
/ 11 pm; closed Mon L; no Amex.

Taberna Etrusca EC4 £30 ④❶❷
9 Bow Churchyard 248 5552 9–2C
"Bustling" City Italian, whose charming outside tables,
in particular, make it "really good for an informal lunch";
the "happy, fast, helpful staff" are much praised, especially
by male reporters. / L only; closed Sat & Sun; no Switch.

Tamarind W1 £34 ❷❷❸
20 Queen St 629 3561 3–3B
"One of the best discoveries of last year", is the sort
of reaction which is creating a strong reputation for this
"sophisticated" Mayfair Indian yearling; "the slightly way-out
décor" generates rather less atmosphere than was
presumably intended. / 11.30 pm; closed Sat L; no Switch;
no smoking area.

Tandoori Lane SW6 £22 ❸❶❸
131a Munster Rd 371 0440 10–1B
"Impeccable" service is the special strength of this darkly
decorated Indian Fulhamite, whose cooking is
"very consistent". / 11 pm; no Amex.

Tandoori of Chelsea SW3 £32 ❸❷❸
153 Fulham Rd 589 7749 5–2C
All-round satisfaction characterises reports on this grand
and comfortable Brompton Cross Indian, whose splendidly
helmeted doorman discourages the incursion of any
evil spirits. / Midnight.

LA TANTE CLAIRE SW3 £ 67 ❶❷❸

68-69 Royal Hospital Rd 352 6045 5–3D
*"Amazing", classic French cuisine and "flawless" service
win universal acclaim for Pierre Koffmann's Chelsea
establishment; as ever, the only real complaints are about
the room, which, though "bright" and "elegant" to some is
merely "really boring" to others; the set lunch here is a well
known bargain (though culinary fireworks are generally
reserved for the hours of darkness).* / 11 pm; closed Sat & Sun;
no Switch; dinner, jacket & tie.

Tao EC4 £ 29 ④④❸

11 Bow Ln 248 5833 9–2C
*"Flash", very '80s City oriental with something of a name
for the "best looking waitresses" in the Square Mile; like one
reporter, we found "horrid" food – perhaps those praising the
cooking were distracted.* / 10 pm; closed Sat & Sun; smart casual.

Tate Gallery SW1 £ 33 ④❷❶

Millbank 887 8877 2–4C
*"Always enjoyable, though the food is unmemorable" –
the undoubted attractions here are the "beautiful" Whistler-
muralled room itself and, more importantly, "the best
reasonably priced wine list in town"; the service – "by school
dinner ladies" – receives general, but not unanimous, praise.*
/ L only; closed Sun; no Amex; no smoking area.

TATSUSO EC2 £ 60 ❶❸④

32 Broadgate Circle 638 5863 9–2D
*"Expensive, very expensive and phenomenally expensive",
the prices may be, but the "sheer quality of ingredients" and
sushi "as good as Tokyo" win a dedicated following for this
Broadgate spot, in spite of the basement's determinedly turgid
atmosphere – upstairs, there is a more glossy teppan-yaki,
popular with western bankers.* / 9.45 pm; closed Sat & Sun;
smart casual.

Tawana W2 £ 21 ❷❸④

3 Westbourne Gr 229 3785 6–1C
*Quality Thai fare draws a surprisingly pukka crowd to this
unpretentious but comfortable spot, a few paces along
from Queensway.* / 10.45 pm.

Tea Rooms des Artistes SW8 £ 19 ❸❸❸

697 Wandsworth Rd 652 6526 10–1D
*"Inexpensive" fare which "steers clear of veggie cliché" is
on offer at this Bohemian bar/café, betwixt Battersea and
Brixton, now, after its refit, a "little less self-consciously gothic"
than of old; "a great place in the summer because of the
cute courtyard".* / Food available until late – licensed to 1 am; D only,
ex Sun open L & D.

The Tenth W8 £ 40 ④④④

Royal Garden Hotel, Ken. High St 361 1910 5–1A
The tenth floor of this Kensington hotel (revamped in airport-executive-lounge-chic) boasts – at least in our experience – the sort of modern British cooking you might fear it would; the wonderful view over the Park defies all distractions – but they try, what with the jazzy carpet and ghastly Musak; service is "friendly but not attentive". / 11.30 pm; closed Sat L & Jul-Aug closed Sun; no smoking area.

Texas Embassy Cantina WC2 £ 24 ⑤④❸

1 Cockspur St 925 0077 2–2C
Though "previously pretty good", this large Tex/Mex by Trafalgar Square looks set to degenerate into the tourist trap which – given its location – always seemed its natural destiny; still, it can be "fun", and it's "great for kids". / 11 pm, midnight (Fri & Sat).

Texas Lone Star SW7 £ 20 ④④❷

154 Gloucester Rd 370 5625 5–2B
"Large burgers, large ribs and loud music" make this long-standing "fun, fun, fun", "loud, brash" American spot "good for kids and people with healthy appetites". / Sun-Wed 11.30 pm, Thu-Sat 12.30 am; no booking.

TGI Friday's £ 25 ⑤④❸

25-29 Coventry St, W1 839 6262 4–4A
6 Bedford St, WC2 379 0585 4–4C
96-98 Bishops Bridge Rd, W2 229 8600 6–1C
"Go, go, go" American theme-diners, lauded by some young-at-heart folk for "an all-round enjoyable evening"; even those who say they "used to be excellent" can now find them "disappointing", however, and, for many, they're just "awful, and not cheap either". / Midnight, W2 11.30 pm; smart casual; no smoking area; no booking.

Thai Bistro W4 £ 18 ❷❸④

99 Chiswick High Rd 0181-995 5774 7–2B
"Very tasty", "light" cooking using "fresh ingredients" earns this Chiswick "canteen-style" oriental newcomer (from the owner of Soho's Chiang Mai) a strong thumbs-up; the "novel seating", is "no good for couples", though, and the setting can be "very noisy". / 11 pm; closed Tue L & Thu L; no Amex & no Switch; no smoking area.

Thai Kitchen W2 £ 22 ❷❸④

108 Chepstow Rd 221 9984 6–1B
"Modest" Bayswater Thai whose "good value" dining wins it fans as a "late supper spot"; though a welcoming place, it lacks the atmosphere to make it more than a standby. / 11 pm; D only; closed Sun.

Thai on the River SW10 £34 ②④❸
15 Lots Rd 351 1151 5–4B
One of the "very few places with tables overlooking the river", this Chelsea oriental delivers excellent, very spicy cooking; service is very "slow", however. / 11 pm, Fri & Sat 11.30 pm; closed Sat L & Sun L.

Thai Pot WC2 £24 ❸⑤④
1 Bedfordbury 379 4580 4–4C
"Consistently good Thai food", is on offer at this "very handy location", just behind the Coliseum; its "good value set menus" make it suitable for groups, but service veers between "efficient" and "stroppy". / 11.15 pm; closed Sun.

Thailand SE14 £29 ❷❷④
15 Lewisham Way 0181-691 4040 1–3D
Some of the best Thai food in London – or near London, if Lewisham is beyond your ken – is still to be had in this cramped, characterful spot (which also boasts one of the most comprehensive ranges of single malts in town); book well ahead. / 10.30 pm; D only; closed Mon & Sun; no Amex & no Switch.

Thierry's SW3 £34 ④④❷
342 King's Rd 352 3365 5–3C
"Cosy and romantic", old-style Chelsea Gallic bistro; it's not without its supporters, but we strongly agree with people who now find it is grossly "overpriced". / 10.45 pm, Fri & Sat 11.15 pm, Sun 10.15 pm.

33 SW1 £44 ❸④⑤
33 St James's St 930 4272 3–4C
Art connoisseur and Masterchef-winner Derek Johns's St James's yearling does have its supporters – "wonderful, wonderful, wonderful all round"; the modern British fare is the strongest point, but it does not please everyone, and – given "service in need of improvement" and the "rather stilted" atmosphere – some find prices "exorbitant". / 11 pm; closed Sat L & Sun; smart casual.

Thistells SE22 £22 ⑤❸❷
65 Lordship Ln 0181-299 1921 1–4D
"Thankfully a decent restaurant in south east London", say enthusiastic local supporters of this East Dulwich spot, with its charming Edwardian tiled premises; given such praise, we felt let down by high prices and iffy results from the French/Middle Eastern menu, but eager-to-please service provided some compensation. / 10.30 pm; closed Sat L & Sun D; no Switch.

Thomas Goode Restaurant W1 £49 ⑤❸❷
19 South Audley St 409 7242 3–3A
This "sumptuous room" is part of a rather vulgar Mayfair glass and porcelain emporium; the victuals are "as dainty as the china on which they are served", making meals here "ideal for anorexics". / L & tea only; closed Sat & Sun; no jeans.

Three Little Pigs SE1 £22 ④❸④
89 Westminster Br Rd 928 5535 2–3D
*An unpretentious English bistro, by Lambeth North tube;
"given the area, it's alright, I suppose". / 11 pm, Fri & Sat midnight;
closed Sat L & Sun.*

Tiger Lil's £22 ④④❸
500 King's Rd, SW3 376 5003 5–3B
15a Clapham Common S'side, SW4 720 5433 10–2D
*The young-at-heart love the "good fun" of choosing their own
ingredients and seeing them flashily fried before their very
eyes; fuddy-duddies proclaim the "DIY nightmare" of a chain
"which should have been strangled at birth" – "no matter
what you pick, it always comes out as overcooked gloop".
/ 11.30 pm, Fri & Sat midnight; D only, ex Sat & Sun when open all day;
no Amex; no smoking areas.*

Toff's N10 £24 ❶❸④
38 Muswell Hl Broadway 0181-883 8656 1–1B
*"Fish and chips as art", "to die for", "the best in town",
"enormous portions", "great food", "highly recommended" –
in Muswell Hill, and be prepared to queue. / 10 pm; closed Mon
& Sun; no Switch; no booking.*

Tokyo Diner WC2 £14 ❷❶④
2 Newport Pl 287 8777 4–3B
*"Excellent bento boxes" and "inexpensive sushi" make this
"centrally located" Japanese – on the fringe of Chinatown –
an all-round good bet; service is "rapid". / Midnight; no Amex;
no smoking area; no booking.*

Tootsies £19 ④❸④
177 New King's Rd, SW6 736 4023 10–1B
107 Old Brompton Rd, SW7 581 8942 5–2B
120 Holland Pk Ave, W11 229 8567 6–2A
148 Chiswick High Rd, W4 0181-747 1869 7–2A
198 Haverstock Hill, NW3 431 7609 8–2A
147 Church Rd, SW13 0181-748 3630 10–1A
*"Consistent" chain offering a "relaxed atmosphere" and
known for good burgers; "my granddaughters rate it highly".
/ 11 pm - 11.30 pm, Fri & Sat midnight; no Amex; no booking.*

Topsy-Tasty W4 £19 ❶❷④
5 Station Parade 0181-995 3407 1–3A
*"Exceptional value, spicy Thai food" justifies the pilgrimage
to the Bedlington Café's sibling (opposite Chiswick Station),
whose setting is reminiscent of a '50s tea-shop. / 10.30 pm;
D only; closed Sun; no credit cards.*

Toto's SW1 £40 ❸❷❷
Lennox Gardens Mews 589 2062 5–2D
*For a "good meal in a lovely setting", this "glamorous"
but "relaxed" trattoria finds much support – its lofty and
atmospheric premises may be just a stone's throw from
Harrods, but the 'attitude' characterising many fashionable
destinations is notably absent. / 11.30 pm; smart casual.*

Troika NW1 £16 ❸❹❸
101 Regents Pk Rd 483 3765 8–2B
*"Cosy", all-day Primrose Hill tea-room (formerly called the
Primrose Brasserie), which serves "a good range of Russian
dishes"; service may now have three horsepower, but it is
still rather "slow". / 10.30 pm; no credit cards; no smoking area.*

Troubadour SW5 £14 ❸❹❶
265 Old Brompton Rd No tel 5–3A
*Very characterful Earl's Court coffee house, whose service
tends to the bolshie; the cakes, omelettes and salads are quite
cheap, but it is as a hang-out for soi-disant Bohemians,
intellectuals and artists that the place excels. / 10.30 pm;
no credit cards; no booking.*

La Truffe Noire SE1 £38 ❷❹❺
29 Tooley St 378 0621 9–4C
*What a curate's egg this place by Blackfriars Bridge is;
the solid Gallic fare is "good, if rather expensive", but on the
service front "it's always amateur day", and the somewhat
frilly room "lacks atmosphere", especially in the evening.
/ 11.30 pm; closed Sat & Sun; smart casual; no smoking area.*

Tui SW7 £26 ❷❸❺
19 Exhibition Rd 584 8359 5–2C
*"Excellent", "fiery" cooking makes this South Kensington spot
"the best Thai in London" for many reporters; given the
prices, however, the setting is a touch rudimentary, and
"don't sit upstairs" is good advice. / 10.45 pm; smart casual.*

Tuk Tuk N1 £20 ❷❸❸
330 Upper St 226 0837 8–3D
*"Cheap, tasty and satisfying", this "basic Thai" in Islington is
now back on its previous consistent form. / 11 pm; closed Sat L
& Sun L.*

Turner's SW3 £55 ❹❹❹
87-89 Walton St 584 6711 5–2C
*Consistency problems are besetting Brian Turner's long-
established Knightsbridge restaurant; perhaps "he should stay
off TV and mind the shop", as the ratings for his formerly fine
modern French fare have fallen dramatically, and neither the
bijou setting ("romantic" to some, "like my gran's front room"
to others) nor the service really compensates; "great lunch
value" continues. / 11 pm, Sun 8.30 pm; closed Sat L; smart casual.*

Tusc SW5   **£ 27**   ④④❸
256 Old Brompton Rd   373 9082   5–3A
*"They didn't really go far enough in the revitalisation of
Pontevecchio" – this once-fashionable Earl's Court trattoria,
now rather superficially made-over as a contemporary Italian
'grazerie', offers OK food and "patchy" service.* / Midnight.

Twenty Trinity Gardens SW9   **£ 26**   ❸④❸
20 Trinity Gdns   733 8838   10–2D
*A "very relaxing" atmosphere make this Brixton
neighbourhood spot "a pleasant change of scene"; but while
some feel it provides "good value, simplish fare", others think
the modern British menu is "definitely more inviting than the
dishes themselves".* / 10.30 pm, Fri & Sat 11 pm; D only, closed Sun;
no Amex; no smoking area.

Twenty two degrees south W1   **£ 31**   ④❷❸
22-25 Dean St   287 0940   4–2A
*New Soho South American steak-house – the prototype of
a new Whitbread concept – with quite a stylish setting and
service which is eager to please; we thought the cooking
expensive and rather mediocre.* / 11 pm; closed Sun; no smoking area.

Two Brothers N3   **£ 21**   ❶❸④
297/303 Regent's Pk Rd   0181-346 0469   1–1B
*Having finally made the pilgrimage to this much vaunted
Finchley fish and chip parlour, we had some difficulty seeing
quite what all the fuss is about; still, its many loyal local fans
hail "the best fish in London" in a "true family restaurant".*
/ 10.15 pm; closed Mon & Sun; no smoking area; book L only.

The Union Café W1   **£ 29**   ❸❷❸
96 Marylebone Ln   486 4860   3–1A
*"Marvellous ingredients" and "simple" modern British
dishes is a recipe which delights fans of this light, "spacious"
establishment, just off Manchester Square; the menu is
"limited" however (with the more interesting items tending
to run out), and the setting is somewhat short on
creature comforts.* / 10 pm; closed Sat D & Sun; no Amex;
no smoking area.

Upper Street Fish Shop N1   **£ 19**   ❷❷④
324 Upper St   359 1401   8–2D
*Islington's "upmarket chippie with a BYO policy" is vaunted
by many for its "great fish and chips" and its "cheerful", if
basic, atmosphere.* / 10.15 pm; closed Mon L & Sun; no credit cards;
no booking.

Valhalla SW11   **£ 22**   ❸④❸
57 Battersea Bridge Rd   978 7272   5–4C
*"Relaxed", new Battersea bar-restaurant (with Sistine Chapel
ceiling), approved by locals for its "reasonable prices";
the modern British cooking is "not brilliant", but
perfectly acceptable.* / 11.15 pm, Thu-Sat 11.45 pm.

Vasco & Piero's Pavilion W1 £27 ❸❷❸
15 Poland St 437 8774 3–1D
The setting may be "a bit dilapidated now", but most "enjoy
the food and staff" in this quirky Soho dining room, rescued
from a now-demolished theatre; the cooking – somewhere
between "so-so" and "reliable" – comes at no great cost.
/ 11 pm; closed Sat & Sun (open one Sat D monthly); no Switch; smart casual.

Veeraswamy W1 £41 ④④❸
99-101 (Victory Hs) Regent St 734 1401 3–3D
London's oldest Indian (established 1926) does not
nowadays raise much enthusiasm from reporters; the
cooking is "average", prices are high, and the (albeit perfectly
comfortable) surroundings, looking down on Regent Street,
have no special charm. / 11.30 pm; closed Sun; no Switch;
smart casual; no smoking area.

The Vegetarian Cottage NW3 £17 ④❸❸
91 Haverstock Hl 586 1257 8–2B
As ever, the enthusiasm this oriental veggie in Belsize Park
inspires from some people – "the only London Chinese I
really like" – leaves us (together with a good number of
reporters) completely baffled. / 11.15 pm; D only ex Sun open L & D;
no Amex.

Vegia Zena NW1 £27 ❶④❸
17 Princess Rd 483 0192 8–3B
"A rare regional Italian in London", this Primrose Hill spot is
"worth the trip" for its "imaginative, flavour-packed cooking",
even if "charming" service can be "slow" and the setting is on
the basic side (especially downstairs); book before you set off
– "once an undiscovered gem, now it's always full". / 11 pm.

Vendôme W1 £33 ❸❸❷
20 Dover St 629 5417 3–3C
Simple, well executed brasserie dishes coupled with
charmingly decadent décor (what bliss to escape all that low
key 'contemporary good taste') has won this Mayfair yearling
some high praise; let's hope they don't throw it all away with
the major expansion that's under way as we go to press.
/ 11.30 pm; closed Sat L & Sun.

Verbanella SW3 £31 ❸❸④
30 Beauchamp Pl 584 1107 5–1D
As a "favourite lunch venue", this "good value" Knightsbridge
trattoria arguably has a rôle; our vote, though, is with those
who find the whole experience depressingly "mechanical".
/ 11.30 pm; no Switch; smart casual.

Veronica's W2 £27 ❸❷④
3 Hereford Rd   229 5079   6–1B
*"Unusual" dishes from the "interesting, historical menu",
and "very friendly service" make this singular Bayswater
English local "a treat" for most reporters; the "home-spun"
atmosphere is not to all tastes, though, and some decry
a place which is "amateur on all counts". / Midnight; closed Sat L
& Sun.*

Vic Naylors EC1 £24 ④⑤❷
40 St John St   608 2181   9–1B
*"Strictly a long lunch place" – partially thanks to its
"appalling service" – this "fun", brick-lined Smithfield spot
offers "good atmosphere" and, rather incidental, English
brasserie fare; "it used to be better". / 10.30 pm; closed Sat L
& Sun.*

Il Vicolo SW1 £27 ❸❷④
3-4 Crown Passage   839 3960   3–4D
*"Friendly" St James's trattoria, the standard of whose cooking
(pasta especially) is a few notches higher than might be
expected, making it a useful standby in an expensive area;
good for an informal business lunch. / 10.15 pm; closed Sat & Sun.*

Vijay NW6 £16 ❷❸④
49 Willesden Ln   328 1087   1–1B
*High quality South Indian vegetarian dishes – as well as some
more standard items – continue to draw a wider than local
following to this obscurely located Kilburn spot. / 10.45 pm, Fri
& Sat 11.45 pm.*

Villa Bianca NW3 £32 ④❸❷
1 Perrins Ct   435 3131   8–2A
*Thanks to its very bijou Hampstead side-street location, this
glossy trattoria gets away with food which is "variable" and
"too expensive"; "great outside tables", though. / 11.30 pm.*

Village Bistro N6 £32 ❷❸❷
38 Highgate High St   0181-340 5165   8–1B
*"Very good", "friendly" English restaurant, cutely located in
a Highgate cottage; it's "very cramped", but some find
it romantic. / 11 pm; Mon-Fri, closed L*

Villandry Dining Rooms W1 £37 ❷④④
89 Marylebone High St   224 3799   2–1A
*"Idiosyncratic French eatery" at the rear of a Marylebone
foodie shop, whose "ever changing menu, always using fresh
ingredients", has quite a reputation; prices (wine in particular)
are high, though, especially given tightly-packed conditions,
"school classroom furniture", and sometimes "appalling"
service; "why are they not open for dinner?" – good question.
/ L only with one dinner monthly; closed Sun; no smoking.*

Vincent's SW15 £22 ❸❷④
147 Upper Richmond Rd   0181-780 3553   10–2B
*Bright and welcoming – if in a very suburban way – this
Putney newcomer provides modern British dishes of which
some, but not all, are very good, and at reasonable prices;
competition isn't exactly fierce thereabouts, however, so it's
undoubtedly a useful addition to the area.* / 10.30 pm; closed Sat L
& Sun.

Vingt-Quatre SW10 £23 ❸❷❸
325 Fulham Rd   376 7224   5–3B
*Those for whom life is a 24-hour party – "a dubious clientele"
– naturally gravitate to this fashionable Chelsea diner, open all
hours; the chief surprise is that the food and service are
actually quite good.* / open 24 hours; no booking.

VONG SW1 £40 ❶❸❷
Wilton Pl   235 1010   5–1D
*"Exciting and innovative" Knightsbridge newcomer, which
has breezed in from the Big Apple to general acclaim for its
"zingy", "dramatically displayed" French/Thai fare; some are
underwhelmed – service can be found "snooty", and the
rather bland setting is "less exciting than its NY sister's".*
/ 11.30 pm; closed Sun; no smoking area.

W11 W11 £29 ④❷❷
123a Clarendon Rd   229 8889   6–2A
*Given the attractions of a "huge fireplace, with a real fire
in winter" and a "lovely outside terrace in summer", it is
perhaps no great shock that the "straightforward" modern
British cooking at this modishly converted pub on the fringe of
Holland Park does not live up to the setting.* / 11.30 pm; no Amex.

Wagamama £15 ❷❷❸
10a Lexington St, W1   292 0990   3–2D
4a Streatham St, WC1   323 9223   2–1C
*"Always fun and fab", say fans of these bare but striking
noodle canteens – the Bloomsbury original now has a
Soho offshoot; some may quibble about the authenticity of
the Japanese-inspired fare, but "incredible value" for
"production-line food which manages to taste personally
cooked" ensures that it's not just students who invest the
time in the queue; once inside, you "take the luck of the draw
as to dining partners".* / 11 pm; no Amex; no smoking; no booking.

Wakaba NW3 £40 ❷❸④
122a Finchley Rd   586 7960   8–2A
*Complaints that this stark Japanese (opposite Finchley Road
tube) is "overpriced" are nothing new, and though it now
strikes some as being "a bit tired", it continues to offer
"excellent food".* / 11 pm; D only; closed Sun; no Switch; no smoking area.

F S A

The Waldorf Meridien WC2 £15 ❸❷❷
Aldwych 836 2400 2–2D

As an afternoon retreat, this grand hotel on the fringe of Covent Garden is a contender as "the best tea place in London", with "inconspicuous service and a tranquil atmosphere"; not so quiet at weekends, though, when the longest-running thé dansant in town takes to the floor. / Tea daily 3.30 pm-6 pm; for tea dance, jacket & tie.

Walton's SW3 £45 ❸❷❸
121 Walton St 584 0204 5–2C

Tired of raucous new mega-brasseries? – head for this "haven of calm" in a "sumptuous" Knightsbridge townhouse; it is not out to startle in any way, but the pricey English food is good, and service is "discreet and unhurried". / 11.30 pm, Sun 10 pm; no Switch; smart casual.

The Waterloo Fire Station SE1 £22 ❸④❸
150 Waterloo Rd 401 3267 9–4A

The "great atmosphere" at this large and airy bar-refectory near the railway station continues to attract a lively twentysomething crowd (and it can be "very noisy" and "smoky"); "interesting", affordable modern British dishes are complemented by an "intelligent wine list", and while service is sometimes "slow" it is "generally very friendly". / 11 pm; closed Sun D; need 15+ to book.

West Zenders WC2 £30 ❷❸④
4a Upper St Martin's Ln 497 0376 4–3B

"Reasonable", "mainly Chinese" oriental, in the heart of Theatreland – very useful before or after a show; though it shares the striking styling of the rest of the Zen group, it is perhaps not atmospheric enough to make an evening of. / 11.15 pm; smart casual.

The Westbourne W2 £21 ❷④❶
101 Westbourne Park Villas 221 1332 6–1B

"Inventive", "Italianate" fare from the "daily changing menu", served in a "young, viby atmosphere" has made this updated Bayswater boozer much more than a flash in the pan – though some bewail its "posers' paradise" popularity with "W11 trendies"; service can take its time. / 10 pm; closed Mon L; no Amex.

White Cross Hotel TW9 £17 ❸④❷
Water Ln 0181-940 6844 1–4A

If you fancy a trip to Richmond, this characterful riverside pub, with its nice beer garden, is excellent for a spot of lunch; the grub (weekend roasts plus some more imaginative fare) is well done, and popularity and overcrowding are the main drawbacks; kids welcome. / L only; no Amex & no Switch.

White Tower W1   £ 38   ❸❸❷

1 Percy St   636 8141   2–1C
This "great" Fitzrovia "time-warp", is now more polished under new ownership; on our visit, we went French on the first floor (finding quality, old-style brasserie fare), but the Greek cuisine for which the place is better known is still served in the green, ground floor dining room; above, there are some of the most atmospheric private rooms in London. / 10.30 pm; closed Sun.

Whittington's EC4   £ 36   ❸④❸

21 College HI   248 5855   9–3B
The "only fairly formal restaurant in the City offering half-decent value", is quite characterfully located in the cellar of Dick's old home; there is a nice neighbouring wine bar. / L only; closed Sat & Sun.

Wilson's W14   £ 27   ④❶❷

236 Blythe Rd   603 7267   7–1C
To its fans, this intimate Brook Green spot is "a great Scottish restaurant", and few doubt the high level of "personal service" from the "friendly, eccentric" patron (whose bagpipes "are an ever-present risk"); on the downside, some fear the fare is becoming "ordinary". / 10 pm; closed Sat L & Sun D.

Wiltons SW1   £ 53   ④❸❸

55 Jermyn St   629 9955   3–3C
"Staid" and "stuffy" – or, if you prefer, "delightfully predictable" – St James's clubland restaurant; "horribly expensive" it may be, but there are those prepared to pay a high premium to see "standards maintained". / 10.30 pm; closed Sat; jacket & tie.

Windows on the World
Park Lane Hilton Hotel W1   £ 64   ④⑤④

22 Park Ln   493 8000   3–4A
The "fantastic views" – from 28 floors above Mayfair – and the "extremely good buffet breakfast" are the only possible excuses to visit this otherwise dismal and expensive restaurant; if you must see the panorama, go for a cocktail. / Mon-Thu 11 pm, Fri & Sat 11.30 pm; closed Sat L & Sun D; dinner, jacket & tie.

Windsor Castle W8   £ 18   ❸❸❶

114 Campden HI Rd   727 8491   6–2B
"The food has its ups and downs but is generally pretty good" at this very "charming pub", just off Notting Hill Gate; the "big garden" is a key attraction (it gets "absolutely packed", but there are fewer moans this year about slow service). / 11 pm; no smoking area (L only); no booking.

Wine & Kebab SW10 £20 ❸❸❸
343 Fulham Rd   352 0967   5–3B
*Recently revamped Chelsea-fringe taverna, offering a warm
welcome to those in search of real food in the early hours.
/ 2 am; D only.*

Wine Gallery £22 ④❷❷
49 Hollywood Rd, SW10   352 7572   5–3B
*Comforting, dated wine bar, owing its continued success
to "straightforward food, pleasant service and a relaxed
atmosphere", and also, perhaps, to the very agreeable
summer garden; for the former W11 branch, see Zah Bar.
/ 11 pm.*

Wódka W8 £32 ④❸④
12 St Alban's Gr   937 6513   5–1B
*Hidden away in Kensington, this cramped and "unusual",
Polish spot produces "heavy" cooking to "variable" standards
– occasionally "superb", sometimes "stodgy"; if the food is
not up to scratch, the large selection of vodkas may offer
some solace. / 11.15 pm; closed Sat L & Sun L; smart casual.*

Wolfe's £25 ❸❷④
30 Gt Queen St, WC2   831 4442   4–1D
25 Basil St, SW3   584 7217   5–1D
*"Good portions and great burgers" maintain the popularity of
these "rather American" diners (located behind Harrods and
on the eastern fringes of Covent Garden); the Knightsbridge
branch, in particular, attracts so many US families that a visit
here is a curiously mid-Atlantic experience. / 11.30 pm-midnight;
WC2 closed Sun.*

Wong Kei W1 £13 ❸⑤④
41-43 Wardour St   437 8408   4–3A
*"Loads of abuse from the staff" is all part of the "fun" at this
vast Chinatown "experience", where "if you choose right, the
food can be very good"; 'cash only' means cash only.
/ 10.30 pm; no credit cards; no booking.*

Woodlands £22 ❸④❸
37 Panton St, SW1   839 7258   4–4A
77 Marylebone Rd, W1   486 3862   3–1A
*The smartest South Indian vegetarians in town offer top
quality cooking, but at prices which make little concession
to the cheapness of the ingredients; the "tables are too close
together", and the Marylebone branch is the nicer of the two.
/ 10.30 pm; no Switch.*

Wren at St James's SW1 £10 ❸④❷
197 Piccadilly   437 9419   3–3D
*This annex to the famous Wren church on Piccadilly provides
"good, staple veggie food", and in summer its outside tables
are particularly pleasant; you may have to queue, though,
and it's a little "pricey". / 7 pm, Sun 5 pm; no credit cards;
no smoking: no booking.*

Wynkyn de Worde EC4 £13 ❸❸❸
1 St Brides Pas, Bride Ln 936 2554 9–3A
Nestling behind the famous 'wedding-cake' church, this
"pleasant" City wine bar provides relief in a thin area;
the adjacent restaurant has long been tipped as a culinary
experience best avoided, but there are signs that it's
somewhat "improved". / L only; closed Sat & Sun; no Switch.

Yoahan Plaza food court NW9 £7 ❷④⑤
399 Edgware Rd no tel 1–1A
For fans of oriental fare or experience-seekers, the frenetic
food hall cum cafeteria at this huge Japanese shopping
mall (ten minutes' walk from Colindale tube) is worth the trip;
many different eastern cuisines are offered, and nothing costs
more than a few quid. / 6 pm; no credit cards; no booking.

Young Turks EC2 £26 ④❸④
7-8 Bishopsgate Pl 628 2826 9–2D
Only in the City could an historic listed basement Turkish bath
(once the characterful Gallipoli Restaurant) be so witlessly
converted, into a mediocre Italo-Ottoman troughing-spot
for local worker-bees; our visit found willing service the only
redeeming feature. / Mon L only – Tue, Wed & Fri 8 pm – Thu 10 pm;
closed Sat & Sun; smart casual.

Yum Yum N16 £23 ❸❸❸
30 Stoke Newington Ch St 254 6751 1–1C
"Consistently good food" and a lively atmosphere ensure the
continued popularity of this well-run Stoke Newington Thai.
/ 10.45 pm, Fri & Sat 11.15 pm.

Zah Bar £22 ④❷❷
294 Westbourne Gr, W11 229 1877 6–1B
Notting Hill's former Wine Gallery was renamed in the late
summer of 1996; it is still under the same ownership, and
apparently no sweeping changes to the old formula (see
Wine Gallery SW10) are planned. / 11 pm; closed Sun; no Amex.

Zafferano SW1 £30 ❶❸❸
16 Lowndes St 235 5800 2–4A
"Excellent ingredients", "quality cooking" and "affordable
prices" have built a strong reputation for this Belgravia
modern Italian; service is occasionally "off-hand" and
"arrogant" however, and the reporter who expressed the
thought that "at 40+, I still feel this is a restaurant for
old people" was not alone. / 11 pm; closed Sun; no Switch.

Zamoyski NW3 £17 ❸❷❷
85 Fleet Rd 794 4792 8–2A
"Good, plain, wholesome Polish food" is served at this
"not expensive" and justifiably popular Hampstead spot;
"one of the best selection of vodkas in London" contributes
to the "fun" atmosphere. / 10.30 pm, Fri & Sat 11 pm; D only ex Sun,
when open all day; no Switch; smart casual.

FSA

Zen SW3 £41 ③④④
Chelsea Cloisters, Sloane Av 589 1781 5–2C
"Expensive Chinese classic", attracting a "glamorous Chelsea crowd"; though some still say the food is "fantastic", there's quite a contingent nowadays which finds "extortionate" bills for fare "which is not wildly inspiring". / 11.15 pm; smart casual.

Zen Central W1 £45 ②③④
20-22 Queen St 629 8089 3–3B
Minimalist Mayfair Chinese which continues to deliver very high quality cooking, tipped by many as the best in town; as ever, though, the décor can seem "sterile", and the overall experience "overpriced". / 11.30 pm; smart casual.

Zen Garden W1 £40 ③②④
15-16 Berkeley St 493 1381 3–3C
Datedly swanky oriental, just off Berkeley Square; though far from bargain basement, it does offer accomplished Chinese cooking (including good dim-sum), and service is "very attentive". / 11 pm; smart casual.

ZeNW3 NW3 £31 ②③③
83 Hampstead High St 794 7863 8–2A
"Consistent", "fresh" cooking continues to win votes for this "fun, modern" Chinese, whose striking glass-fronted premises look on to Hampstead's main drag. / 11.30 pm; smart casual.

Ziani SW3 £31 ③②②
45-47 Radnor Wk 352 2698 5–3C
A "local favourite", this small Chelsea back street Italian offers reliably "OK" food, and the staff are generally "pleased to see you"; there are "too many tables crammed in", though, and it's "very noisy". / 11.30 pm.

Zoe W1 £31 ④⑤④
3-5 Barrett St 224 1122 3–1A
Brightly decorated modern café-restaurant, just off Oxford Street, whose "trying to be sophisticated", "eclectic" menu pleases some ("always successful taste combinations") and horrifies others ("feed not food"); service can be "very slow". / 11.30 pm; closed Sun D; smart casual; no smoking area.

INDEXES

INDEXES

Breakfast
(with opening times)

Central
Atrium *(8)*
Aurora *(8)*
Balans *(8)*
Bank *(6.30)*
Bar Italia *(7)*
Brown's Hotel *(7, Sat & Sun 7.30)*
Café Bohème *(8)*
Café Flo –
    WC2 (10); W1 (9, Sat & Sun 10)
Café Nico *(7)*
Café Pasta – *both WC2 (9.30)*
Café Rouge – *all branches (10)*
Café Sofra – *W1 (7)*
Chez Gérard –
    Chancery Ln, WC2 (8, not Sat & Sun)
Claridges Restaurant *(7, Sun 8)*
Connaught *(7.30)*
Cranks – *all branches (8-10)*
Dôme – *WC2 (8)*
Dorchester Grill *(7, Sun 7.30)*
Fifth Floor (Café) *(10)*
Food for Thought
    (9.30 Mon-Sat, 10.30 Sun)
Häagen-Dazs – *WC2 (10)*
The Halkin *(7)*
The Heights *(7)*
Hyde Park Hotel
    Park Room *(7)*
The Lanesborough *(7)*
Maison Bertaux *(8)*
Marché Mövenpick –
    W1 (8, Sun 9)
Nicole's *(10)*
Oriel *(8.30, Sun 9)*
Pâtisserie Valerie –
    all branches (7.30-9)
Pizza On The Park *(8.30)*
Pret A Manger – *all branches (7-8)*
Randall & Aubin *(10)*
Ranoush *(8)*
The Ritz *(7)*
Savoy River Room *(7)*
Simpsons-in-the-Strand *(7)*
Sotheby's Café *(9)*
Star Café *(7.30)*
Stock Pot – *SW1, W1 (8)*
Villandry *(8.30, Sat 9.30)*
Windows on the World *(7)*
Wren at St James's
    (6.30, Sat & Sun 9)

West
All Saints *(10, Sun 10.30)*
Balans *(8)*
Basil St Hotel *(7.30)*
Bistrot 190 *(7)*
Blakes Hotel *(7.30)*
Blenheim Bis *(8.30)*

La Bouchée *(9.30)*
La Brasserie *(8)*
Brasserie du Marché
    (10, Sun 11)
Café Flo – *SW6, W8 (9)*
Café Grove
    (summer 9, winter 10, Sun 10.30)
Café Montpeliano *(8)*
Café Pasta – *W4 (9); W8 (9.30)*
Café Rouge – *all branches (10)*
Calzone – *SW10, W11 (10)*
Capital Hotel *(7)*
Chelsea Bun Diner *(7, Sun 8)*
Chelsea Kitchen *(8.30, Sun 10)*
Conrad Hotel *(7)*
The Crescent *(8.30)*
Dôme – *SW3, W8 (8)*
Ed's Easy Diner –
    SW3 (Sat & Sun 9)
Fat Boy's *(6.30)*
Fileric – *SW7 (8)*
First Floor *(Mon-Sat 10.30)*
Francofill *(Sat & Sun 10)*
Häagen-Dazs –
    SW7 (10); SW10 (9.30)
Halcyon Hotel *(7, Sun 8)*
I Thai *(7)*
King's Road Café *(10)*
Lisboa Patisserie *(8)*
Mackintosh's Brasserie *(8)*
Manzara *(8, Sun 10)*
Le Metro *(7.30)*
Mona Lisa *(7)*
Palms-on-the-Hill
    (Sat & Sun 9.45)
Pâtisserie Valerie – *both
    SW3 (7.30-9)*
Picasso *(7)*
Pret A Manger – *all branches (7-8)*
Raoul's Café *(9, Sun 9.30)*
Le Shop *(Sat & Sun 10)*
Stock Pot – *SW3 (8); SW3 (9.30)*
Troubadour *(8.30)*
Vingt-Quatre *(always available)*
Zah Bar – *W11 (9 Sat only)*

North
Banners *(10)*
Bar Gansa *(9.30)*
Café Delancey *(8)*
Café Flo –
    NW3 (10); N1 (9, Sat & Sun 8.30)
Café Pasta – *NW3 (9); N1 (9.30)*
Café Rouge – *all branches (10)*
Calzone – *N1 (9)*
Cosmo *(8.30)*
Ed's Easy Diner –
    NW3 (Sat & Sun 9)
House on Rosslyn
    Hill *(Sat & Sun, 10)*
Iznik *(Sun 9)*
Nontas *(8)*

Pret A Manger – *all branches (7-8)*
Ruby in the Dust – *NI, NWI (10)*
Troika *(9)*

South

Boiled Egg *(9, Sun 10)*
Le Bouchon Bordelais *(10)*
Le Bouchon Lyonnais *(10.30)*
Café de la Place
  (8, Sat 9, Sun 9.30)
Café on the Common *(10)*
Café Rouge – *all branches (10)*
Fileric – *SW8 (8)*
Gastro *(8)*
The Grafton *(10)*

East

Al's *(7, Sat & Sun 10)*
Beauchamp's *(9.30)*
Brick Lane Beigel Bake *(24 hr)*
Café Rouge – *EC4 (10)*
Café Sofra – *EC4 (7)*
Carnevale *(10)*
Fox & Anchor *(7)*
Futures – *EC2, EC3 (7.30)*
Hope & Sir Loin *(7)*
Mustards Brasserie *(9.30)*
The Place Below *(7.30)*
Pret A Manger – *all branches (7-8)*

Brunch menus

Central

Balans
Le Caprice
Christopher's
Coast
The Ivy
Joe Allen

West

All Saints
Balans
Beach Blanket Babylon
Bistrot 190
La Brasserie
Café Grove
Chelsea Bun Diner
Conrad Hotel
The Crescent
Jimmy Beez
Joe's Brasserie
Joe's Café
Kartouche
Mas Café
Montana
Palms-on-the-Hill
PJ's
Raoul's Café
Tabac
Vingt-Quatre

North

Banners
The Big Night Out
Café Delancey
Camden Brasserie
The Engineer
House on Rosslyn Hill

South

Boiled Egg
Le Pont de la Tour
Ransome's Dock
The Stepping Stone

East

Al's

Business

Central

Atelier
Atrium
Au Jardin des Gourmets
The Avenue
Bentley's
Beotys
Café Royal Grill
Le Caprice
Cave
Cecconi's
Chez Gérard – *all branches*
Chez Nico
Christopher's
Claridges Restaurant
Connaught
The Criterion
Diverso
Dorchester Grill
Dorchester, Oriental
Efes Kebab House I
Elena's L'Etoile
L'Escargot
Four Seasons
Le Gavroche
Green's
Greenhouse
The Guinea
The Halkin
The Heights
Hodgson's
L'Incontro
Interlude de Chavot
The Ivy
Ken Lo's Memories
Langan's Brasserie
Malabar Junction
Mitsukoshi
Miyama
Mon Plaisir
Neal Street

INDEXES

Nico Central
O'Conor Don
Oak Room
L'Odéon
Odin's
L'Oranger
Orso
Quaglino's
Restaurant MPW
Rib Room
The Ritz
Rules
Santini
Les Saveurs
Savoy Grill
Savoy River Room
Scott's
Shepherd's
Simply Nico
Simpsons-in-the-Strand
Le Soufflé
The Square
Stephen Bull
Suntory
33
Veeraswamy
Il Vicolo
Vong
White Tower
Wiltons
Windows on the World
Zen Central

West
Aubergine
Basil St Hotel
Bibendum
Clarke's
Fulham Road
Grill St Quentin
Launceston Place
Leith's
La Tante Claire
The Tenth
Walton's

North
Frederick's
Odette's

South
Bengal Clipper
Blue Print Café
The Butlers Wharf Chop-
house
Oxo Tower
Le Pont de la Tour
RSJ
La Truffe Noire

East
Ashtons
Aykoku-Kaku
Bleeding Heart
Bubb's
Café du Marché
Le Champenois
City Brasserie
City Miyama
Gladwins
Hothouse Bar & Grill
Imperial City
Leith's at the Institute
Luc's Brasserie
Le Quai
Singapura – EC3
Sri Siam City
Sweetings
Whittington's

BYO
(Bring you own wine)

Central
Café Sofra – W1, WC2
Food for Thought
India Club
Neal's Yard Dining Rooms

West
Adams Café
Alounak
Bedlington Café
Blah! Blah! Blah!
Café 209
Café Grove
Chelsea Bun Diner
Fat Boy's
El Gaucho
Kalamaras, Micro
Mandola
Rôtisserie Jules – SW7
Topsy-Tasty

North
Afghan Kitchen
Ali Baba
Diwana Bhel-Poori House
Troika
Upper St Fish Shop

South
Café on the Common
The Cook House

East
Café Sofra – EC4
Carnevale
F Cooke & Sons
Lahore Kebab House

Children

(h – high or special chairs
m – children's menu
p – children's portions
e – weekend entertainments
o – other facilities)

Central

Ajimura *(h)*
Al Bustan *(hp)*
Al Sultan *(h)*
Alastair Little *(h)*
Alfred *(h)*
Atelier *(p)*
Au Jardin des Gourmets *(p)*
Bahn Thai *(h)*
Browns – *W1, WC2 (hm)*
Café de Colombia *(h)*
Café des Amis du Vin *(hp)*
Café Emm *(h)*
Café Flo – *W1, WC2 (h)*
Café Nico *(hm)*
Café Pacifico *(hm)*
Café Pasta – *both WC2 (hpo)*
Café Rouge – *Frith St, W1 (hm)*
Caffè Uno – *all branches (hm)*
Chiaroscuro *(o)*
Chicago Pizza Pie Factory *(he)*
Chimes *(m)*
China Court *(h)*
Chuen Cheng Ku *(h)*
Claridges Restaurant *(h)*
Como Lario *(h)*
Cranks – *W1, WC2 (h)*
The Criterion *(h)*
Deals – *W1 (hm)*
Diverso *(h)*
Dorchester Grill *(hm)*
Dorchester, Oriental *(h)*
Down Mexico Way *(h)*
Dragon Inn *(h)*
Ed's Easy Diner – *W1*
81 *(h)*
L'Escargot *(h)*
Fakhreldine *(h)*
Fashion Café *(h)*
Fifth Floor (Café) *(o)*
Four Seasons *(hm)*
Fung Shing *(h)*
Gourmet Pizza Co. – *W1 (hm)*
Häagen-Dazs – *WC2 (h)*
The Halkin *(h)*
Hard Rock Café *(h)*
Italian Kitchen *(mo)*
Jade Garden *(h)*
Kettners *(h)*
The Lancers *(m)*
The Lanesborough *(hm)*
Marché Mövenpick – *SW1,
W1 (p)*

Matsuri *(m)*
Melati *(h)*
New World *(h)*
Oak Room *(h)*
Pélican – *WC2 (h)*
Pizza On The Park *(ho)*
PizzaExpress – *all branches (h)*
Pizzeria Condotti *(h)*
Planet Hollywood *(hm)*
Porters *(hmo)*
Rib Room *(h)*
The Ritz *(h)*
Rock Island Diner *(hme)*
Savoy River Room *(h)*
Seafresh *(hp)*
Signor Sassi *(h)*
Smollensky's Balloon *(hmeo)*
Smollensky's, Strand *(hmwo)*
Sofra – *all branches (h)*
Sol e Luna *(hmeo)*
Sol e Stella *(hme)*
Tate Gallery *(h)*
Texas Embassy Cantina *(hm)*
TGI Friday's – *W1, WC2 (hme)*
Wagamama – *W1, WC1 (h)*
The Waldorf Meridien *(m)*
Windows on the World *(h)*
Wolfe's – *WC2 (hm)*
Zoe *(h)*

West

Al Basha *(h)*
Alastair Little W11 *(hp)*
L'Altro *(p)*
Basil St Hotel *(h)*
Benihana – *SW3 (h)*
Big Easy *(h)*
Bistrot 190 *(h)*
Blakes Hotel *(h)*
Blue Elephant *(e)*
Bombay Brasserie *(h)*
The Brackenbury *(h)*
Brady's – *SW6 (p)*
Café Flo – *SW6, W4, W8 (h)*
Café Lazeez *(hm)*
Café Pasta – *W4, W8 (hpo)*
Café Rouge – *W11, W2,
W4, W8 (hm); SW3, SW6 (hmo);
W9 (hp)*
Caffè Uno – *all branches (hm)*
Calzone – *SW10 (hmo); W11 (mo)*
Chicago Rib Shack *(hmo)*
Conrad Hotel *(h)*
Da Pierino *(p)*
Deals – *SW10, W6 (hme)*
Downstairs at 190 *(h)*
Ed's Easy Diner – *SW3*
La Fenice *(p)*
Ffiona's *(p)*
Francofill *(h)*

INDEXES

The Gate (h)
Geale's (h)
Glaisters – SW10 (p)
Grill St Quentin (hm)
Halcyon Hotel (h)
Halepi (p)
Jimmy Beez (p)
Joe's Brasserie (m)
Julie's (h)
Julie's Bar (h)
Kalamaras, Micro (p)
Khan's (h)
Khun Akorn (h)
Lazy Jack's (h)
Leonardo's (h)
Mackintosh's Brasserie (h)
Malabar (h)
Mandarin Kitchen (h)
Manzara (h)
Mas Café (h)
Montpeliano (h)
Nachos – SW10 (hm); W4 (hp)
Nippon-Tuk (o)
Oliver's Island (h)
Palms-on-the-Hill (hm)
Paparazzi Café (h)
Park Inn (h)
Parsons (hm)
Phoenicia (h)
Picasso (h)
Pitcher & Piano – SW10, W4 (hm)
Pizza Chelsea (hme)
Pizza the Action (h)
PizzaExpress – SW10, SW3, W14,
   W2, W4, W8 (h); SW6 (ho)
PJ's (h)
Poons at Whiteleys (h)
The River Café (hp)
Rôtisserie Jules – SW3,
   SW7, W11 (h)
Royal China (h)
Sabai Sabai (o)
San Martino (h)
Sandrini (h)
Scalini (h)
Le Shop (hp)
Sticky Fingers (hmeo)
Sushi Bar Gen (h)
Tabac (p)
The Tenth (h)
Texas Lone Star (hm)
TGI Friday's – W2 (hme)
Tiger Lil's – SW3 (hp)
Tootsies – SW6, SW7,
   W11, W4 (hmo)
Wilson's (h)
Wolfe's – SW3 (hm)
Zen (h)

North
Abeno (hm)

Banners (ho)
Belgo Noord (h)
Benihana – NW3 (hme)
Billboard Café (ph)
Bu San (h)
Byron's (hp)
Café des Arts (h)
Café Flo – N1, NW3 (h)
Café Pasta – N1, NW3 (hpo)
Café Rouge – N6 (hm)
Caffe Graffiti (o)
Caffè Uno – all branches (hm)
Calzone – N1, NW3 (hmo)
Cosmo (h)
Czech Club (p)
Don Pepe (hm)
Ed's Easy Diner – NW3
The Engineer (o)
La Finca – N1 (he)
The Fox Reformed (ho)
Frederick's (hm)
Greek Valley (m)
Laurent (m)
Manna (h)
Mezzaluna (h)
Nachos – N1, NW3 (hm)
Nautilus (h)
La Piragua (h)
PizzaExpress – all branches (h)
Rani – N3 (hm)
Rasa (h)
Rôtisserie – N1 (h)
Ruby in the Dust – N1, NW1 (h)
Le Sacré-Coeur (h)
Seashell (hm)
Solly's (h)
Tootsies – NW3 (hmo)
Troika (p)
Tuk Tuk (m)
Upper St Fish Shop (h)
Vijay (h)
Village Bistro (hp)
Yum Yum (h)
Zamoyski (p)

South
Alma (h)
Antipasto e Pasta (h)
Battersea Rickshaw (hp)
Bellinis (h)
Boiled Egg (hme)
Le Bouchon Bordelais (hm)
Le Bouchon Lyonnais (hm)
La Bouffe (hm)
Brady's – SW18 (p)
Buona Sera (h)
The Butlers Wharf
   Chop-house (h)
Café on the Common (mpo)

Café Rouge – *SE1, SW14, SW15 (hm)*
Caffè Uno – *SW13 (hm)*
Cantina del Ponte *(h)*
The Depot *(h)*
Eco *(h)*
Enoteca Turi *(h)*
La Finca – *SE11 (he)*
Le Gothique *(hcp)*
Gourmet Pizza Co. – *SE1 (hm)*
Hoults *(h)*
The Lavender *(hp)*
Ma Goa *(p)*
Mezzanine *(h)*
Naked Turtle *(hm)*
Newton's *(m)*
C Notarianni & Sons *(m)*
The People's Palace *(p)*
PizzaExpress – *SE1, SW11, SW14, SW15, SW18 (h); SW11, SW4 (ho)*
Pizzeria Castello *(h)*
Le Pont de la Tour Bar & Grill *(h)*
Prego *(h)*
Ransome's Dock *(hp)*
Riva *(hm)*
Scoffers *(hm)*
Sonny's *(h)*
South Bank Brasserie *(h)*
Tea Rooms des Artistes *(h)*
Tiger Lil's – *SW4 (hp)*
Tootsies – *SW13 (hmo)*
The Waterloo Fire Station *(hp)*
White Cross Hotel *(h)*

East

Babe Ruth's *(hm)*
The Clerkenwell *(p)*
The Eagle *(p)*
Frocks *(h)*
George & Vulture *(p)*
Gourmet Pizza Co. – *E14 (hm)*
Japanese Canteen *(p)*
Lahore Kebab House *(h)*
PizzaExpress – *EC2 (h)*
St John *(h)*

Entertainment
(Check times before you go)

Central

Atlantic Bar & Grill
(chess & jazz club, Sun)
Balans
(music, nightly not Sun)
Bar Madrid
(DJ & dancing, Mon, Wed & Thu)
Blues
(downstairs sports bar)
Boulevard
(blues/jazz, Wed-Fri)

Café Bohème
(jazz, nightly)
Calabash
(Arican band, Fri or Sat)
Chicago Pizza Pie Factory
(music, Fri & Sun)
Claridges Restaurant
(dinner dance, Fri & Sat)
Deals – *W1*
(music, Fri & Sat)
Dover St Wine Bar
(band, DJ & dancing, nightly)
Down Mexico Way
(DJ in bar Thu-Sat; 2nd floor, resident band)
Efes Kebab House – *W1*
(belly dancer, nightly)
Fifth Floor (Café)
(jazz nightly)
Football Football
(sports screens)
The Halkin
(music, nightly)
Kaspia
(Russian Music, Thu)
The Lanesborough
(supper dances, Thu - Sat; jazz Sun brunch)
Langan's Brasserie
(jazz, nightly)
The Lexington
(pianist, nightly)
Mezzo
(music, Thu-Sat)
Mondo
(DJ nightly)
O'Conor Don
(duo in bar, Sat eve and Sun afternoon)
Pélican – *WC2*
(jazz, nightly)
Pizza On The Park
(cabaret, nightly)
PizzaExpress – *W1*
(jazz, nightly)
PizzaExpress – *W1*
(music, Wed-Sat)
La Porte des Indes
(folk dancing, Sun brunch)
Quaglino's
(bar-jazz, Fri & Sat)
The Ritz
(band, Fri & Sat; harpist, Sun L)
Rock Island Diner
(DJ, nightly)
Savoy River Room
(dinner dance, nightly ex Sun)
Smollensky's Balloon
(music, nightly)
Smollensky's, Strand
(music, nightly; dancing, Thu-Sat)
Sofra – *W1, WC2*
(music, Mon-Sat)
Soho Soho
(music, rôtisserie nightly)
Le Soufflé
(string trio, Sun L)
Il Vicolo
(music, Fri)
Windows on the World
(dinner dance, Thu-Sat)

INDEXES

West

Al Basha
(music, nightly; belly dancing, Fri & Sat)

Big Easy
(music, nightly)

Bombay Brasserie
(piano & singer nightly and wknd lunch)

Café Lazeez
(music, Wed, Fri & Sat)

Café O
(Greek music, Fri & Sat)

Cambio de Tercio
(guitarist, regularly)

Da Mario
(disco, nightly ex Sun)

Ffiona's
(music, Sat)

First Floor
(jazz, Sun)

The Fulham Tup
(DJ Wed, band Tue & Thu)

Jim Thompson's
(jazz, Sun eve)

Jimmy Beez
(jazz & DJ, weekends)

Los Remos
(guitarist, Thu, Fri & Sat)

Mackintosh's Brasserie
(jazz Duo, Sun)

Maroush – W2
(music & dancing, nightly)

Montana
(jazz, Thu-Sat)

Palio
(jazz, Tue & Thu eves)

Paparazzi Café
(music, nightly)

The Pen
(jazz, Sun pm)

Pizza Pomodoro
(music, nightly)

PizzaExpress – W14
(jazz, Sat)

PizzaExpress – W2
(jazz, Thu)

Shoeless Joe's
(video screens)

606 Club
(jazz, nightly)

Star of India
(music, Tue-Fri)

The Westbourne
(music, Mon eve)

Wine & Kebab
(music, Sat)

North

All Bar One – NW8
(jazz, Sun)

Banners
(music, Mon D)

China Jazz
(jazz, nightly)

Cuba Libre
(dancing, Fri & Sat)

Don Pepe
(singing & organist, nightly)

La Finca – N1
(rhumba & flamenco, Wed; Salsa some Fri)

South

The Fox Reformed
(regular wine tastings, and backgammon evenings)

Greek Valley
(bouzouki music, Fri)

House on Rosslyn Hill
(karaoke, Mon; music, Fri & Sat)

Troika
(Russian gypsy music, Fri & Sat)

Villa Bianca
(guitar twice weekly)

Zamoyski
(gypsy music, Wed, Fri & Sat)

Archduke Wine Bar
(jazz, Tue-Sat)

Batt. Barge Bistro
(guitarist, Thu-Sat)

Le Bouchon Lyonnais
(jazz, Thu-Sat)

Côte à Côte
(music, Wed, Fri & Sat)

Fina Estampa
(music, Fri & Sat)

La Finca – SE11
(latin music, Sat)

Meson Don Felipe
(flamenco guitar, nightly)

Naked Turtle
(jazz, nightly & Sun L)

PizzaExpress – SW18
(large sports TV)

Pizzeria Castello
(guitarist, nightly)

Rebato's
(music, Wed-Sat)

Tea Rooms des Artistes
(jazz, Sun brunch)

La Truffe Noire
(jazz bar, Thu & Fri)

East

Babe Ruth's
(basketball; games area)

Café du Marché
(music, nightly)

The Fence
(music, Thu)

Fuego
(music nightly, Disco Thu-Fri)

Futures – EC2
(jazz, Tue)

Hothouse Bar & Grill
(jazz & blues, Wed - Sat)

Mange 2
(jazz, nightly in bar)

Pizza Pomodoro – E1, EC1
(music, nightly)

Sri Siam City
(music, Thu)

Sri Thai
(music, Wed)

Vic Naylors
(jazz, Sat)

Young Turks
(jazz, Thu)

Late
(open till midnight or later as shown; may be earlier Sunday)

Central

Alwaha *(1 am, summer 3 am)*
Atlantic Bar & Grill *(midnight, bar food until 2.30 am)*
Balans *(Mon-Thu 4 am, Fri & Sat 6 am, Sun 1 am)*
Bank
Bar Italia *(6 am)*
Bar Madrid *(2.30 am)*
Benihana – *W1 (Fri & Sat only)*
Blues *(Thu-Sat 12.45 am)*
Boulevard
Café Bohème *(2.45 am, Thu-Sat open 24 hours)*
Café du Jardin
Café Emm *(Fri & Sat 12.30 am)*
Café Sofra – *all branches*
Caffè Uno – *all branches*
Le Caprice
Chicago Pizza Pie Factory *(Fri 1 am)*
Coast
Cork & Bottle
The Criterion *(Midnight, not Sun)*
Deals – *W1 (Fri & Sat 1 am)*
dell'Ugo
Detroit *(ex Sun)*
Dover St Wine Bar *(2 am)*
Dragon Inn *(Fri & Sat)*
Ed's Easy Diner – *W1 (Midnight, Fri & Sat 1 am)*
Efes Kebab House – *W1 (Fri & Sat 3 am)*
Fakhreldine
Football Football
Garlic & Shots
The Gaucho Grill *(ex Sun)*
Häagen-Dazs – *WC2 (Midnight, Fri & Sat); WC2 (Midnight, Fri & Sat 1 am)*
Hamine *(2.30 am, Sat 1.30 am, Sun midnight)*
Hard Rock Café *(12.30 am, Fri & Sat 1 am)*
Hujo's
The Ivy
Joe Allen *(12.45 am)*
Kettners
The Lancers
The Lanesborough
Langan's Brasserie *(11.45 pm, Sat 12.45 am)*
Lindsay House *(Midnight, not Sun)*
Little Italy *(4 am, Sun midnight)*
Marché Mövenpick – *SW1, W1*
Maroush – *W1 (1 am)*
Maze *(Fri & Sat only)*
Melati *(Fri & Sat 12.30 am)*
Mezzo *(Mon-Wed midnight, Thu-Sat 1 am (crustacea till 3 am), not Sun)*

Mezzonine *(Mon-Wed 12.30 am, Thu-Sat 2.30 am, not Sun)*
Mondo *(snacks till 2 am)*
Mr Kong *(1.45 am)*
L'Odéon
Orso
Le Palais du Jardin
Pélican – *WC2 (12.30 am, Sun 10.30 pm)*
Pizza On The Park
PizzaExpress – *SW1, W1, WC1, WC2*
PizzaExpress – *W1 (Midnight, Wed-Sat 1 am)*
Pizzeria Condotti
Planet Hollywood *(1 am)*
Pollo
La Porte des Indes *(Midnight, Sun 10.30 pm)*
Quaglino's *(Midnight, Fri & Sat 1 am, not Sun)*
Ranoush *(3 am)*
Smollensky's Balloon *(ex Sun)*
Smollensky's, Strand *(Midnight, Thu - Sat 12.30 am, not Sun)*
Sofra – *all branches*
Soho Soho *(rotisserie 12.45 am)*
Sol e Luna *(ex Sun)*
Texas Embassy Cantina *(Fri & Sat)*
TGI Friday's – *W1, WC2*
Tokyo Diner
Wolfe's – *WC2*

West

Al Basha
Albero & Grana, Bar
Balans *(1 am)*
Bersagliera
Big Easy *(Midnight, Fri & Sat 12.30 am)*
Bistrot 190 *(12.30 am)*
Blakes Hotel
Blue Elephant *(12.30 am ex Sun)*
Bombay Brasserie
La Brasserie
Café Lazeez *(12.30 am)*
Caffè Uno – *W2, W8*
Calzone – *W11; SW10 (Midnight, Fri & Sat 12.45 am)*
The Canteen *(Fri & Sat only)*
Cappadoccia *(Fri & Sat only)*
Ciabatta
Da Mario
La Delizia – *SW3, SW5*
Ed's Easy Diner – *SW3*
Ffiona's
Häagen-Dazs – *SW7; W2 (12.30 am)*
Halepi *(12.30 am)*
The Jam *(1 am)*
Kalamaras, Mega
Kartouche
Los Remos

Lou Pescadou
Mackintosh's Brasserie
Maroush – W2 (1 am); SW3 (5 am)
Montpeliano
Mr Wing
Nachos – W11; SW10 (1 am); W4 (Thu-Sat 2 am)
Paparazzi Café (1 am)
Parsons (12.30 am)
Pizza Pomodoro (1 am)
Pizza the Action
PizzaExpress – SW10, SW3, W14, W2, W4, W8
Riccardo's
Rôtisserie Jules – SW3
Le Shop
606 Club (Mon-Thu 1.30 am, Fri & Sat 2 am)
Spago
Lo Spuntino
Stock Pot – SW3
Tandoori of Chelsea
Texas Lone Star (Thu-Sat 12.30 am)
Tiger Lil's – SW3 (Fri & Sat only)
Tootsies – SW6, SW7, W11, W4 (Fri & Sat only)
Tusc
Veronica's
Wine & Kebab (2 am)
Wine Gallery – SW10, W11
Wolfe's – SW3

North
Afghan Kitchen
Ali Baba
Anglo Asian Tandoori (Fri & Sat 12.45 am)
Benihana – NW3
Blakes (Fri & Sat only)
Caffè Uno – N1, N6, NW1, NW8
Calzone – N1, NW3
China Jazz
Cuba Libre (Fri & Sat 12.30 am)
Don Pepe (12.15 am)
Ed's Easy Diner – NW3
La Finca – N1 (1.30 am, Fri & Sat)
Greek Valley
Haandi (Sat & Sun only)
House on Rosslyn Hill
Le Mercury (1 am)
Nachos – N1, NW3
Pasha (Fri & Sat)
La Piragua
PizzaExpress – N1, NW3
Rasa (Fri & Sat)
Le Sacré-Coeur (Fri & Sat only)
Sarcan
Tootsies – NW3 (Fri & Sat only)

South
Buona Sera

Caffè Uno – SW13
Côte à Côte
Gastro
Haweli
PizzaExpress – SW11, SW14, SW15, SW18
Tea Rooms des Artistes (Food available until late - licensed to 1am)
Three Little Pigs (Fri & Sat Midnight)
Tiger Lil's – SW4 (Fri & Sat Midnight)
Tootsies – SW13 (Fri & Sat)

East
Brick Lane Beigel Bake (24 hr)
Clifton (1 am)
Lahore Kebab House
Pizza Pomodoro – E1 (1 am)

No-smoking areas
(* completely no smoking)

Central
Ajimura
Alwaha
Atrium
Au Jardin des Gourmets
Bertorelli's – WC2
Café de Colombia*
Café Fish
Café Nico
Café Pacifico
Café Sofra – W1
Caldesi
Caravan Serai
Chez Gérard – all branches
Chiaroscuro
Chicago Pizza Pie Factory
Chimes
China City
Connaught*
Cranks – all branches*
Fashion Café
Food for Thought*
Football Football
Footstool
The Foundation
Gopal's of Soho
Gourmet Pizza Co. – W1
Häagen-Dazs – WC2*
Hanover Square
Hard Rock Café
Ikkyu – WC2
Joe Allen
The Lancers
Maison Bertaux
Malabar Junction
Mandeer*
Marché Mövenpick – W1
Mildreds*
Museum St Café*

Neal's Yard Dining Rooms*
Nicole's
L'Odéon
Oriel
Orso
Pizza On The Park
Planet Hollywood
La Porte des Indes
Pret A Manger – *all branches*
Ristorante Italiano
Soho Soho
Sol e Luna
Sol e Stella
Star Café
Tamarind
Tate Gallery
TGI Friday's – *W1, WC2*
Tokyo Diner
22° South
The Union Café
Veeraswamy
Villandry*
Vong
Wagamama – *W1, WC1**
Wren at St James's*
Zoe

West
The Ark
Big Easy
Bombay Palace
Café Lazeez
Café Pasta – *W4, W8*
Chelsea Kitchen
Chicago Rib Shack
Chutney Mary
Clarke's
Daquise
Francofill
Häagen-Dazs – *SW7, W2**; *SW10*
James R
King's Road Café
Mackintosh's Brasserie
Mamta
Manzara
Mr Wing
Nayab
Nikita's
Noughts 'n' Crosses
192
Orsino
Parsons
Pizza Chelsea
Pret A Manger – *all branches*
Raoul's Café
San Martino
Standard Tandoori
Stock Pot – *SW3*
The Sugar Club
Sushi Bar Gen

TGI Friday's – *W2*
Thai Bistro
Tiger Lil's – *SW3*
Windsor Castle

North
The Blenheim
La Brasserie Highgate
Byron's
Café des Arts
Café Pasta – *NW3*
Casale Franco
China Jazz
Cottons
Diwana Bhel-Poori House*
Euphorium
Frederick's
Gresslin's
Manna
Marine Ices
Pret A Manger – *all branches*
Rani – *N3*
Rasa*
San Carlo
Seashell
Solly's
Troika
Two Brothers
Wakaba

South
The Depot
Eco
Gastro
The Grafton
Hoults
Mezzanine
Naked Turtle
Newton's
Oxo Tower
The Pepper Tree
Prego
Rani – *TW9*
The Stepping Stone
Tiger Lil's – *SW4*
La Truffe Noire
Twenty Trinity Gdns

East
Babe Ruth's
Café Spice Namaste
Futures – *EC3**, *EC2*
Gourmet Pizza Co. – *E14*
Japanese Canteen
Leith's at the Institute
Moshi Moshi Sushi – *EC2**
The Place Below*
Pret A Manger – *EC4**, *EC1, EC2*
Rupee Room

INDEXES

Outside tables
(* particularly recommended)

Central
Al Bustan
Al Hamra*
Alfred
All Bar One – WC2
Andrew Edmunds
L'Artiste Musclé*
Aurora*
Bahn Thai
Bar Italia
Boisdale
Boudin Blanc*
Brahms*
Café Bohème
Café des Amis du Vin*
Café du Jardin
Café Emm
Café Flo – W1
Café Pasta – both WC2
Café Rouge – Frith St W1, James St W1, Wellington St WC2
Café Sofra – Shepherd Mkt, W1*
Caffè Uno – W1, WC2
Caldesi
Caraffini
Caravan Serai
Chez Gérard – W1 (Dover St)*, WC2 (The Piazza)*; W1 (Charlotte St), WC2 (Chancery Ln)
Chiaroscuro
Chimes
Cork & Bottle
Cranks – all branches but Adelaide St
Deals – W1
dell'Ugo
Ed's Easy Diner – W1
Efes Kebab House – W1
Fifth Floor (Café)
La Finezza
Food for Thought
Garlic & Shots
Gordon's Wine Bar*
Gourmet Pizza Co. – W1
Grumbles
Häagen-Dazs – WC2
Hard Rock Café
Hardy's
Italian Kitchen
Little Italy
Maison Bertaux
Marché Mövenpick – W1
Mars
Maze
Mekong
Mildreds
Motcomb's
Oriel
Le Palais du Jardin

Pâtisserie Valerie – W1 (RIBA)*; Sagne W1, Russel St WC2
Pélican – WC2
Pierre Victoire – SW1
Pizza On The Park
PizzaExpress – Baker St, Charlotte St, Barrett St W1; Coptic St WC1
Porters
La Poule au Pot
Pret A Manger – Baker St, Regent's St, Tottenham Ct Rd W1, High Holborn WC1, St Martin's Ln WC2
Randall & Aubin
Ristorante Italiano
The Ritz*
Santini
Scott's
Sheekey's*
Silks & Spice
Sofra – St Christopher's Pl, Shepherd Mkt (both Sofra and Bistro Sofra) W1*
Soho Soho
Sol e Luna
Sol e Stella
Texas Embassy Cantina
Toto's*
Wolfe's – WC2
Wren at St James's*
Zoe*

West
The Abingdon*
L'Accento Italiano*
Alastair Little W11
L'Altro
Anglesea Arms
The Ark
L'Artiste Assoiffé
Ask – W4
Au Bon Accueil*
Balans
Bar Central – SW3
Bedlington Café
Belvedere*
Big Easy
Blakes Hotel*
Blenheim Bis
La Bouchée
The Brackenbury
La Brasserie
Brasserie du Marché
Brinkley's*
Busabong Tree*
Café Flo – SW6
Café Grove*
Café Lazeez*
Café Med
Café Montpeliano
Café O
Café Pasta – W4, W8

172

Café Rouge – SW3, WII, W4, W8, W9
Caffé Uno – W2
Calzone – SW10, WII
Cambio de Tercio
Charco's
Chelsea Bun Diner*
Chelsea Ram
Chinon
Chiswick
Cibo
Conrad Hotel*
Costa's Grill*
Da Pierino
Dan's*
Daphne's*
De Cecco*
Deals – SW10*; W6
La Delizia – SW3*
La Dordogne
Dove
Emile's – SW6
The Enterprise
L'Escargot Doré
The Establishment
Il Falconiere
La Famiglia*
Fat Boy's*
Fats
Formula Veneta*
The Gate*
El Gaucho*
Geale's
La Giara
Gilbert's
Glaisters – SW10*
Halcyon Hotel*
The Havelock Tavern
Henry J Beans*
Jason's*
Jim Thompson's*
Jimmy Beez*
Joe's Brasserie
Joe's Café
Julie's Bar*
Khan's of Kensington
The Ladbroke Arms*
Lisboa Patisserie
Lou Pescadou
Luigi's Delicatessen
Mackintosh's Brasserie
Mon Petit Plaisir*
Montpeliano*
Mr Frascati
Nachos – W4
Nippon-Tuk
Noughts 'n' Crosses
Ognisko Polskie*
Oliver's Island
192

Osteria Basilico
Palio
Palms-on-the-Hill
Paparazzi Café
Pâtisserie Valerie – SW3
Paulo's
Picasso
Pizza Chelsea
PizzaExpress – SW6, WI4, W2, W4, W8
Poissonnerie de l'Avenue
Pret A Manger – SW3
Princess of Wales
Pucci Pizza
Raoul's Café
The Red Pepper
Riccardo's
The River Café*
Rôtisserie Jules – SW3
San Frediano
Sandrini
The Scarsdale*
Shaw's
Le Shop
Spago
Sporting Page
Lo Spuntino
The Stamford
Stick & Bowl
Stock Pot – SW3
The Sugar Club*
Thai Bistro
Thai on the River*
Tootsies – SW6, SW7, WII, W4
Topsy-Tasty
Tusc*
Veronica's
WII*
The Westbourne*
Windsor Castle*
Wine Gallery – SW10*; WII
Wolfe's – SW3

North
Ali Baba
Anna's Place*
Ask – NW3
L'Aventure*
Bar Gansa
The Big Night Out
The Blenheim*
Byron's
Café Delancey
Café des Arts
Café Flo – NI, NW3
Café Pasta – NI, NW3
Café Rouge – N6
Caffe Graffiti
Caffé Uno – NI, N6, NW8
La Cage Imaginaire*

INDEXES

Calzone – N1, NW3
Casale Franco*
Cottons
Crown & Goose
Cuba Libre
Czech Club
Daphne*
Ed's Easy Diner – NW3
The Engineer*
Florians
The Fox Reformed*
Frederick's*
Greek Valley
House on Rosslyn Hill
Kavanagh's
Lansdowne
Nachos – N1
Nontas*
Odette's
La Piragua
PizzaExpress – NW3
Ruby in the Dust – N1, NW1
Le Sacré-Coeur
San Carlo*
Sarcan
Singapore Garden
Solly's
Soulard
Troika
Vegia Zena
Villa Bianca*

South
Antipasto e Pasta
Archduke Wine Bar*
B Square
The Bank
Bar Central – TW9*; SE1
Battersea Rickshaw
Bellinis
Blue Print Café*
Boiled Egg*
Le Bouchon Bordelais
Le Bouchon Lyonnais
La Bouffe
Buchan's
Buona Sera
The Butlers Wharf
  Chop-house*
Café de la Place*
Café Jeune*
Café on the Common*
Café Rouge – SW15
Caffé Uno – SW13*
Cantina del Ponte*
Côte à Côte
The Depot*
Dixie's Bar & Grill
Glaisters – SW11
Le Gothique*

Gourmet Pizza Co. – SE1*
The Grafton
Hoults*
The Lavender
Livebait
The Mason's Arms
Naked Turtle
Newton's
C Notarianni & Sons
Ost. Antica Bologna
Oxo Tower*
Phoenix
Pitcher & Piano – SW12
PizzaExpress – SE1, SW15, SW4
Le Pont de la Tour*
Le Pont de la Tour Bar*
Prego
Ransome's Dock*
RSJ
The Ship*
South Bank Brasserie
Tea Rooms des Artistes*
Tootsies – SW13
La Truffe Noire
Twenty Trinity Gdns
White Cross Hotel*

East
Al's
All Bar One – E14*
Bar Etrusca*
Bleeding Heart*
The Bow Wine Vaults*
Brasserie Rocque*
Café Rouge – EC4
Café Spice Namaste
Carnevale*
The Eagle
The Fence*
Frocks*
Future1 – EC2*
Gourmet Pizza Co. – E14
Japanese Canteen
Maison Novelli
Mange 2
The Place Below*
Poons in the City
Pret A Manger – EC1
Singapura – EC4
Taberna Etrusca*
Tao*
Wynkyn de Worde

Private rooms

(for the most comprehensive
listing of venues for functions –
from palaces to pubs – see
Harden's London Party Guide,
available in all good bookshops)
* particularly recommended

Central

Ajimura *(20)*
Al Bustan *(10)*
Alastair Little *(14)*
Arirang *(35)*
Arisugawa *(20,8)*
L'Artiste Musclé *(30)*
Atelier *(16)*
Atlantic Bar & Grill *(70)**
Atrium *(12,24)*
Au Jardin des
  Gourmets *(8-55)*
Bahn Thai *(20;30)*
Bar Madrid *(50)*
Belgo Centraal *(25,30)*
Benihana *– W1 (10)*
Bentley's *(16)**
Beotys *(6-60)*
Bice *(22)*
Blues *(30)*
Boisdale *(20)*
Boudin Blanc *(35)*
Boulevard *(40)*
Browns *– W1 (16,8,8)*
Café du Jardin *(70)*
Café Flo *– W1 (30)*
Caldesi *(22)*
La Capannina *(12-30)*
Caravan Serai *(20)*
Chez Gérard *– Dover St W1 (30);*
  Chancery Ln WC2 (35)
Chez Nico *(20)**
Chiang Mai *(22)*
Chiaroscuro *(16)*
Chicago Pizza Pie
  Factory *(50)*
Chimes *(30)*
China City *(20,30,50)*
China Court *(10-400)*
Christopher's *(32)*
Chuen Cheng Ku *(20-300)*
Claridges Restaurant *(14)*
Como Lario *(20)*
Connaught *(22)**
Cork & Bottle *(30)*
dell'Ugo *(16,12)*
Dorchester, Oriental *(6,10,16)**
Dover St Wine Bar *(36)*
Elena's L'Etoile *(6-28)*
L'Escargot *(24,60)**
L'Estaminet *(22)*
Fashion Café *(40)*

Football Football *(50)*
Fung Shing *(28,40)*
Garbo's *(50)*
Garlic & Shots *(25)*
Le Gavroche *(20)**
Gay Hussar *(12,24)**
Golden Dragon *(30)*
Green's *(34)*
The Guinea *(10-30)*
The Halkin *(26)*
Hanover Square *(120)*
Harbour City *(40,60,70)*
Hardy's *(15)*
The Heights *(11)*
Hodgson's *(20)*
Hollihead *(16)*
Ikeda *(8)*
Ikkyu *– W1 (10)*
L'Incontro *(35)*
Interlude de Chavot *(16)*
The Ivy *(20-60)**
Jin *(25)*
Kaspia *(12)*
Ken Lo's Memories *(20)*
Kettners *(12-70)*
The Lancers *(20)*
The Lexington *(20)*
Lindsay House *(12,20)*
Little Italy *(35)*
Luigi's *(35)*
Malabar Junction *(40)*
Mars *(30)*
Masako *(16)*
Matsuri *(18)*
Mekong *(14/24)*
Mimmo d'Ischia *(30,12)*
Mitsukoshi *(12,24)*
Miyama *(17)*
Mon Plaisir *(28)*
Motcomb's *(24)*
Mr Chow *(70)*
Neal Street *(26)**
New World *(200)*
Nico Central *(12)*
L'Odéon *(20)*
L'Oranger *(25)*
Pied à Terre *(12)*
Pitcher & Piano *– WC2 (20,40);*
  W1 (30,60)
Pizza On The Park *(100)*
PizzaExpress *– Wardour St W (40)*
  Dean St W1 (70); WC2 (50)
Pizzeria Condotti *(40)*
Planet Hollywood *(100)*
Pomegranates *(12)*
La Porte des Indes *(12-80)*
Quaglino's *(40)**
Red Fort *(60)*
Rib Room *(16)*
Ristorante Italiano *(25,40)*

INDEXES

Rodos *(40)*
Rules *(48,25,12)**
Saga *(12)*
Saigon *(50)*
Santini *(30)*
Les Saveurs *(11)**
Scott's *(14)*
Shampers *(45)*
Sheekey's *(12)*
Shepherd's *(32)**
Signor Sassi *(30)*
Simpsons-in-the-
    Strand *(150,45)**
Sofra – *Bistro (20);*
    Taviscock St WC2 (70)
Soho Soho *(60)**
The Square *(20)*
Sri Siam *(32)*
Suntory *(4)**
Texas Embassy Cantina *(180)*
Vasco & Piero's Pavilion *(32)*
West Zenders *(30)*
White Tower *(8,10,18)**
Wiltons *(16)**
Zen Garden *(30,12)*

West
Adams Café *(24)*
Al Basha *(60)*
All Saints *(20)*
The Ark *(28)*
L'Artiste Assoiffé *(35)*
Au Bon Accueil *(32)*
Beach Blanket Babylon *(35-50)*
Benihana – *SW3 (12)*
Bistrot 190 *(28)*
Blah! Blah! Blah! *(30)*
Blakes Hotel *(16)*
Blue Elephant *(200)*
Bombay Palace *(30)*
Bonjour Vietnam *(20,100)*
Brasserie du Marché *(30)*
Brasserie St Quentin *(20)*
Brinkley's *(46,18)*
Bucci *(10,15,25)*
Busabong Too *(25)*
Busabong Tree *(25-50)*
Café Lazeez *(50)*
Café Rouge – *W8 (20)*
Cambio de Tercio *(40)*
Capital Hotel *(24)**
Chaba *(18)*
Chelsea Ram *(12)*
Conrad Hotel *(16)*
Coopers Arms *(30)*
Costa's Grill *(25)*
The Crescent *(80)*
The Cross Keys *(50)*
Dan's *(34,12)**
Daquise *(35)*

La Dordogne *(30)*
Downstairs at 190 *(24)**
Emile's – *SW6 (42)*
English Garden *(30)**
English House *(12,8,12)*
L'Escargot Doré *(25)*
Fables *(25)*
Il Falconiere *(30)*
La Famiglia *(40)*
First Floor *(35,55)**
Formula Veneta *(30)*
Foxtrot Oscar *(35)*
Front Page *(22)*
Fulham Road *(16)*
The Green Olive *(20-25)*
Halcyon Hotel *(10)*
I Thai *(20)*
James R *(30)*
Jimmy Beez *(20)*
Julie's *(16,32,45)**
Launceston Place *(30)*
Leith's *(36)**
Lou Pescadou *(35)*
Made in Italy *(30)*
Malabar *(24)*
Mao Tai *(40)*
Memories of India *(30)*
Mr Wing *(30)*
Nachos – *SW10 (100);*
    W4 (200); W11 (30)
Nam Long *(20)*
Nikita's *(14,10,6)**
Nineteen *(26)*
Nizam *(25)*
Oliver's Island *(36)*
Orsino *(16-32)**
Palio *(60)*
Paulo's *(20)*
Phoenicia *(36)*
Pitcher & Piano – *SW10 (30)*
Pizza Chelsea *(80)*
PizzaExpress – *SW3 (20); SW6 (30)*
PJ's *(60)*
Poissonnerie de l'Avenue *(22)*
La Pomme d'Amour *(35)*
Princess of Wales *(30)*
Prost *(36)*
Red *(20)*
Royal China *(15,20)*
San Lorenzo *(30)*
San Martino *(32)*
Sash *(14)*
755 *(40)*
Shoeless Joe's *(40)*
Le Shop *(40)*
Snows on the Green *(24)*
Spago *(30)*
Lo Spuntino *(40)*
The Stamford *(25)*
Standard Tandoori *(55)*

Stick & Bowl (20)
Stratford's (30)
Le Suquet (16)*
Tabac (45)
Tawana (50)
Thierry's (30)
Verbanella (30)
Veronica's (40)
W11 (50)
Walton's (10,24)*
Wine Gallery (40,18)
Wódka (30)
Wolfe's – SW3 (40)
Zah Bar (25)
Zen (24)

North
Afghan Kitchen (20)
Benihana – NW3 (8)
The Big Night Out (30)
The Blenheim (16,35)
Café des Arts (25)
Caffé Uno – NW8 (60)
Camden Brasserie (80)
Chutneys (120)
Cottons (30)
Crown & Goose (20)
Czech Club (20,100)
Daphne (35)
Diwana Bhel-Poori
   House (40)
Don Pepe (25)
The Engineer (32)
Feng Shang (45)
La Finca – N1 (150)
Frederick's (30)
Geeta (10-30)
Greek Valley (30)
Gresslin's (16)
Lansdowne (30)
Lemonia (40)
Le Mercury (50)
Nachos – N1 (200)
Nachos – NW3 (40)
Odette's (8,30)*
PizzaExpress – N1 (30)
Quincy's (16)
Rani – N3 (60)
Ruby in the Dust – N1 (50)
Singapore Garden (50)
Solly's (100)
Soulard (16)
The Vegetarian Cottage (20)
Vegia Zena (15)
Villa Bianca (75)
Village Bistro (25)
ZeNW3 (25)

South
Alma (70)

Archduke Wine Bar (50)
Batt. Barge Bistro (10)
Bellinis (30)
Bombay Bicycle Club (22)
Le Bouchon Bordelais (40)
Buchan's (50-60)
Café Jeune (40)
Chez Bruce (25)
Côte à Côte (80)
Emile's – SW15 (45,30)
Enoteca Turi (45)
Fina Estampa (20-60)
Glaisters – SW11 (40)
Mezzanine (12)
Naked Turtle (36)
Le P'tit Normand (20)
Phoenix (30)
Phuket (25)
PizzaExpress – SW11,
   SW15 (30); SE1 (80)
Le Pont de la Tour (20)*
Prego (16)
RSJ (16)
The Ship (14-20)
Shree Krishna (60)
Sonny's (20)
South Bank Brasserie (55)
Tea Rooms des
   Artistes (45,70)
Three Little Pigs (35)
La Truffe Noire (16,30,40)

East
Ashtons (12)
Aykoku-Kaku (8,4)
Babe Ruth's (100-120)
Beauchamp's (20;30)
Bleeding Heart (50)
The Bow Wine Vaults (70)
Bubb's (22)
Café du Marché (60)
Café Spice Namaste (35)
City Miyama (10,8,4)
F Cooke & Sons (40)
Fox & Anchor (20)
Frocks (30)
Gow's (100)
Hope & Sir Loin (30,25)
Hothouse Bar & Grill (20)
Imperial City (16)*
Inmala (30)
Japanese Canteen (70)
Leadenhall Tapas Bar (45)
Leith's at the Institute (8-230)
The Lobster Trading
   Co (25,10)
Maison Novelli (50)
Mange 2 (22)
PizzaExpress – EC2 (200)
The Place Below (40)

INDEXES

Poons in the City *(10-40)*
St John *(20)*
Singapura – *EC3 (12)*
Tao *(16)*
Tatsuso *(6,8)*
Wynkyn de Worde *(12)*

Romantic

Central
Al Bustan
Andrew Edmunds
Bentley's
Boudin Blanc
Café Royal Grill
Le Caprice
Christopher's
Claridges Restaurant
Connaught
The Criterion
Dover St Wine Bar
La Fontana
French House
Le Gavroche
Gay Hussar
Greenhouse
The Guinea
Hodgson's
L'Incontro
The Ivy
Joe Allen
Kaspia
Kettners
Langan's Brasserie
Lindsay House
Mimmo d'Ischia
Mon Plaisir
Motcomb's
Le Muscadet
Neal Street
O'Conor Don
Odin's
L'Oranger
Orso
La Porte des Indes
La Poule au Pot
The Ritz
Sale e Pepe
Salloos
Santini
Savoy Grill
Savoy River Room
Shogun
Tate Gallery
White Tower
Windows on the World

West
L'Artiste Assoiffé
Au Bon Accueil

Belvedere
Bibendum
Blakes Hotel
Blue Elephant
Brasserie St Quentin
Chez Moi
Christoph's
Clarke's
The Cow
Dan's
Daphne's
La Dordogne
English House
Fables
La Famiglia
First Floor
Gilbert's
Glaisters – *SW10*
The Green Olive
Halcyon Hotel
Julie's
Julie's Bar
Kalamaras, Mega
Launceston Place
Maggie Jones's
Mon Petit Plaisir
Monkeys
Mr Wing
Nam Long
Nikita's
Oliver's Island
La Pomme d'Amour
San Lorenzo
Sandrini
Scalini
Shaw's
Le Suquet
Thai on the River
Thierry's
Turner's
Walton's

North
Anna's Place
L'Aventure
Byron's
Café des Arts
La Cage Imaginaire
The Engineer
Frederick's
House on Rosslyn Hill
Odette's
Oslo Court

South
Rebato's
RSJ

East
Bleeding Heart

Café du Marché
Hothouse Bar & Grill

Rooms with a view

Central
Fakhreldine
The Fifth Floor
The Heights
The Ritz
Savoy River Room
Windows on the World

West
Belvedere
Conrad Hotel
The Tenth
Thai on the River

South
Bar Central – TW9
Batt. Barge Bistro
Blue Print Café
The Butlers Wharf Chop-
  house
Cantina del Ponte
The Depot
Gourmet Pizza Co. – SE1
Oxo Tower
The People's Palace
Le Pont de la Tour
Le Pont de la Tour Bar &
  Grill
South Bank Brasserie

East
Le Quai

Vegetarian
(* particularly recommended)

Central
Chiang Mai
Cranks
Dorchester Grill*
The Fifth Floor
Food for Thought*
India Club*
The Lanesborough
Malabar Junction*
Mandeer*
Mildreds
Neal's Yard Dining Rooms
Ragam
Savoy River Room
Woodlands
Wren at St James's

West
Blah! Blah! Blah!*
Blue Elephant*

The Gate*
Halcyon Hotel*
Leith's
Mamta*

North
Chutneys*
Diwana Bhel-Poori House*
Geeta*
Manna
Rani
Rasa*
The Vegetarian Cottage
Vijay*
Yum Yum

South
Bangles*
Café on the Common
Kastoori*
Le Pont de la Tour
Rani
Shree Krishna*
Tea Rooms des Artistes

East
Carnevale*
Futures – EC3
The Place Below*

CUISINES – EUROPE

An asterisk (*) after an entry indicates exceptional or very good cooking.

EUROPE

Belgian

Central
Belgo Centraal *(WC2)*

North
Belgo Noord *(NW1)*

British, Modern

Central
Alastair Little *(W1)*
Alfred *(WC2)**
All Bar One *(W1, WC2)*
Andrew Edmunds *(W1)*
Atelier *(W1)**
Atlantic Bar & Grill *(W1)*
Atrium *(SW1)*
Aurora *(W1)**
The Avenue *(SW1)*
Bank *(WC2)*
Blues *(W1)*
Café du Jardin *(WC2)*
Café Nico *(W1)*
Le Caprice *(SW1)**
Chiaroscuro *(WC1)**
Coast *(W1)*
Delicious Blue *(W1)*
dell'Ugo *(W1)*
Detroit *(WC2)*
Drones *(SW1)*
Ebury Street Wine Bar *(SW1)*
81 *(SW1)*
Euten's *(WC2)*
Exxo *(W1)*
The Fifth Floor *(SW1)*
Fifth Floor (Café) *(SW1)*
The Foundation *(SW1)*
French House *(W1)**
The Heights *(W1)**
Hodgson's *(WC2)*
Hollihead *(W1)*
Hujo's *(W1)*
The Ivy *(WC2)**
The Lanesborough *(W1)*
Langan's Brasserie *(W1)*
The Lexington *(W1)*
Lindsay House *(W1)*
Mars *(WC2)*
Maze *(W1)*
Mezzo *(W1)*

Mondo *(W1)*
Museum St Café *(WC1)**
Nicole's *(W1)*
Plummers *(WC2)*
Quaglino's *(W1)*
Saint *(WC2)*
Sotheby's Café *(W1)*
The Square *(W1)**
Stephen Bull *(W1)**
Tate Gallery *(SW1)*
33 *(SW1)*
Thomas Goode *(W1)*
The Union Café *(W1)*
Zoe *(W1)*

West
The Abingdon *(W8)*
Alastair Little W11 *(W11)**
All Bar One *(SW6, W4)*
All Saints *(W11)*
Anglesea Arms *(W6)*
L'Artiste Assoiffé *(W11)*
Bar Central *(SW3)*
Beach Blanket Babylon *(W11)*
Belvedere *(W8)*
Bistrot 190 *(SW7)*
Blenheim Bis *(W11)*
Boyd's *(W8)**
The Brackenbury *(W6)**
Brinkley's *(SW10)*
Café Med *(W11)*
The Canteen *(SW10)**
Charco's *(SW3)**
Chelsea Ram *(SW10)*
Chiswick *(W4)*
Christoph's *(SW10)**
Clarke's *(W8)**
The Collection *(SW3)*
The Cow *(W11)*
The Crescent *(SW3)*
The Cross Keys *(SW3)*
Dan's *(SW3)*
Daphne's *(SW3)*
Downstairs at 190 *(SW7)*
English Garden *(SW3)*
English House *(SW3)*
The Establishment *(SW7)*
Fables *(SW6)**
Ffiona's *(W8)**
First Floor *(W11)*
Fulham Road *(SW3)*
The Fulham Tup *(SW10)*
Gilbert's *(SW7)*
Halcyon Hotel *(W11)**
The Havelock Tavern *(W14)*
Hilaire *(SW7)*
The Imperial Arms *(SW6)**
James R *(SW6)*
Jimmy Beez *(W10)**
Joe's Brasserie *(SW6)*

Joe's Café (SW3)
Kartouche (SW10)
Kensington Place (W8)
The Ladbroke Arms (W11)*
Launceston Place (W8)*
Lazy Jack's (W12)
Leith's (W11)
Mas Café (W11)
Le Metro (SW3)
Noughts 'n' Crosses (W5)
Oliver's Island (W4)
192 (W11)
The Pen (SW6)
The Prince Bonaparte (W2)
Princess of Wales (SW3)
Raoul's Café (W9)
755 (SW6)*
Shaw's (SW7)
606 Club (SW10)
Snows on the Green (W6)
The Stamford (W6)
The Sugar Club (W11)*
Tabac (W10)*
The Tenth (W8)
Vingt-Quatre (SW10)
W11 (W11)
Walton's (SW3)
The Westbourne (W2)*
Wilson's (W14)

North
All Bar One (N1, NW8)
Bar Central (N1)
The Big Night Out (NW1)
Blakes (NW1)*
The Blenheim (NW8)
Byron's (NW3)
Café des Arts (NW3)
Crown & Goose (NW1)
Cucina (NW3)*
The Engineer (NW1)
Euphorium (N1)*
Granita (N1)*
Gresslin's (NW3)*
Kavanagh's (N1)
Lansdowne (NW1)*
Odette's (NW1)*
Quincy's (NW2)

South
The Apprentice (SE1)*
B Square (SW11)
The Bank (SW11)
Bar Central (SE1, TW9)
Blue Print Café (SE1)
Buchan's (SW11)
Café dell'Ugo (SE1)
Chez Bruce (SW17)*
The Cook House (SW15)
Glaisters (SW11)

The Grafton (SW4)*
The Lavender (SW11)
The Mason's Arms (SW8)*
Mezzanine (SE1)
Oxo Tower (SE1)
The People's Palace (SE1)
Phoenix (SW15)
Le Pont de la Tour (SE1)
Ransome's Dock (SW11)
RSJ (SE1)*
Scoffers (SW11)
Sonny's (SW13)
The Stepping Stone (SW8)*
Three Little Pigs (SE1)
Valhalla (SW11)
Vincent's (SW15)
The Waterloo Fire
    Station (SE1)
White Cross
    Hotel (RICHMOND)

East
All Bar One (E14, EC4)
City Brasserie (EC3)
The Fence (EC1)
Frocks (E9)
Gladwins (EC3)
Hothouse Bar & Grill (E1)
Leith's at the Institute (EC2)
The Peasant (EC1)
The Quality Chop Hs (EC1)*
St John (EC1)
Stephen Bull Bistro (EC1)
Whittington's (EC4)

British, Traditional

Central
Chimes (SW1)
Claridges Restaurant (W1)
Connaught (W1)
Dorchester Grill (W1)*
Green's (SW1)
Greenhouse (W1)*
Grenadier (SW1)
The Guinea (W1)
Porters (WC2)
Rib Room (SW1)*
Rules (WC2)
Savoy Grill (WC2)
Savoy River Room (WC2)
Scott's (W1)
Seafresh (SW1)*
Shepherd's (SW1)
Simpsons-in-the-Strand (WC2)
Wiltons (SW1)

West
Basil St Hotel (SW3)
Brady's (SW6)*

Costa's Fish (W8)*
Geale's (W8)*
Maggie Jones's (W8)
Veronica's (W2)
Windsor Castle (W8)

North
Nautilus (NW6)*
Seashell (NW1)*
Toff's (N10)*
Two Brothers (N3)*
Upper St Fish Shop (N1)*

South
Brady's (SW18)*
The Butlers Wharf Chop-
  house (SE1)

East
The Bow Wine Vaults (EC4)
F Cooke & Sons (E8)
Fox & Anchor (EC1)*
George & Vulture (EC3)
Reynier (EC3)
Simpson's of Cornhill (EC3)

Czech

North
Czech Club (NW6)

East/West

Central
Mezzonine (W1)
Vong (SW1)*

West
I Thai (W2)

Fish & seafood

Central
Bank (WC2)
Belgo Centraal (WC2)
Bentley's (W1)
Café Fish (SW1)
Cave (W1)
Fung Shing (WC2)*
Green's (SW1)
Manzi's (WC2)*
Motcomb's (SW1)*
Quaglino's (W1)
Randall & Aubin (W1)*
Scott's (W1)
Sheekey's (WC2)
Wiltons (SW1)

West
L'Altro (W11)
Bibendum Oyster Bar (SW3)*

Big Easy (SW3)
Downstairs at 190 (SW7)
Ghillies (SW6)
Jason's (W9)*
Lou Pescadou (SW5)
Mandarin Kitchen (W2)*
Poissonnerie de l'Ave (SW3)*
Stratford's (W8)*
Le Suquet (SW3)

North
Belgo Noord (NW1)
Chez Liline (N4)*

South
Livebait (SE1)*
Lobster Pot (SE11)*
Le Pont de la Tour Bar &
  Grill (SE1)

East
Beauchamp's (EC3)
F Cooke & Sons (E8)
Gow's (EC2)
The Lobster Trading
  Co (EC2)*
Rudland & Stubbs (EC1)
Sheekey's (EC4)
Sweetings (EC4)

French

Central
L'Artiste Musclé (W1)
Au Jardin des Gourmets (W1)
Beotys (WC2)
Boudin Blanc (W1)*
Café Bohème (W1)
Café des Amis du Vin (WC2)
Café Flo (W1, WC2)
Café Rouge (W1, WC2)
Café Royal Grill (W1)
Chez Gérard (W1, WC2)
Chez Nico (W1)*
Claridges Restaurant (W1)
Connaught (W1)
The Criterion (W1)
Elena's L'Etoile (W1)
L'Escargot (W1)
L'Estaminet (WC2)
Four Seasons (W1)*
Le Gavroche (W1)*
Interlude de Chavot (W1)*
Langan's Bistro (W1)
Magno's Brasserie (WC2)
Mirabelle (W1)
Mon Plaisir (WC2)
Le Muscadet (W1)
Nico Central (W1)
Oak Room (W1)
L'Odéon (SW1)

Odin's *(W1)*
L'Oranger *(SW1)**
Le Palais du Jardin *(WC2)**
Pélican *(WC2)*
Pied à Terre *(W1)*
Pierre Victoire *(SW1, W1, WC1)*
La Poule au Pot *(SW1)*
Quo Vadis *(W1)*
Restaurant MPW *(SW1)*
The Ritz *(W1)*
Les Saveurs *(W1)*
Savoy River Room *(WC2)*
Simply Nico *(SW1)**
Soho Soho *(W1)*
Le Soufflé *(W1)**
Villandry *(W1)**
White Tower *(W1)*
Windows on the World *(W1)*

West
The Ark *(W8)*
Au Bon Accueil *(SW3)*
Aubergine *(SW10)**
Bibendum *(SW3)**
Le Bon Choix *(SW10)*
La Bouchée *(SW7)*
La Brasserie *(SW3)*
Brasserie du Marché *(W10)**
Brasserie St Quentin *(SW3)**
Café Flo *(SW6, W4, W8)*
Café Rouge *(SW3, SW6, SW7, W11, W2, W4, W6, W8, W9)*
Capital Hotel *(SW3)**
Chez Max *(SW10)**
Chez Moi *(W11)*
Chinon *(W14)**
La Dordogne *(W4)**
Emile's *(SW6)*
L'Escargot Doré *(W8)*
Francofill *(SW7)**
The Green Olive *(W9)*
Grill St Quentin *(SW3)*
Jigsaw *(W12)*
Lou Pescadou *(SW5)*
Mon Petit Plaisir *(W8)**
Monkeys *(SW3)**
Pierre Victoire *(SW6, W11)*
Poissonnerie de
  l'Avenue *(SW3)**
La Pomme d'Amour *(W11)*
Stratford's *(W8)**
Le Suquet *(SW3)*
La Tante Claire *(SW3)**
Thierry's *(SW3)*
Turner's *(SW3)*

North
L'Aventure *(NW8)**
Café Flo *(N1, NW3)*
Café Rouge *(N6, NW3, NW8)*
La Cage Imaginaire *(NW3)*

Camden Brasserie *(NW1)**
Frederick's *(N1)*
Le Mercury *(N1)*
Oslo Court *(NW8)**
Pierre Victoire *(N1, NW1)*
Le Sacré-Coeur *(N1)*
Soulard *(N1)*
Village Bistro *(N6)**

South
Le Bouchon Bordelais *(SW11)*
Le Bouchon Lyonnais *(SW8)*
La Bouffe *(SW11)*
Café de la Place *(SW11)*
Café Rouge *(SE1, SW11, SW14, SW15, SW4)*
Café Tabac *(SW15)*
Emile's *(SW15)*
Gastro *(SW4)*
Le Gothique *(SW18)*
Lobster Pot *(SE11)**
Newton's *(SW4)*
Le P'tit Normand *(SW18)**
Pierre Victoire *(SW15)*
La Truffe Noire *(SE1)**
Twenty Trinity Gdns *(SW9)*

East
Ashtons *(EC3)*
Bleeding Heart *(EC1)**
Bubb's *(EC1)**
Café du Marché *(EC1)**
Café Rouge *(EC4)*
Le Champenois *(EC2)*
Luc's Brasserie *(EC3)*
Maison Novelli *(EC1)*
Mange 2 *(EC1)*
Le Mesurier *(EC1)**
Pélican *(E14)*
Pierre Victoire *(EC1)*
Le Quai *(EC4)*
Sheekey's *(EC4)*

Game

Central
Rules *(WC2)*
Wiltons *(SW1)*

West
Monkeys *(SW3)**

German

West
Prost *(W11)*

North
Cosmo *(NW3)*

CUISINES – EUROPE

Greek

Central
Beotys (WC2)
Epicuria (W1)*
Rodos (WC2)
White Tower (W1)

West
Café O (SW3)*
Costa's Grill (W8)
Halepi (W2)
Kalamaras, Mega/Micro (W2)
Wine & Kebab (SW10)

North
Daphne (NW1)*
Greek Valley (NW8)*
Lemonia (NW1)
Nontas (NW1)*

East
Kolossi Grill (EC1)*

Hungarian

Central
Gay Hussar (W1)

Italian

Central
Bertorelli's (W1, WC2)
Bice (W1)
Café Pasta (WC2)
Caffè Uno (W1, WC2)
Caldesi (W1)
La Capannina (W1)
Caraffini (SW1)
Cecconi's (W1)
Como Lario (SW1)
Diverso (W1)
La Finezza (SW1)
La Fontana (SW1)
The Halkin (SW1)
L'Incontro (SW1)
Italian Kitchen (WC1)
Little Italy (W1)
Luigi's (WC2)
Mimmo d'Ischia (SW1)
Neal Street (WC2)
Oliveto (SW1)
Olivo (SW1)*
Orso (WC2)
Il Passetto (WC2)*
Pollo (W1)
Ristorante Italiano (W1)
Sale e Pepe (SW1)
Santini (SW1)
Signor Sassi (SW1)
Sol e Luna (WC2)
Sol e Stella (W1)
Toto's (SW1)
Vasco & Piero's Pavilion (W1)
Il Vicolo (SW1)
Zafferano (SW1)*

West
L'Accento Italiano (W2)
Al San Vincenzo (W2)*
L'Altro (W11)
Assaggi (W2)*
Bersagliera (SW3)
Bucci (SW3)*
Café Montpeliano (SW3)
Café Pasta (W4, W8)
Caffè Uno (W2, W8)
Calzone (SW10, W11)*
Cento 50 (W11)
Ciabatta (SW3)
Cibo (W14)
Da Pierino (SW7)
De Cecco (SW6)*
La Delizia (SW3, SW5)*
Elistano (SW3)*
Il Falconiere (SW7)
La Famiglia (SW10)
La Fenice (W11)
Formula Veneta (SW10)
La Giara (SW3)
The Jam (SW3)
Leonardo's (SW10)*
Luigi's Delicatessen (SW10)*
Made in Italy (SW3)
Mona Lisa (SW10)
Montpeliano (SW7)
Mr Frascati (W2)
Orsino (W11)
Osteria Basilico (W11)*
Osteria Le Fate (SW3)
Palio (W11)
Paparazzi Café (SW3)
Picasso (SW3)
The Red Pepper (W9)*
Riccardo's (SW3)
The River Café (W6)*
Sambuca (SW3)
San Frediano (SW3)
San Lorenzo (SW3)
San Martino (SW3)
Sandrini (SW3)
Scalini (SW3)
Spago (SW7)
Lo Spuntino (SW3)*
Tusc (SW5)
Verbanella (SW3)
Ziani (SW3)

North
A Tavola (NW8)
Billboard Café (NW6)

La Brasserie Highgate *(N6)**
Café Pasta *(N1, NW3)*
Caffè Uno *(N1, N6, NW1, NW8)*
Calzone *(N1, NW3)**
Casale Franco *(N1)*
Florians *(N8)**
Luna *(NW1)*
Marine Ices *(NW3)*
Mezzaluna *(NW2)*
San Carlo *(N6)*
Vegia Zena *(NW1)**
Villa Bianca *(NW3)*

South

Antipasto e Pasta *(SW4)*
Bellinis *(SW13)*
Buona Sera *(SW11)**
Caffè Uno *(SW13)*
Cantina del Ponte *(SE1)*
Del Buongustaio *(SW15)**
Enoteca Turi *(SW15)**
C Notarianni & Sons *(SW11)**
Ost. Antica Bologna *(SW11)**
Prego *(TW9)*
Riva *(SW13)**

East

Alba *(EC1)*
Bar Etrusca *(EC4)*
The Clerkenwell *(EC1)**
Taberna Etrusca *(EC4)*
Young Turks *(EC2)*

Irish

Central

O'Conor Don *(W1)**

Mediterranean

Central

Bruno Soho *(W1)*

East

The Eagle *(EC1)**

Polish

West

Daquise *(SW7)*
Ognisko Polskie *(SW7)*
Wódka *(W8)*

North

Zamoyski *(NW3)*

Russian

Central

Kaspia *(W1)**

West

Nikita's *(SW10)*

North

Troika *(NW1)*

Scandinavian

Central

Garbo's *(W1)*
Scandinavian Restaurant *(SW1)*

North

Anna's Place *(N1)**

Steaks & grills

Central

Chez Gérard *(W1, WC2)*
Christopher's *(WC2)*
The Gaucho Grill *(W1)*
The Guinea *(W1)*
Kettners *(W1)*
Quaglino's *(W1)*
Rib Room *(SW1)**
Rowley's *(SW1)*
Smollensky's Balloon *(W1)*
Smollensky's, Strand *(WC2)*
Soho Soho *(W1)*
22° South *(W1)*

West

El Gaucho *(SW3)**
Popeseye *(W14)**
Rôtisserie *(W12)*
Rôtisserie Jules *(SW3, SW7, W11)*

North

Camden Brasserie *(NW1)**
Rôtisserie *(N1)*

South

Le Pont de la Tour Bar *(SE1)*

East

Fox & Anchor *(EC1)**
Hope & Sir Loin *(EC1)**
Simpson's of Cornhill *(EC3)*

Spanish

Central

Bar Madrid *(W1)*

West

Albero & Grana *(SW3)*
Albero & Grana, Bar *(SW3)**
Cambio de Tercio *(SW5)*
Galicia *(W10)*
Los Remos *(W2)*

North

Bar Gansa *(NW1)**

CUISINES – EUROPE

Don Pepe *(NW8)*
La Finca *(N1)*

South
La Finca *(SE11)*
Meson Don Felipe *(SE1)*
Rebato's *(SW8)**
La Rueda *(SW4)*

East
Barcelona Tapas *(EC3)**
Barcelona Tapas Bar *(E1)**
Fuego *(EC3)*
Leadenhall Tapas Bar *(EC3)*

Swiss

Central
St Moritz *(W1)*

International

Central
Balans *(W1)*
Boisdale *(SW1)*
Boulevard *(WC2)*
Brahms *(SW1)*
Browns *(W1, WC2)*
Cork & Bottle *(WC2)*
Deals *(W1)*
Dôme *(W1, WC2)*
Dover St Wine Bar *(W1)*
Footstool *(SW1)*
Garlic & Shots *(W1)*
Gordon's Wine Bar *(WC2)*
Grumbles *(SW1)*
Hanover Square *(W1)*
Hardy's *(W1)*
Marché Mövenpick *(SW1, W1)*
Motcomb's *(SW1)**
Oriel *(SW1)*
Pitcher & Piano *(W1, WC2)*
Pomegranates *(SW1)*
Sarastro *(WC2)*
Shampers *(W1)**
Stock Pot *(SW1, W1)*
Vendôme *(W1)*

West
Balans *(SW5)*
Blakes Hotel *(SW7)*
Café Grove *(W11)*
Chelsea Bun Diner *(SW10)*
Chelsea Kitchen *(SW3)*
Conrad Hotel *(SW10)**
Coopers Arms *(SW3)*
Deals *(SW10, W6)*
Dôme *(SW3, SW5, W8)*
Dove *(W6)*
The Enterprise *(SW3)*
Foxtrot Oscar *(SW3)*

Front Page *(SW3)**
The Gasworks *(SW6)*
Glaisters *(SW10)*
Julie's *(W11)*
Julie's Bar *(W11)*
Mackintosh's Brasserie *(W4)*
Nineteen *(SW3)*
Palms-on-the-Hill *(W8)*
Pitcher & Piano *(SW10, SW6, W4)*
PJ's *(SW3)*
The Scarsdale *(W8)*
Sporting Page *(SW10)**
Stock Pot *(SW3)*
Windsor Castle *(W8)*
Wine Gallery *(SW10, W11)*

North
Banners *(N8)*
Café Delancey *(NW1)*
Caffe Graffiti *(NW3)*
Cosmo *(NW3)*
Dôme *(N1, NW1, NW3)*
The Fox Reformed *(N16)*
House on Rosslyn Hill *(NW3)*
The Little Bay *(NW6)*
Parks *(N5)*
Ruby in the Dust *(N1, NW1)*

South
Alma *(SW18)*
Archduke Wine Bar *(SE1)*
Batt. Barge Bistro *(SW8)*
Café Jeune *(SW9)*
Côte à Côte *(SW11)*
The Depot *(SW14)*
Hoults *(SW17)*
Naked Turtle *(SW14)*
Pitcher & Piano *(SW12)*
The Ship *(SW18)*
South Bank Brasserie *(SE1)*
Thistells *(SE22)*
Tiger Lil's *(SW4)*

East
Al's *(EC1)**
Brasserie Rocque *(EC2)*
Dôme *(EC1)*
Mustards Brasserie *(EC1)*
Vic Naylors *(EC1)*
Wynkyn de Worde *(EC4)*

'SNACK' FOOD

Afternoon tea

Central
Aurora (W1)*
Brown's Hotel (W1)
Fifth Floor (Café) (SW1)
The Heights (W1)*
Hyde Park Hotel
  Park Room (SW1)
The Lanesborough (W1)
Simpsons-in-the-Strand (WC2)
Thomas Goode (W1)
Villandry (W1)*
The Waldorf Meridien (WC2)

West
Basil St Hotel (SW3)
Daquise (SW7)
Julie's Bar (W11)
Ognisko Polskie (SW7)

Burgers, etc

Central
Deals (W1)
Ed's Easy Diner (W1)
Fashion Café (W1)
Football Football (SW1)
Hard Rock Café (W1)
Joe Allen (WC2)
Planet Hollywood (W1)
Rock Island Diner (W1)
Wolfe's (WC2)

West
Big Easy (SW3)
Deals (SW10, W6)
Ed's Easy Diner (SW3)
Foxtrot Oscar (SW3)
Henry J Beans (SW3)
Luigi Malones (SW7)
Parsons (SW10)
Sticky Fingers (W8)
Tootsies (SW6, SW7, W11, W4)
Wolfe's (SW3)

North
Ed's Easy Diner (NW3)
Ruby in the Dust (N1, NW1)
Tootsies (NW3)

South
Tootsies (SW13)

East
Babe Ruth's (E1)

Fish & chips

Central
Le Palais du Jardin (WC2)*
Seafresh (SW1)*

West
Brady's (SW6)*
Costa's Fish (W8)*
Geale's (W8)*

North
Nautilus (NW6)*
Seashell (NW1)*
Toff's (N10)*
Two Brothers (N3)*
Upper St Fish Shop (N1)*

South
Brady's (SW18)*

Ice cream

Central
Häagen-Dazs (WC2)

West
Häagen-Dazs (SW10, SW7, W2)

North
Marine Ices (NW3)

South
C Notarianni & Sons (SW11)*

Pizza

Central
Ask (W1)
Chicago Pizza Pie Fact'y (W1)
Gourmet Pizza Co. (W1)
Kettners (W1)
Oliveto (SW1)
Pizza On The Park (SW1)
PizzaExpress (SW1, W1, WC1, WC2)
Pizzeria Condotti (W1)
Sol e Luna (WC2)
Sol e Stella (W1)

West
Ask (SW6, SW7, W4)
Calzone (SW10, W11)*
Ciabatta (SW3)
Da Mario (SW7)*
La Delizia (SW3, SW5)*
Paparazzi Café (SW3)
Pizza Chelsea (SW3)
Pizza Pomodoro (SW3)
Pizza the Action (SW6)
PizzaExpress (SW10, SW3, SW6, W14, W2, W4, W8)
Pucci Pizza (SW3)

The Red Pepper *(W9)**
Spago *(SW7)*

North
Ask *(N1, NW3)*
Calzone *(N1, NW3)**
Casale Franco *(N1)*
Marine Ices *(NW3)*
PizzaExpress *(N1, NW3)*

South
Bellinis *(SW13)*
Buona Sera *(SW11)**
Eco *(SW4)**
Gourmet Pizza Co. *(SE1)*
C Notarianni & Sons *(SW11)**
Pizza Metro *(SW11)**
PizzaExpress *(SE1, SW11, SW14, SW15, SW18, SW4)*
Pizzeria Castello *(SE1)**

East
Gourmet Pizza Co. *(E14)*
Pizza Pomodoro *(E1, EC1)*
PizzaExpress *(EC2)*

Sandwiches, cakes, etc

Central
Bar Italia *(W1)*
Café de Colombia *(W1)*
Café Emm *(W1)*
Maison Bertaux *(W1)*
Pâtisserie Valerie *(W1, WC2)**
Pret A Manger
  (SW1, W1, WC1, WC2)
Star Café *(W1)*

West
Café Grove *(W11)*
Fileric *(SW7)*
King's Road Café *(SW3)*
Lisboa Patisserie *(W10)**
Manzara *(W11)**
Pâtisserie Valerie *(SW3)**
Pret A Manger *(SW3, W6, W8)*
Le Shop *(SW3)*
Troubadour *(SW5)*

North
Pret A Manger *(N1, NW1)*

South
Boiled Egg *(SW11)*
Fileric *(SW8)*

East
Brick Lane Beigel Bake *(E1)**
Pret A Manger *(EC1, EC2, EC4)*

AMERICAS

American

Central
Christopher's *(WC2)*
Joe Allen *(WC2)*
Smollensky's Balloon *(W1)*
Smollensky's, Strand *(WC2)*
TGI Friday's *(W1, WC2)*

West
Big Easy *(SW3)*
Chicago Rib Shack *(SW7)*
Montana *(SW6)**
Shoeless Joe's *(SW6)*
TGI Friday's *(W2)*

East
Babe Ruth's *(E1)*

Argentinian

Central
The Gaucho Grill *(W1)*

Brazilian

West
Paulo's *(W6)*

Cajun/creole

West
Fats *(W9)*

Mexican/TexMex

Central
Café Pacifico *(WC2)*
Down Mexico Way *(W1)*
Texas Embassy Cantina *(WC2)*

West
Nachos *(SW10, W11, W4)*
Texas Lone Star *(SW7)*

North
Nachos *(N1, NW3)*

South
Dixie's Bar & Grill *(SW11)*

South American

Central
Bar Madrid *(W1)*
22° South *(W1)*

West
El Gaucho *(SW3)**

North
Cuba Libre (N1)
La Piragua (N1)

South
Fina Estampa (SE1)*

AFRICA

Afro-Caribbean

Central
Calabash (WC2)

West
Fats (W9)

North
Cottons (NW1)

South African

West
Springbok Café (W4)*

Sudanese

West
Mandola (W11)*

Tunisian

West
Adams Café (W12)*

North
Laurent (NW2)*

MIDDLE EAST

Egyptian

North
Ali Baba (NW1)*

Israeli

North
Solly's (NW11)*

Kosher

North
Nautilus (NW6)*
Solly's (NW11)*

Lebanese

Central
Al Bustan (SW1)*
Al Hamra (W1)*
Al Sultan (W1)*
Alwaha (W1)
Fakhreldine (W1)
Maroush (W1)
Ranoush (W1)*

West
Al Basha (W8)
Maroush (SW3, W2)
Phoenicia (W8)

Persian

West
Alounak (W14)*

Turkish

Central
Café Sofra (W1, WC2)
Cappadoccia (SW10)
Efes Kebab House (W1)
Bistro Sofra (W1, W1, WC2)

North
Manzara (W11)*
Iznik (N5)*
Pasha (N1)
Sarcan (N1)*

South
Beyoglu (SW11)*

East
Café Sofra (EC4)
Young Turks (EC2)

ASIA

Afghani

Central
Caravan Serai (W1)

North
Afghan Kitchen (N1)*

Burmese

West
Mandalay (W2)*

Chinese

Central
China City (WC2)
China Court (W1)
Chuen Cheng Ku (W1)
Dorchester, Oriental (W1)*
Dragon Inn (W1)*
Fung Shing (WC2)*
Golden Dragon (W1)*
Harbour City (W1)*
Jade Garden (W1)
Ken Lo's Memories (SW1)*
Mekong (SW1)
Mr Chow (SW1)
Mr Kong (WC2)
New World (W1)
Poons (WC2)*
Poons, Lisle Street (WC2)*
Princess Garden (W1)
West Zenders (WC2)*
Wong Kei (W1)
Zen Central (W1)*
Zen Garden (W1)

West
The Four Seasons (W2)
Good Earth (SW3)*
Mandarin Kitchen (W2)*
Mao Tai (SW6)*
Mr Wing (SW5)
Nam Long (SW5)
Nanking (W6)
New Culture Rev'n (SW3)
Park Inn (W2)*
Poons at Whiteleys (W2)
Red (SW3)
Royal China (W2)*
Stick & Bowl (W8)
Zen (SW3)

North
Abeno (NW9)
Cheng Du (NW1)
China Jazz (NW1)
Feng Shang (NW1)
Gung-Ho (NW6)
New Culture Rev'n (N1, NW1)
Singapore Garden (NW6)*
The Vegetarian
  Cottage (NW3)
Yoahan Plaza (NW9)*
ZeNW3 (NW3)*

South
Royal China (SW15)*

East
Imperial City (EC3)*
Poons in the City (EC3)

Chinese, Dim-sum

Central
China Court (W1)
Chuen Cheng Ku (W1)
Dorchester, Oriental (W1)*
Dragon Inn (W1)*
Golden Dragon (W1)*
Harbour City (W1)*
Jade Garden (W1)
New World (W1)
Zen Central (W1)*

West
Poons at Whiteleys (W2)
Royal China (W2)*
Zen (SW3)

South
Royal China (SW15)*

Indian

Central
Gopal's of Soho (W1)
India Club (WC2)*
Kundan (SW1)
The Lancers (W1)*
Malabar Junction (WC1)*
Mandeer (W1)*
La Porte des Indes (W1)
Ragam (W1)
Red Fort (W1)*
Salloos (SW1)
Tamarind (W1)*
Veeraswamy (W1)
Woodlands (SW1, W1)

West
Bombay Brasserie (SW7)
Bombay Palace (W2)
Café Lazeez (SW7)
Chutney Mary (SW10)*
Khan's (W2)
Khan's of Kensington (SW7)*
Khyber Pass (SW7)*
Malabar (W8)*
Mamta (SW6)*
Memories of India (SW7)
Nayab (SW6)*
Nizam (SW5)
Noor Jahan (SW5)*
Standard Tandoori (W2)*
Star of India (SW5)*
Tandoori Lane (SW6)
Tandoori of Chelsea (SW3)

North
Anglo Asian Tandoori (N16)*
Chutneys (NW1)*

Diwana Bhel-Poori
   House *(NW1)**
Geeta *(NW6)**
Great Nepalese *(NW1)**
Haandi *(NW1)*
Karahi *(NW6)**
Rani *(N3)*
Rasa *(N16)**
Vijay *(NW6)**

South
Battersea Rickshaw *(SW11)*
Bengal Clipper *(SE1)**
Bombay Bicycle Club *(SW12)**
Haweli *(SW13)**
Indian Ocean *(SW17)**
Kastoori *(SW17)**
Ma Goa *(SW15)*
Rani *(TW9)*
Shree Krishna *(SW17)**

East
Café Spice Namaste *(E1)**
Clifton *(E1)**
Lahore Kebab House *(E1)**
Rupee Room *(EC2)*

Indian, Southern

Central
India Club *(WC2)**
Malabar Junction *(WC1)**
Mandeer *(W1)**
Ragam *(W1)*
Woodlands *(SW1, W1)*

West
Mamta *(SW6)**

North
Chutneys *(NW1)**
Diwana Bhel-Poori Hs *(NW1)**
Geeta *(NW6)**
Rani *(N3)*
Rasa *(N16)**
Vijay *(NW6)**

South
Kastoori *(SW17)**
Rani *(TW9)*
Shree Krishna *(SW17)**

Indonesian

East
Inmala *(EC2)*

Japanese

Central
Ajimura *(WC2)*

Arisugawa *(W1)*
Benihana *(W1)*
Café Sogo *(SW1)*
Hamine *(W1)*
Ikeda *(W1)*
Ikkyu *(W1, WC2)**
Masako *(W1)**
Matsuri *(SW1)**
Mitsukoshi *(SW1)**
Miyama *(W1)**
Saga *(W1)*
Shogun *(W1)**
Suntory *(SW1)*
Tokyo Diner *(WC2)**
Wagamama *(W1, WC1)**

West
Benihana *(SW3)*
Inaho *(W2)**
Nippon-Tuk *(SW3)*
Sumos *(W6)**
Sushi Bar Gen *(SW6)**

North
Abeno *(NW9)*
Benihana *(NW3)*
Bu San *(N7)**
Café Japan *(NW11)*
Jin Kichi *(NW3)**
Wakaba *(NW3)**

East
Aykoku-Kaku *(EC4)*
City Miyama *(EC4)*
Japanese Canteen *(EC1)*
Moshi Moshi Sushi *(EC2, EC4)**
Noto *(EC2, EC4)*
Tatsuso *(EC2)**

Japanese, Teppan-yaki

Central
Benihana *(W1)*
Matsuri *(SW1)**
Miyama *(W1)**
Suntory *(SW1)*

West
Benihana *(SW3)*

North
Benihana *(NW3)*

East
Aykoku-Kaku *(EC4)*
Tatsuso *(EC2)**

Korean

Central
Arirang *(W1)*
Jin *(W1)**

North
Bu San (N7)*

Malaysian

Central
Melati (W1)*

West
Jim Thompson's (SW6)

North
Singapore Garden (NW6)*

East
Singapura (EC3, EC4)

Misc oriental

Central
Mongolian Barbecue (WC2)

West
Bonjour Vietnam (SW6)
Mongolian Barbecue (SW6, SW7, W4)
Sash (SW6)
Tiger Lil's (SW3)

North
Mongolian Barbecue (NW1)
Yoahan Plaza (NW9)*

South
Mongolian Barbecue (SW11)

East
East One (EC1)
Tao (EC4)

Thai

Central
Bahn Thai (W1)
Blue Jade (SW1)*
Chiang Mai (W1)
Silks & Spice (W1)*
Sri Siam (W1)*
Thai Pot (WC2)

West
Bangkok (SW7)*
Bedlington Café (W4)*
Ben's Thai (W9)*
Blue Elephant (SW6)*
Busabong Too (SW10)*
Busabong Tree (SW10)*
Café 209 (SW6)
Chaba (SW10)*
Chokdee (SW5)
Churchill (W8)*
Dove (W6)
Esarn Kheaw (W12)*

Fat Boy's (W4)*
Jim Thompson's (SW6)
Khun Akorn (SW3)
Krungtap (SW10)
Latymers (W6)*
Sabai Sabai (W6)*
Sash (SW6)
Tawana (W2)*
Thai Bistro (W4)*
Thai Kitchen (W2)*
Thai on the River (SW10)*
Topsy-Tasty (W4)*
Tui (SW7)*

North
Tuk Tuk (N1)*
Yum Yum (N16)

South
Chada (SW11)
The Pepper Tree (SW4)
Phuket (SW11)
Thailand (SE14)*

East
Sri Siam City (EC2)*
Sri Thai (EC4)*

Vietnamese

Central
Mekong (SW1)
Saigon (W1)

West
Nam Long (SW5)

AREA OVERVIEWS

CENTRAL

Soho, Covent Garden & Bloomsbury
(Parts of W1, all WC2 and WC1)

£60+	Savoy River Room	*French*	❸❸❷
£50+	Savoy Grill	*British, Traditional*	❸❷❸
	Café Royal Grill	*French*	❸❷❶
	Neal Street	*Italian*	④④❸
£40+	The Ivy	*British, Modern*	❷❷❶
	Lindsay House	*"*	⑤❸❶
	Sheekey's	*Fish & seafood*	④❷④
	Christopher's	*American*	④④❷
£35+	Atlantic Bar & Grill	*British, Modern*	④④❷
	Mezzo	*"*	④④❸
	Simpsons-in-the-Strand	*British, Traditional*	④❸❸
	Bank	*Fish & seafood*	——
	Manzi's	*"*	❷④④
	Au Jardin des Gourmets	*French*	——
	The Criterion	*"*	❸④❶
	L'Escargot	*"*	❸❷❸
	Luigi's	*Italian*	④④❸
£30+	Alastair Little	*British, Modern*	❸④⑤
	Alfred	*"*	❷❸⑤
	Atelier	*"*	❷❸④
	Café du Jardin	*"*	❸❸❸
	Chiaroscuro	*"*	❷❸④
	Delicious Blue	*"*	④❸❷
	dell'Ugo	*"*	④⑤❸
	Museum St Café	*"*	❷❷④
	Saint	*"*	④④❶
	Rules	*British, Traditional*	❸❷❷
	Beotys	*French*	④❶❷
	L'Estaminet	*"*	❸❷④
	Magno's Brasserie	*"*	④❸④
	Mon Plaisir	*"*	❸❷❷
	Le Palais du Jardin	*"*	❷❷❷
	Soho Soho	*"*	❸④❷
	Gay Hussar	*Hungarian*	④❸❸
	Bertorelli's	*Italian*	④④④
	Orso	*"*	④④❸
	Il Passetto	*"*	❷❷❸
	22° South	*Steaks & grills*	④❷❸
	Fung Shing	*Chinese*	❶④⑤
	West Zenders	*"*	❷❸④
	Red Fort	*Indian*	❷❸④

			Ratings
	Ajimura	*Japanese*	③④④
£25+	Belgo Centraal	*Belgian*	④④❷
	Blues	*British, Modern*	❸❷❷
	Detroit	"	❸⑤❸
	Euten's	"	❸❷④
	French House	"	❷❷❷
	Hodgson's	"	④❸❸
	The Lexington	"	④❷④
	Mondo	"	❸④❶
	Mezzonine	*East/West*	❸❸❸
	Café Bohème	*French*	④❸❷
	Café des Amis du Vin	"	❸④❸
	Chez Gérard	"	❸❸④
	Pélican	"	❸❸❷
	La Capannina	*Italian*	❸❷④
	Italian Kitchen	"	❸❸④
	Little Italy	"	❸❷❶
	Sol e Luna	"	④❷❸
	Vasco & Piero's Pavilion	"	❸❷❸
	Bruno Soho	*Mediterranean*	—
	St Moritz	*Swiss*	❸❷❸
	Boulevard	*International*	❸❷❷
	Deals	"	④⑤④
	Garlic & Shots	"	❸❸❸
	Sarastro	"	④⑤❸
	Shampers	"	❷❸❸
	Fashion Café	*Burgers, etc*	④❷❸
	Planet Hollywood	"	④❸❷
	Wolfe's	"	❸❷④
	Joe Allen	*American*	④④❷
	Smollensky's, Strand	"	④❸❸
	TGI Friday's	"	⑤④❸
	Café Pacifico	*Mexican/TexMex*	❸❷❷
	Alwaha	*Lebanese*	④❸④
	China Court	*Chinese*	❸④❸
	Harbour City	"	❷④⑤
	Malabar Junction	*Indian*	❷❷❸
	Ikkyu	*Japanese*	❶❸❷
	Bahn Thai	*Thai*	❸⑤⑤
	Chiang Mai	"	❸⑤⑤
	Sri Siam	"	❷❷❸
£20+	Andrew Edmunds	*British, Modern*	❸❷❶
	Hujo's	"	❸⑤❸
	Mars	"	❸④❷
	Plummers	"	❸❷④
	Café Flo	*French*	④④❸
	Café Rouge	"	⑤④④
	Randall & Aubin	"	❷⑤❸

195

Soho & Covent Garden (continued)

Rodos	Greek	③③⑤
Caffé Uno	Italian	③③④
Balans	International	④③③
Brown's	"	⑤⑤③
Cork & Bottle	"	④④③
Dôme	"	④⑤④
Rock Island Diner	Burgers, etc	③③③
Kettners	Pizza	⑤⑤③
Texas Embassy Cantina	Mexican/TexMex	⑤④③
Sofra	Turkish	④④④
China City	Chinese	③③③
Chuen Cheng Ku	"	③④④
Golden Dragon	"	②③④
Jade Garden	"	③③③
New World	"	④⑤⑤
Gopal's of Soho	Indian	③④④
Arirang	Korean	③②④
Jin	"	②②④
Melati	Malaysian	②③④
Mongolian Barbecue	Misc oriental	④④③
Thai Pot	Thai	③⑤④
Saigon	Vietnamese	③③③

£15+

All Bar One	British, Modern	③③②
Aurora	"	②③③
Porters	British, Traditional	④④④
Pierre Victoire	French	⑤④④
Café Pasta	Italian	④②③
Marché Mövenpick	International	④④④
Pitcher & Piano	"	④③②
The Waldorf Meridien	Afternoon tea	③②②
Ed's Easy Diner	Burgers, etc	④②③
PizzaExpress	Pizza	③②③
Café Emm	S'wiches, cakes, etc	③③④
Pâtisserie Valerie	"	②②②
Cranks	Vegetarian	③⑤⑤
Mildreds	"	③③③
Calabash	Afro-Caribbean	③④⑤
Dragon Inn	Chinese	②③④
Mr Kong	"	③③④
Poons	"	②④④
Poons, Lisle Street	"	①③④
India Club	Indian	②③④
Wagamama	Japanese	②②③

£10+

Pollo	Italian	③③④
Gordon's Wine Bar	International	③④②
Stock Pot	"	④②④

	Star Café	S'wiches, cakes, etc	③④③
	Neal's Yard Dining Rooms	Vegetarian	③③③
	Café Sofra	Turkish	③④④
	Wong Kei	Chinese	③⑤④
	Hamine	Japanese	③④④
	Tokyo Diner	"	②①④
£5+	Häagen-Dazs	Ice cream	③④③
	Bar Italia	S'wiches, cakes, etc	④④①
	Maison Bertaux	"	③③②
	Pret A Manger	"	③①③
	Food for Thought	Vegetarian	②③④

Mayfair & St James's
(Parts of W1 and SW1)

£70+	Chez Nico	French	②③④
	Le Gavroche	"	②②②
	Suntory	Japanese	③②④
£60+	Connaught	British, Traditional	③①②
	The Ritz	French	④②①
	Windows on the World	"	④⑤④
£50+	The Lanesborough	British, Modern	⑤③②
	The Square	"	②③–
	Wiltons	British, Traditional	④③③
	Claridges Restaurant	French	④②②
	Four Seasons	"	②③④
	Oak Room	"	③①②
	Les Saveurs	"	④②③
	Le Soufflé	"	②②④
	Cecconi's	Italian	④④④
	Dorchester, Oriental	Chinese	②②③
	Ikeda	Japanese	③②④
	Mitsukoshi	"	①③④
	Miyama	"	②②⑤
£40+	Le Caprice	British, Modern	②①①
	Coast	"	③④③
	Quaglino's	"	④④②
	33	"	③④⑤
	Thomas Goode	"	⑤③②
	Dorchester Grill	British, Traditional	②①②
	Green's	"	④③④
	Greenhouse	"	②②③
	Cave	Fish & seafood	—
	L'Odéon	French	③④④

Mayfair & St James's (continued)

Diverso	Italian		④②③
Signor Sassi	"		③④②
Kaspia	Russian		②③④
The Guinea	Steaks & grills		③④④
Princess Garden	Chinese		④③④
Zen Central	"		②③④
Zen Garden	"		③②④
Veeraswamy	Indian		④④③
Benihana	Japanese		④④③
Matsuri	"		②①④
Saga	"		③③④
Shogun	"		②②③

£35+	The Avenue	British, Modern	④④③
	Café Nico	"	⑤④④
	81	"	④④⑤
	Langan's Brasserie	"	④③②
	Nicole's	"	③④④
	Scott's	British, Traditional	——
	Bentley's	Fish & seafood	③③③
	L'Oranger	French	①①②
	Bice	Italian	④④⑤
	Dover St Wine Bar	International	⑤⑤④
	Fakhreldine	Lebanese	③③③

£30+	Maze	British, Modern	④④③
	Café Fish	Fish & seafood	④④④
	The Gaucho Grill	Steaks & grills	④④②
	Rowley's	"	⑤③④
	Vendôme	International	③③②
	Al Hamra	Lebanese	②⑤⑤
	Tamarind	Indian	②②③

£25+	Sotheby's Café	British, Modern	③③③
	Boudin Blanc	French	②④③
	Chez Gérard	"	③③④
	Ristorante Italiano	Italian	③②③
	Il Vicolo	"	③②④
	Hanover Square	International	③③④
	Hard Rock Café	Burgers, etc	③④③
	Smollensky's Balloon	American	③③②
	Al Sultan	Lebanese	②③③
	The Lancers	Indian	②③④

£20+	L'Artiste Musclé	French	④④②
	Caffé Uno	Italian	③③④
	Browns	International	⑤⑤③
	Football Football	Burgers, etc	⑤③④
	Café de Colombia	S'wiches, cakes, etc	③③⑤

	Down Mexico Way	*Mexican/TexMex*	⑤④❷
	Sofra	*Turkish*	❷❸❸
	Bistro Sofra	"	④④④
	Woodlands	*Indian*	❸④❸
	Café Sogo	*Japanese*	❸❷④
£15+	All Bar One	*British, Modern*	❸❸❷
	Pierre Victoire	*French*	⑤④④
	Brown's Hotel	*Afternoon tea*	❸❸❷
	Chicago Pizza Pie Factory	*Pizza*	❸❷④
	Gourmet Pizza Co.	"	❸④❸
	PizzaExpress	"	❸❷❸
	Pizzeria Condotti	"	❸❶❸
£10+	Stock Pot	*International*	④❷④
	Ask	*Pizza*	❸❷❸
	Wren at St James's	*Vegetarian*	❸④❷
	Café Sofra	*Turkish*	❸④④
£5+	Pret A Manger	*S'wiches, cakes, etc*	❸❶❸

**Fitzrovia & Marylebone
(Part of W1)**

£60+	Pied à Terre	*French*	❸④–
£50+	Interlude de Chavot	*French*	❷❸❸
	Masako	*Japanese*	❷❷❸
£40+	The Heights	*British, Modern*	❷❶④
	La Porte des Indes	*Indian*	④④❷
£35+	Stephen Bull	*British, Modern*	❷❶❸
	Elena's L'Etoile	*French*	❸❷❷
	Le Muscadet	"	❸❸❸
	Nico Central	"	❸④④
	Villandry	"	❷④④
	White Tower	*Greek*	❸❸❷
	Arisugawa	*Japanese*	❸❷④
£30+	Zoe	*British, Modern*	④⑤④
	Odin's	*French*	❸❶❶
	Bertorelli's	*Italian*	④④④
	Maroush	*Lebanese*	❸❸④
£25+	Exxo	*British, Modern*	④④⑤
	Hollihead	"	—
	The Union Café	"	❸❷❸
	Langan's Bistro	*French*	④❷④
	Caldesi	*Italian*	❸❷④

Fitzrovia & Marylebone (continued)

			Rating	
	O'Conor Don	Irish	② ① ①
	Garbo's	Scandinavian	④ ③ ③
	Hardy's	International	③ ③ ②
	Caravan Serai	Afghani	③ ③ ②
	Ikkyu	Japanese	① ③ ②
£20+	Café Flo	French	④ ④ ③
	Café Rouge	"	⑤ ④ ④
	Epicuria	Greek	② ④ ③
	Caffé Uno	Italian	③ ③ ④
	Sol e Stella	"	④ ② ③
	Bar Madrid	Spanish	④ ③ ③
	Sofra	Turkish	④ ④ ④
	Woodlands	Indian	③ ④ ③
	Silks & Spice	Thai	② ③ ③
£15+	Pierre Victoire	French	⑤ ④ ④
	PizzaExpress	Pizza	③ ② ③
	Pâtisserie Valerie	S'wiches, cakes, etc	② ② ②
	Cranks	Vegetarian	③ ⑤ ⑤
	Efes Kebab House	Turkish	③ ④ ②
	Mandeer	Indian	② ③ ③
	Ragam	"	③ ④ ⑤
£10+	Stock Pot	International	④ ② ④
	Ask	Pizza	③ ③ ③
	Ranoush	Lebanese	① ④ ④
£5+	Pret A Manger	S'wiches, cakes, etc	③ ① ③

Belgravia, Victoria & Pimlico (SW1, except St James's)

			Rating	
£90+	Restaurant MPW	French	③ ④ ⑤
£50+	The Halkin	Italian	④ ④ ③
	L'Incontro	"	④ ⑤ ⑤
	Santini	"	④ ④ ④
£40+	The Fifth Floor	British, Modern	④ ② ②
	Vong	East/West	① ③ ②
	Mimmo d'Ischia	Italian	③ ③ ②
	Toto's	"	③ ② ②
	Rib Room	Steaks & grills	② ② ③
	Mr Chow	Chinese	⑤ ④ ④
	Salloos	Indian	③ ⑤ ⑤
£35+	Drones	British, Modern	④ ② ③
	La Poule au Pot	French	④ ③ ①

	Simply Nico	*French*	②②④
	La Fontana	*Italian*	③③③
	Sale e Pepe	*"*	③③①
	Motcomb's	*International*	②②②
	Pomegranates	*"*	③②③
	Al Bustan	*Lebanese*	②②③
	Ken Lo's Memories	*Chinese*	②②④
£30+	Atrium	*British, Modern*	⑤⑤④
	Ebury Street Wine Bar	*"*	③④③
	The Foundation	*"*	③③⑤
	Tate Gallery	*"*	④②①
	Shepherd's	*British, Traditional*	③①③
	Caraffini	*Italian*	③②③
	Como Lario	*"*	③④④
	La Finezza	*"*	④③③
	Olivo	*"*	②②③
	Zafferano	*"*	①③③
	Boisdale	*International*	③③②
£25+	Fifth Floor (Café)	*British, Modern*	③②③
	Scandinavian Restaurant	*Scandinavian*	③④④
	Footstool	*International*	④④③
	Grumbles	*"*	③③③
	Oriel	*"*	③④②
	Oliveto	*Pizza*	③③③
£20+	Kundan	*Indian*	③③④
	Blue Jade	*Thai*	②③④
£15+	Chimes	*British, Traditional*	⑤③④
	Marché Mövenpick	*International*	④④④
	Hyde Park Hotel Park Room	*Afternoon tea*	③②②
	Seafresh	*Fish & chips*	②③④
	Pizza On The Park	*Pizza*	③④②
	PizzaExpress	*"*	③②③
	Mekong	*Vietnamese*	④③④
£10+	Brahms	*International*	④④③
£5+	Grenadier	*British, Traditional*	⑤②①
	Pret A Manger	*S'wiches, cakes, etc*	③①③

WEST

Chelsea, South Kensington, Kensington, Earl's Court & Fulham (SW3, SW5, SW6, SW7, SW10 & W8)

			Ratings
£80+	Blakes Hotel	International	③④❶
£60+	Capital Hotel	French	②③③
	La Tante Claire	"	❶②③
£50+	Aubergine	French	❶②②
	Bibendum	"	②③②
	Turner's	"	④④④
	San Lorenzo	Italian	⑤⑤④
£40+	Clarke's	British, Modern	❶②③
	English Garden	"	④③③
	English House	"	⑤③③
	Fulham Road	"	③③④
	Hilaire	"	③②③
	Shaw's	"	③②③
	The Tenth	"	④④④
	Walton's	"	③②③
	Poissonnerie de l'Avenue	Fish & seafood	❶③③
	San Frediano	Italian	⑤④④
	Albero & Grana	Spanish	④④②
	Zen	Chinese	③④④
	Benihana	Japanese	④④③
	Blue Elephant	Thai	②③❶
£35+	The Canteen	British, Modern	②③②
	Daphne's	"	④④②
	Downstairs at 190	"	③④③
	Joe's Café	"	③③③
	Kensington Place	"	③③②
	Launceston Place	"	②②②
	Stratford's	Fish & seafood	②②④
	Chez Max	French	②③④
	Lou Pescadou	"	③⑤④
	Monkeys	"	②②②
	Le Suquet	"	③⑤③
	La Famiglia	Italian	③④②
	Montpeliano	"	⑤③③
	Scalini	"	④③②
	Conrad Hotel	International	②③③
	Bombay Brasserie	Indian	③③②
	Khun Akorn	Thai	④⑤④
£30+	The Abingdon	British, Modern	③②③

	Name	Cuisine	Rating
	Belvedere	British, Modern	4 3 1
	Boyd's	"	2 1 3
	Charco's	"	2 3 4
	Christoph's	"	2 2 3
	The Collection	"	4 4 2
	Dan's	"	4 2 1
	The Establishment	"	5 3 4
	Gilbert's	"	3 2 3
	Kartouche	"	4 4 2
	755	"	2 3 4
	Basil St Hotel	British, Traditional	3 3 2
	Maggie Jones's	"	3 3 2
	Brasserie St Quentin	French	2 2 2
	L'Escargot Doré	"	3 2 5
	Grill St Quentin	"	3 3 4
	Mon Petit Plaisir	"	2 2 2
	Thierry's	"	4 4 2
	La Giara	Italian	3 2 4
	Osteria Le Fate	"	3 5 2
	Sambuca	"	3 1 4
	San Martino	"	3 3 3
	Sandrini	"	4 4 3
	Verbanella	"	3 3 4
	Ziani	"	3 2 2
	Wódka	Polish	4 3 4
	Nikita's	Russian	4 3 2
	PJ's	International	5 4 3
	Montana	American	2 2 2
	Al Basha	Lebanese	3 3 3
	Maroush	"	3 3 4
	Mr Wing	Chinese	4 2 1
	Chutney Mary	Indian	2 3 3
	Star of India	"	2 4 2
	Tandoori of Chelsea	"	3 2 3
	Thai on the River	Thai	2 4 3
£25+	Bar Central	British, Modern	4 3 3
	Bistrot 190	"	3 4 3
	Brinkley's	"	4 3 3
	The Cross Keys	"	4 4 3
	Fables	"	2 2 3
	James R	"	3 4 4
	Joe's Brasserie	"	3 3 3
	Le Metro	"	3 4 3
	The Pen	"	3 3 2
	606 Club	"	4 2 2
	Bibendum Oyster Bar	Fish & seafood	1 2 2
	Ghillies	"	3 3 3
	The Ark	French	4 3 4
	Au Bon Accueil	"	4 1 2

Chelsea, South Kensington, etc (continued)

La Bouchée	*French*	❸❹❶
La Brasserie	*"*	❹❹❷
Café O	*Greek*	❷❷❷
Bucci	*Italian*	❷❸❷
De Cecco	*"*	❷❸❷
Elistano	*"*	❷❷❸
Il Falconiere	*"*	❸❶❹
Formula Veneta	*"*	❹❷❷
Leonardo's	*"*	❷❷❸
Lo Spuntino	*"*	❷❸❹
Tusc	*"*	❹❹❸
Ognisko Polskie	*Polish*	❸❸❷
Cambio de Tercio	*Spanish*	❹❸❹
Deals	*International*	❹❺❹
The Enterprise	*"*	❸❷❶
Foxtrot Oscar	*"*	❹❹❹
The Gasworks	*"*	❹❸❷
Wolfe's	*Burgers, etc*	❸❷❹
Big Easy	*American*	❹❷❷
Shoeless Joe's	*"*	❹❹❷
Phoenicia	*Lebanese*	❸❶❹
Good Earth	*Chinese*	❷❷❸
Mao Tai	*"*	❷❷❸
Red	*"*	❸❸❹
Café Lazeez	*Indian*	❸❸❷
Nizam	*"*	❸❷❹
Busabong Too	*Thai*	❷❸❹
Busabong Tree	*"*	❷❸❹
Tui	*"*	❷❸❺
Nam Long	*Vietnamese*	❸❸❶
£20+ Chelsea Ram	*British, Modern*	❸❸❸
The Crescent	*"*	❸❷❸
Ffiona's	*"*	❷❷❷
The Imperial Arms	*"*	❶❹❹
Princess of Wales	*"*	❸❸❸
Vingt-Quatre	*"*	❸❷❸
Le Bon Choix	*French*	❸❸❺
Café Flo	*"*	❹❹❸
Café Rouge	*"*	❺❹❹
Emile's	*"*	❸❷❸
Wine & Kebab	*Greek*	❸❸❸
Bersagliera	*Italian*	❸❷❹
Café Montpeliano	*"*	❸❸❷
Caffé Uno	*"*	❸❸❹
The Jam	*"*	❹❸❸
Made in Italy	*"*	❸❸❸
Paparazzi Café	*"*	❹❹❸

			Rating
	Riccardo's	Italian	3 4 2
	Albero & Grana, Bar	Spanish	2 3 1
	Balans	International	3 2 2
	Dôme	"	4 5 4
	Glaisters	"	4 4 3
	Nineteen	"	3 3 3
	Palms-on-the-Hill	"	4 4 3
	Wine Gallery	"	4 2 2
	Luigi Malones	Burgers, etc	3 2 2
	Parsons	"	3 2 3
	Sticky Fingers	"	4 3 3
	Da Mario	Pizza	2 3 3
	Pizza Chelsea	"	3 4 4
	Pizza Pomodoro	"	3 4 1
	Chicago Rib Shack	American	4 4 4
	Nachos	Mexican/TexMex	4 3 3
	Texas Lone Star	"	4 4 2
	El Gaucho	South American	2 4 1
	Cappadoccia	Turkish	3 1 3
	Khan's of Kensington	Indian	2 1 2
	Malabar	"	2 2 3
	Memories of India	"	3 2 3
	Nayab	"	2 2 4
	Noor Jahan	"	2 3 4
	Tandoori Lane	"	3 1 3
	Sushi Bar Gen	Japanese	2 4 4
	Jim Thompson's	Malaysian	4 5 2
	Bonjour Vietnam	Misc oriental	4 4 3
	Mongolian Barbecue	"	4 4 3
	Tiger Lil's	"	4 4 3
	Bangkok	Thai	2 3 4
	Chaba	"	2 3 4
	S&P	"	2 1 4
£15+	All Bar One	British, Modern	3 3 2
	Francofill	French	2 4 3
	Pierre Victoire	"	5 4 4
	Café Pasta	Italian	4 2 3
	Calzone	"	2 1 3
	Da Pierino	"	3 3 4
	Picasso	"	3 3 3
	Spago	"	3 4 3
	Rôtisserie Jules	Steaks & grills	3 3 4
	Coopers Arms	International	3 2 3
	Front Page	"	2 4 2
	Pitcher & Piano	"	4 3 2
	The Scarsdale	"	4 3 2
	Sporting Page	"	2 3 2
	Windsor Castle	"	3 3 1
	Ed's Easy Diner	Burgers, etc	4 2 3

Chelsea, South Kensington, etc (continued)

Henry J Beans	Burgers, etc	(4)(4)(3)
Tootsies	"	(4)(3)(4)
Brady's	Fish & chips	(2)(4)(4)
Geale's	"	(2)(4)(5)
La Delizia	Pizza	(2)(4)(2)
Pizza the Action	"	(3)(2)(3)
PizzaExpress	"	(3)(2)(3)
Pucci Pizza	"	(3)(4)(2)
King's Road Café	S'wiches, cakes, etc	(3)(3)(3)
Pâtisserie Valerie	"	(2)(2)(2)
Le Shop	"	(3)(3)(3)
Khyber Pass	Indian	(2)(3)(4)
Mamta	"	(2)(2)(5)
Nippon-Tuk	Japanese	(3)(2)(4)
Sash	Misc oriental	(3)(3)(3)
Chokdee	Thai	(3)(3)(4)

£10+	The Fulham Tup	British, Modern	(3)(3)(4)
	Costa's Grill	Greek	(3)(3)(4)
	Luigi's Delicatessen	Italian	(1)(4)(3)
	Mona Lisa	"	(3)(2)(4)
	Daquise	Polish	(3)(2)(3)
	Chelsea Bun Diner	International	(3)(4)(3)
	Chelsea Kitchen	"	(3)(3)(3)
	Stock Pot	"	(4)(2)(4)
	Costa's Fish	Fish & chips	(2)(3)(4)
	Ask	Pizza	(3)(2)(3)
	Ciabatta	"	(3)(4)(3)
	Troubadour	S'wiches, cakes, etc	(3)(4)(1)
	New Culture Rev'n	Chinese	(3)(4)(4)
	Stick & Bowl	"	(3)(3)(4)
	Café 209	Thai	(4)(3)(3)
	Churchill	"	(2)(4)(2)
	Krungtap	"	(3)(3)(3)

£5+	Häagen-Dazs	Ice cream	(3)(4)(3)
	Fileric	S'wiches, cakes, etc	(3)(3)(4)
	Pret A Manger	"	(3)(1)(3)

Notting Hill, Holland Park, Bayswater, North Kensington & Maida Vale (W2, W9, W10, W11)

£80+	1 Thai	East/West	——
£50+	Leith's	British, Modern	(3)(3)(3)
£40+	Halcyon Hotel	British, Modern	(1)(2)(2)

			Ratings
£35+	First Floor	British, Modern	③④❶
	L'Artiste Assoiffé	French	③⑤❷
	Chez Moi	"	❸❶❸
	Al San Vincenzo	Italian	❶❷④
	L'Altro	"	❸④❸
	Orsino	"	④④❸
	Julie's	International	④❸❶
£30+	All Saints	British, Modern	❸⑤❸
	Beach Blanket Babylon	"	⑤⑤❷
	192	"	④④❷
	The Sugar Club	"	❷❷❸
	Jason's	Fish & seafood	❶❷❸
	The Green Olive	French	❸❸❸
	Assaggi	Italian	❷❸④
	Mr Frascati	"	❸❸④
	Maroush	Lebanese	❸❸④
	Bombay Palace	Indian	❸❷❸
£25+	Alastair Little	British, Modern	❷❸❸
	Café Med	"	④❷❷
	Jimmy Beez	"	❷④❷
	Mas Café	"	④⑤④
	Tabac	"	❶❷❸
	W11	"	④❷❷
	Veronica's	British, Traditional	❸❸④
	Brasserie du Marché	French	❷❷❷
	La Pomme d'Amour	"	❸❶❷
	Prost	German	❸❷⑤
	Halepi	Greek	❸❷④
	L'Accento Italiano	Italian	❸④④
	Cento 50	"	⑤④⑤
	La Fenice	"	❸❷❷
	Palio	"	④❸❸
	The Red Pepper	"	❷④❸
	Julie's Bar	International	④④❶
	TGI Friday's	American	⑤④❸
	Mandarin Kitchen	Chinese	❶④④
	Poons at Whiteleys	"	❸④④
	Royal China	"	❷④❸
£20+	Blenheim Bis	British, Modern	❸④④
	The Ladbroke Arms	"	❷❸❷
	Raoul's Café	"	❸❸❸
	The Westbourne	"	❷④❶
	Café Rouge	French	⑤④④
	Kalamaras, Mega	Greek	❸❸❸
	Caffé Uno	Italian	❸❸④
	Osteria Basilico	"	❷❸❶

Notting Hill, Holland Park, etc (continued)

	Galicia	Spanish	③④❸
	Zah Bar	International	④❷❷
	Nachos	Mexican/TexMex	④❸❸
	Mandola	Sudanese	❷❸❸
	Park Inn	Chinese	❷❸④
	Inaho	Japanese	❶❷④
	Tawana	Thai	❷❸④
	Thai Kitchen	"	❷❸④
£15+	The Prince Bonaparte	British, Modern	❸④❷
	Pierre Victoire	French	⑤④④
	Kalamaras, Micro	Greek	❸❸④
	Calzone	Italian	❷❶❸
	Rôtisserie Jules	Steaks & grills	❸❸④
	Los Remos	Spanish	❸❷④
	Café Grove	International	❸④❷
	Tootsies	Burgers, etc	④❸④
	PizzaExpress	Pizza	❸❷❸
	Fats	Cajun/creole	❸④④
	Manzara	Turkish	❷❸④
	The Four Seasons	Chinese	❸④⑤
	Standard Tandoori	Indian	❷❷④
	Ben's Thai	Thai	❷❸❸
£10+	Mandalay	Burmese	❷❷④
	Khan's	Indian	❸⑤❷
£5+	Häagen-Dazs	Ice cream	❸④❸
	Lisboa Patisserie	S'wiches, cakes, etc	❶❸❸

Hammersmith, Shepherd's Bush
Chiswick & Olympia
(W4, W5, W6, W12, W14)

£40+	Cibo	Italian	❸❸④
	The River Café	"	❶❸❷
£35+	Chinon	French	❶④④
	La Dordogne	"	❷❶❷
£30+	Noughts 'n' Crosses	British, Modern	④④❸
	Oliver's Island	"	④❸❷
	Snows on the Green	"	④❸④
£25+	Chiswick	British, Modern	❸④④
	The Stamford	"	④❷❷
	Wilson's	"	④❶❷
	Popeseye	Steaks & grills	❷④④

	Rôtisserie	*Steaks & grills*	③③④
	Deals	*International*	④⑤④
	Springbok Café	*South African*	②②③
	Nanking	*Chinese*	③③③
£20+	Anglesea Arms	*British, Modern*	③⑤④
	The Brackenbury	"	②③③
	Lazy Jack's	"	③③④
	Café Flo	*French*	④④③
	Café Rouge	"	⑤④④
	Mackintosh's Brasserie	*International*	④②②
	Blah! Blah! Blah!	*Vegetarian*	②③③
	The Gate	"	①②③
	Paulo's	*Brazilian*	③③③
	Nachos	*Mexican/TexMex*	④③③
	Adams Café	*Tunisian*	②②④
	Sumos	*Japanese*	②③④
	Mongolian Barbecue	*Misc oriental*	④④③
	Esarn Kheaw	*Thai*	②③④
	Fat Boy's	"	②③③
	Sabai Sabai	"	②③⑤
£15+	All Bar One	*British, Modern*	③③②
	The Havelock Tavern	"	③④③
	Jigsaw	*French*	③③③
	Café Pasta	*Italian*	④②③
	Pitcher & Piano	*International*	④③②
	Tootsies	*Burgers, etc*	④③④
	PizzaExpress	*Pizza*	③②③
	Bedlington Café	*Thai*	①④④
	Latymers	"	②③⑤
	Thai Bistro	"	②③④
	Topsy-Tasty	"	①②④
£10+	Dove	*International*	③③③
	Ask	*Pizza*	③②③
	Alounak	*Persian*	①③④
£5+	Pret A Manger	*S'wiches, cakes, etc*	③①③

NORTH

Hampstead, West Hampstead, St John's Wood, Regent's Park, Kilburn & Camden Town (NW postcodes)

£40+	Benihana	*Japanese*	④④③
	Wakaba	*"*	②③④
£35+	Odette's	*British, Modern*	②②①
	L'Aventure	*French*	②②①
£30+	The Big Night Out	*British, Modern*	③④③
	Quincy's	*"*	③②④
	Oslo Court	*French*	②①②
	Mezzaluna	*Italian*	③③④
	Villa Bianca	*"*	④③②
	Feng Shang	*Chinese*	③②③
	ZeNW3	*"*	②③③
£25+	Belgo Noord	*Belgian*	③④②
	The Blenheim	*British, Modern*	④③④
	Byron's	*"*	③④③
	Café des Arts	*"*	④③②
	Cucina	*"*	②②③
	The Engineer	*"*	③⑤②
	Gresslin's	*"*	②②⑤
	La Cage Imaginaire	*French*	④①④
	Camden Brasserie	*"*	②②②
	A Tavola	*Italian*	④⑤②
	Vegia Zena	*"*	①④③
	Café Delancey	*International*	④⑤②
	Caffe Graffiti	*"*	③②③
	House on Rosslyn Hill	*"*	④④②
	Cottons	*Afro-Caribbean*	⑤⑤②
	Solly's	*Israeli*	②④③
	Cheng Du	*Chinese*	③②③
	China Jazz	*"*	④④③
	Gung-Ho	*"*	③②③
	Singapore Garden	*Malaysian*	②③③
£20+	Blakes	*British, Modern*	②④②
	Crown & Goose	*"*	③④③
	Lansdowne	*"*	②④②
	Café Flo	*French*	④④③
	Café Rouge	*"*	⑤④④
	Daphne	*Greek*	②②③
	Lemonia	*"*	③②②
	Billboard Café	*Italian*	③③④
	Caffè Uno	*"*	③③④
	Luna	*"*	③③④

Marine Ices	Italian	❸❸❷
Don Pepe	Spanish	❸❶❷
Cosmo	International	❸❷④
Dôme	"	④⑤④
Ruby in the Dust	"	④❸❷
Seashell	Fish & chips	❶❸⑤
Nachos	Mexican/TexMex	④❸❸
Laurent	Tunisian	❶❸④
Great Nepalese	Indian	❷❸④
Café Japan	Japanese	❸❷❸
Jin Kichi	"	❷❸④
Mongolian Barbecue	Misc oriental	④④❸

£15+	All Bar One	British, Modern	❸❸❷
	Czech Club	Czech	❸❸④
	Greek Valley	Greek	❷❸❸
	Nontas	"	❷❸❷
	Café Pasta	Italian	④❷❸
	Calzone	"	❷❶❸
	Zamoyski	Polish	❸❷❷
	Troika	Russian	❸④❸
	Bar Gansa	Spanish	❷❸❷
	Ed's Easy Diner	Burgers, etc	④❷❸
	Tootsies	"	④❸④
	Nautilus	Fish & chips	❷❸④
	PizzaExpress	Pizza	❸❷❸
	Manna	Vegetarian	❸❸④
	Ali Baba	Egyptian	❷❸④
	The Vegetarian Cottage	Chinese	④❸❸
	Haandi	Indian	❸❸④
	Karahi	"	❷❸④
	Vijay	"	❷❸④
	Abeno	Japanese	❸❷④

£10+	The Little Bay	International	❸❸❸
	Ask	Pizza	❸❷❸
	New Culture Rev'n	Chinese	❸④④
	Chutneys	Indian	❷⑤④
	Diwana B.-Poori Hs	"	❷❸④
	Geeta	"	❷④⑤

£5+	Pret A Manger	S'wiches, cakes, etc	❸❶❸
	Yoahan Plaza	Misc oriental	❷④⑤

AREA OVERVIEWS

Islington, Highgate, Crouch End, Stoke Newington, Finsbury Park, Muswell Hill & Finchley (N postcodes)

£35+	San Carlo	*Italian*	④❸④
£30+	Euphorium	*British, Modern*	❷❶❷
	Frederick's	*French*	❸❷❷
	Village Bistro	"	❷❸❷
	La Brasserie Highgate	*Italian*	❷❸④
	Casale Franco	"	❸④❸
£25+	Bar Central	*British, Modern*	④❸❸
	Granita	"	❷❸④
	Kavanagh's	"	❸❸④
	Chez Liline	*Fish & seafood*	❶④④
	Florians	*Italian*	❷❷❸
	Anna's Place	*Scandinavian*	❷❷❸
	Rôtisserie	*Steaks & grills*	❸❸④
	Cuba Libre	*South American*	❸❸❷
£20+	Café Flo	*French*	④④❸
	Café Rouge	"	⑤④④
	Soulard	"	❸❷❸
	Caffé Uno	*Italian*	❸❸④
	Banners	*International*	④④❷
	Dôme	"	④⑤④
	The Fox Reformed	"	❸❷❷
	Parks	"	④❷❸
	Ruby in the Dust	"	④❸❷
	Toff's	*Fish & chips*	❶❸④
	Two Brothers	"	❶❸④
	Nachos	*Mexican/TexMex*	④❸❸
	Pasha	*Turkish*	❸❸❸
	Rani	*Indian*	❸④④
	Tuk Tuk	*Thai*	❷❸❸
	Yum Yum	"	❸❸❸
£15+	All Bar One	*British, Modern*	❸❸❷
	Le Mercury	*French*	④❷❷
	Pierre Victoire	"	⑤④④
	Le Sacré-Coeur	"	❸❸④
	Café Pasta	*Italian*	④❷❸
	Calzone	"	❷❶❸
	La Finca	*Spanish*	❸④❸
	Upper St Fish Shop	*Fish & chips*	❷❷④
	PizzaExpress	*Pizza*	❸❷❸
	La Piragua	*South American*	❸❷❷
	Iznik	*Turkish*	❷❸❷
	Sarcan	"	❷❷❸
	Anglo Asian Tandoori	*Indian*	❷❸❷

	Rasa	*Indian*	❶❷❸
	Bu San	*Korean*	❷❸④
£10+	Ask	*Pizza*	❸❷❸
	Afghan Kitchen	*Afghani*	❶④④
	New Culture Rev'n	*Chinese*	❸④④
£5+	Pret A Manger	*S'wiches, cakes, etc*	❸❶❸

SOUTH

**South Bank
(SE1)**

£50+	Le Pont de la Tour	British, Modern	③④②
£40+	Oxo Tower	British, Modern	④④❶
	The Butlers Wharf Chop-house	British, Traditional	④④❸
£35+	Blue Print Café	British, Modern	❸❸②
	La Truffe Noire	French	②④⑤
£30+	Café dell'Ugo	British, Modern	④④❸
	Livebait	Fish & seafood	❶②④
	Cantina del Ponte	Italian	⑤⑤④
	Le Pont de la Tour Bar & Grill	Steaks & grills	❸❸②
	Bengal Clipper	Indian	❶②❸
£25+	Bar Central	British, Modern	④❸❸
	Mezzanine	"	❸❸④
	The People's Palace	"	❸❸④
	RSJ	"	②②❸
	South Bank Brasserie	International	④❸②
£20+	The Apprentice	British, Modern	②④④
	Three Little Pigs	"	④❸④
	The Waterloo Fire Station	"	❸④❸
	Café Rouge	French	⑤④④
	Meson Don Felipe	Spanish	❸②②
	Archduke Wine Bar	International	⑤④❸
	Fina Estampa	South American	②②❸
£15+	Gourmet Pizza Co.	Pizza	❸④❸
	PizzaExpress	"	❸②❸
	Pizzeria Castello	"	❶④❸

**Battersea, Clapham, Wandsworth,
Barnes, Putney, Brixton & Lewisham
(All postcodes south of the river except SE1)**

£35+	Lobster Pot	Fish & seafood	②②②
£30+	Chez Bruce	British, Modern	❶❶②
	Ransome's Dock	"	❸②②
	Sonny's	"	❸②②
	Le Gothique	French	④④②
	Antipasto e Pasta	Italian	❸❸❸

			Rating
	Riva	*Italian*	❶❷④
£25+	B Square	*British, Modern*	❸❸❸
	The Bank	"	❸❸❸
	Bar Central	"	④❸❸
	Buchan's	"	④❸④
	The Cook House	"	❸❸④
	Phoenix	"	❸❷❸
	The Stepping Stone	"	❶❶❷
	Le Bouchon Bordelais	*French*	❸④❷
	Le Bouchon Lyonnais	"	④④❸
	La Bouffe	"	❸❸❸
	Le P'tit Normand	"	❷❷⑤
	Twenty Trinity Gdns	"	❸④❸
	Del Buongustaio	*Italian*	❶❸❷
	Enoteca Turi	"	❷❷④
	Ost. Antica Bologna	"	❷❸❷
	Prego	"	④④❸
	The Depot	*International*	④④❷
	Hoults	"	④④❷
	Naked Turtle	"	❸❷❷
	Royal China	*Chinese*	❷❸❸
	Bombay Bicycle Club	*Indian*	❷❸❸
	Chada	*Thai*	❸❷❸
	Thailand	"	❷❷④
£20+	Glaisters	*British, Modern*	④④❸
	The Grafton	"	❷❸❸
	The Lavender	"	④⑤❸
	Scoffers	"	④④❷
	Valhalla	"	❸④❸
	Vincent's	"	❸❷④
	Café de la Place	*French*	❸⑤❸
	Café Rouge	"	⑤④④
	Café Tabac	"	④❸❸
	Emile's	"	❸❷❸
	Gastro	"	❸④❸
	Newton's	"	④❸❷
	Buona Sera	*Italian*	❷❸❷
	Caffé Uno	"	❸❸④
	Rebato's	*Spanish*	❷❷❶
	La Rueda	"	④❸❶
	Alma	*International*	④④❸
	Café Jeune	"	❸❸❸
	The Ship	"	❸④❷
	Thistells	"	⑤❸❷
	Tiger Lil's	"	④④❸
	Eco	*Pizza*	❶❸❷
	Battersea Rickshaw	*Indian*	❸❸❸
	Haweli	"	❷❸④

Battersea, Clapham, etc (continued)

	Ma Goa	*Indian*	③②③
	Rani	"	③④④
	Mongolian Barbecue	*Misc oriental*	④④❸
£15+	The Mason's Arms	*British, Modern*	②④②
	White Cross Hotel	"	③④②
	Pierre Victoire	*French*	⑤④④
	La Finca	*Spanish*	③④❸
	Batt. Barge Bistro	*International*	④②②
	Pitcher & Piano	"	④❸②
	Tootsies	*Burgers, etc*	④❸④
	Brady's	*Fish & chips*	②④④
	C Notarianni & Sons	*Pizza*	②④❸
	Pizza Metro	"	②②④
	PizzaExpress	"	❸②❸
	Boiled Egg	*S'wiches, cakes, etc*	❸④❸
	Café on the Common	*Vegetarian*	❸❸④
	Tea Rooms des Artistes	"	❸❸❸
	Dixie's Bar & Grill	*Mexican/TexMex*	④④②
	Indian Ocean	*Indian*	②②④
	Shree Krishna	"	❶⑤⑤
	The Pepper Tree	*Thai*	❸❸④
	Phuket	"	❸②④
£10+	Côte à Côte	*International*	④④④
	Bellinis	*Pizza*	❸❸②
	Bangles	*Vegetarian*	②❸④
	Beyoglu	*Turkish*	❶❸④
	Kastoori	*Indian*	❶❶❸
£5+	Fileric	*S'wiches, cakes, etc*	❸❸④

EAST

Smithfield & Farringdon (EC1)

Price	Restaurant	Cuisine	Rating
£40+	Maison Novelli	*French*	③④④
£35+	Bubb's	*French*	②③③
	Mange 2	*"*	④④③
£30+	The Fence	*British, Modern*	④④③
	Stephen Bull Bistro	*"*	③③④
	Rudland & Stubbs	*Fish & seafood*	③③④
	Café du Marché	*French*	②②①
	Le Mesurier	*"*	②③④
	Hope & Sir Loin	*Steaks & grills*	②③②
£25+	The Peasant	*British, Modern*	③④④
	The Quality Chop House	*"*	②②③
	St John	*"*	④③④
	Bleeding Heart	*French*	②②②
	Alba	*Italian*	③②④
	The Clerkenwell	*"*	①③④
	Mustards Brasserie	*International*	④③③
£20+	The Eagle	*Mediterranean*	②④③
	Dôme	*International*	④⑤④
	Vic Naylors	*"*	④⑤②
	Pizza Pomodoro	*Pizza*	③④③
	Carnevale	*Vegetarian*	②②③
	East One	*Misc oriental*	④⑤③
£15+	Pierre Victoire	*French*	⑤④④
	Kolossi Grill	*Greek*	②②③
	Al's	*International*	②③③
	Japanese Canteen	*Japanese*	④④④
£10+	Fox & Anchor	*British, Traditional*	②②②
£5+	Pret A Manger	*S'wiches, cakes, etc*	③①③

The City & East End
(All E and EC postcodes, except EC1)

Price	Name	Cuisine	Ratings
£60+	Tatsuso	Japanese	❶③④
£50+	City Miyama	Japanese	❸③④
£40+	City Brasserie	British, Modern	④④❸
	Gladwins	"	❸❸❸
	Beauchamp's	Fish & seafood	④❸④
	Le Champenois	French	④❸❸
	Le Quai	"	④④④
	Aykoku-Kaku	Japanese	❸④④
£35+	Whittington's	British, Modern	❸④❸
	Gow's	Fish & seafood	❸❸④
	Sheekey's	"	⑤④❸
	Ashtons	French	④❸❸
£30+	Leith's at the Institute	British, Modern	④❸❸
	The Lobster Trading Co	Fish & seafood	❷❸❸
	Sweetings	"	❸❸❷
	Luc's Brasserie	French	❸❸④
	Taberna Etrusca	Italian	④❶❷
	Brasserie Rocque	International	④④❸
£25+	Hothouse Bar & Grill	British, Modern	❸❸❷
	George & Vulture	British, Traditional	④❸❷
	Pélican	French	❸❸❷
	Young Turks	Italian	④❸④
	Babe Ruth's	American	④❸❷
	Imperial City	Chinese	❷❷❸
	Poons in the City	"	④④④
	Café Spice Namaste	Indian	❶❷❸
	Inmala	Indonesian	❸❸④
	Tao	Misc oriental	④④❸
	Sri Siam City	Thai	❷❷❸
	Sri Thai	"	❷❸❸
£20+	Frocks	British, Modern	❸④❷
	The Bow Wine Vaults	British, Traditional	④❸❸
	Café Rouge	French	⑤④④
	Bar Etrusca	Italian	❸④❸
	Fuego	Spanish	④④❸
	Pizza Pomodoro	Pizza	❸④❸
	Futures	Vegetarian	❸❷❷
	Rupee Room	Indian	❸❸④
	Singapura	Malaysian	❸❸❸
£15+	All Bar One	British, Modern	❸❸❷
	Simpson's of Cornhill	British, Traditional	❸❸❶

	Barcelona Tapas	*Spanish*	②❸❸
	Barcelona Tapas Bar	*Spanish*	❷❸④
	Leadenhall Tapas Bar	"	❸❸❸
	Gourmet Pizza Co.	*Pizza*	❸④❸
	PizzaExpress	"	❸❷❸
	Clifton	*Indian*	❷❸❸
	Noto	*Japanese*	❸❷⑤
£10+	Reynier	*British, Traditional*	❸④❸
	Wynkyn de Worde	*International*	❸❸❸
	The Place Below	*Vegetarian*	❷❷❸
	Café Sofra	*Turkish*	❸④④
	Lahore Kebab House	*Indian*	❶④④
	Moshi Moshi Sushi	*Japanese*	❶❷❸
£5+	F Cooke & Sons	*Fish & seafood*	④❸❷
	Pret A Manger	*S'wiches, cakes, etc*	❸❶❸
	Futures, take-away	*Vegetarian*	❸❷❷
£1+	Brick Lane Beigel Bake	*S'wiches, cakes, etc*	❷❷⑤

MAPS

MAP 1 – LONDON OVERVIEW

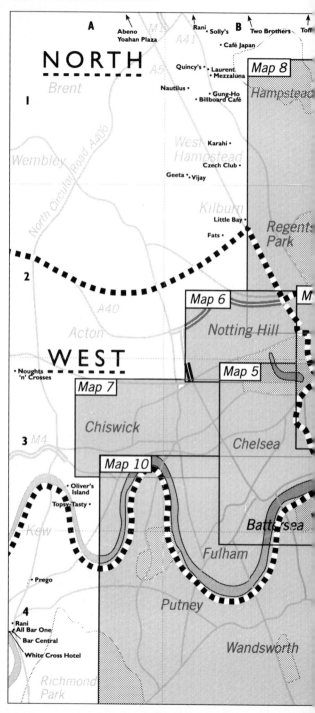

MAP 1 – LONDON OVERVIEW

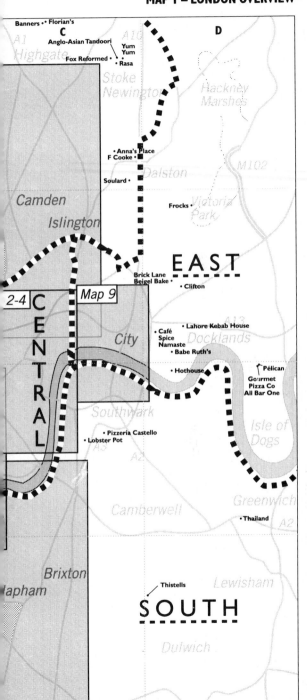

Banners • Florian's
C
D
Highgate
A1
A10
Anglo-Asian Tandoori
Yum
Yum
Fox Reformed •
• Rasa
Stoke
Newington
Hackney
Marshes
• Anna's Place
F Cooke •
Dalston
M102
Soulard •
Camden
Frocks •
Victoria
Park
Islington
EAST
Brick Lane
Beigel Bake •
• Clifton
2-4
Map 9
C
City
• Lahore Kebab House
E
A13
Café
Docklands
N
Spice
Namaste
T
• Babe Ruth's
• Pélican
R
• Hothouse
Gourmet
Pizza Co
A
All Bar One
Southwark
L
Isle of
• Pizzeria Castello
Dogs
• Lobster Pot
A5
A2
Camberwell
Greenwich
• Thailand
A2
Brixton
Lewisham
Clapham
Thistells
SOUTH
Dulwich

MAP 2 – WEST END OVERVIEW

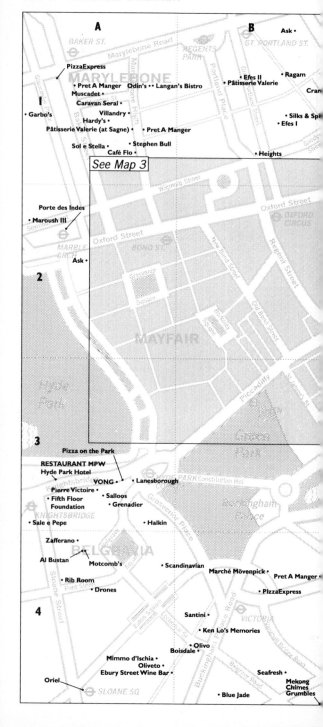

A

B

Ask •

BAKER ST.

Marylebone Road

GT. PORTLAND ST.

REGENTS PARK

PizzaExpress

MARYLEBONE

1

• Pret A Manger   Odin's • • Langan's Bistro

• Efes II   • Ragam

Muscadet •   • Pâtisserie Valerie

Caravan Serai •   Cran

• Garbo's

Villandry •

Hardy's •   • Silks & Spi

Pâtisserie Valerie (at Sagne) •   • Efes I

• Pret A Manger

Sol e Stella •

• Stephen Bull

Café Flo •   • Heights

See Map 3

Wigmore Street

Oxford Street

OXFORD CIRCUS

Porte des Indes

• Maroush III

Oxford Street

BOND ST.

2

MARBLE ARCH

New Bond Street

Regent Street

Old Bond Street

Ask •

MAYFAIR

Grosvenor Square

Hyde Park

Piccadilly

Green Park

3

Pizza on the Park

RESTAURANT MPW

Hyde Park Hotel

VONG   • Lanesborough

HYDE PARK Constitution Hill

Pierre Victoire •

• Fifth Floor   • Salloos

Foundation   • Grenadier

Buckingham Palace

KNIGHTSBRIDGE

• Sale e Pepe   • Halkin

Zafferano •

BELGRAVIA

Al Bustan   Motcomb's

• Scandinavian   Marché Mövenpick •   • Pret A Manger

• Rib Room

• Drones   • PizzaExpress

4

VICTORIA

Santini •

• Ken Lo's Memories

Boisdale • • Olivo

Mimmo d'Ischia •

Oliveto •

Ebury Street Wine Bar •   Seafresh •

Oriel •   Mekong

SLOANE SQ.   Chimes

Grumbles

• Blue Jade

MAP 2 –WEST END OVERVIEW

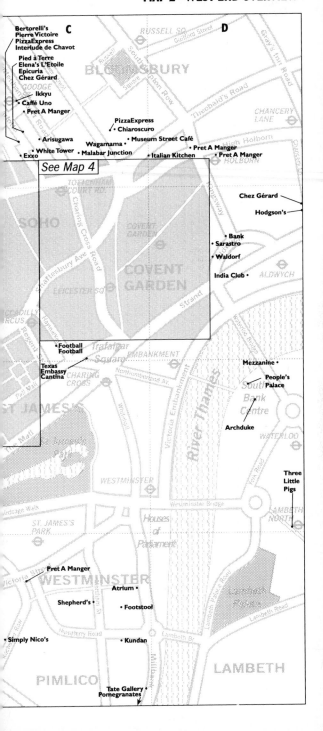

MAP 3 – MAYFAIR, ST JAMES'S & WEST SOHO

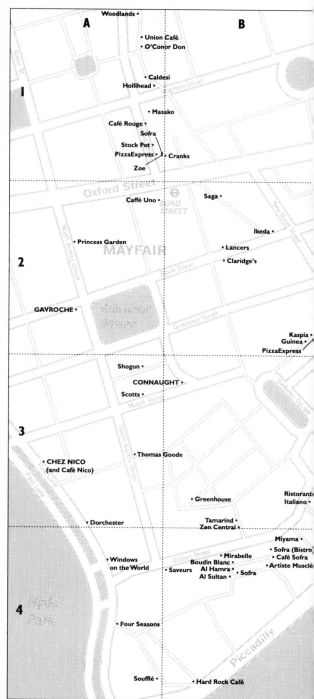

MAP 3 – MAYFAIR, ST JAMES'S & WEST SOHO

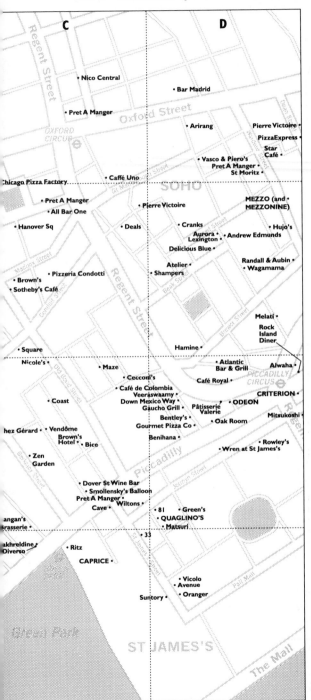

C

D

Regent Street

• Nico Central

• Bar Madrid

• Pret A Manger

Oxford Street

• Arirang

Pierre Victoire •

OXFORD CIRCUS

PizzaExpress •

Star Café •

• Vasco & Piero's
Pret A Manger •
St Moritz •

Chicago Pizza Factory

• Caffé Uno

SOHO

MEZZO (and •
MEZZONINE)

• Pret A Manger

• Pierre Victoire

• All Bar One

• Hanover Sq

• Cranks

• Hujo's

• Deals

Aurora •
Lexington •

• Andrew Edmunds

Delicious Blue •

Randall & Aubin •

Atelier •

• Wagamama

• Shampers

• Pizzeria Condotti

Regent Street

• Brown's

• Sotheby's Café

Melati •

Rock
Island
Diner

• Square

Hamine •

Nicole's •

• Atlantic
Bar & Grill

Alwaha •

PICCADILLY
CIRCUS

• Maze

• Ceccoñi's

Café Royal •

CRITERION •

• Café de Colombia
Veeraswaamy •
Down Mexico Way •

• Coast

• ODEON

Mitsukoshi •

Gaucho Grill •

Pâtisserie
Valerie

Bentley's •

• Oak Room

hez Gérard •

• Vendôme

Gourmet Pizza Co •

Brown's
Hotel •

Benihana •

• Bice

• Rowley's

• Zen
Garden

•Wren at St James's

Piccadilly

• Dover St Wine Bar

• Smollensky's Balloon

Pret A Manger •

angan's

Cave •

Wiltons •

rasserie •

• 81

• Green's

• QUAGLINO'S

akhreldine •
Diverso

• 33

• Ritz

• Matsuri

CAPRICE •

• Vicolo
• Avenue

Suntory •

• Oranger

Green Park

ST JAMES'S

The Mall

MAP 4 – EAST SOHO, CHINATOWN & COVENT GARDEN

A

B

Pierre Victoire •

Mandeer •

New Oxford Street

Pret A Manger •

Oxford Street

Dyott St

TOTTENHAM CT. RD

I

Soho St

Rodos •

Charing Cross Road

Soho Square

• Gay Hussar

• Au Jardin des Gourmets

Café Pasta •

SOHO

Mildreds •

Mon Plaisir

Bruno Soho • • Café Rouge

Shaftesbury Avenue

• 22° South

Euten's

• Quo Vadis • dell'Ugo

2 • All Bar One • Soho Soho • Mondo

Dean St

• PizzaExpress

Escargot • Stock Pot •

Jin •

Great St

Red

• Gopal's Garlic Sri Siam •

Fort

Saigon & Shots Pollo •

Monmouth St

• Pitcher & Piano • Café Emm

• Saigon • Bahn Thai

Alastair Little • • Little Italy • Ed's

Cambridge

Chiang Mai • • Bar Italia

Circus

Blues • Pâtisserie • Café Bôhème

Valerie • • Maison Bertaux

Old Compton St

Café Sofra •

Kettners •

Balans • Capannina • Epicure

• French House

IVY •

• Dôme • Lindsay House

• New World

Shaftesbury Avenue

• Harbour City

3 Dragon Inn • Ikkyu •

WestZenders •

CHINATOWN

• Saint

• Tokyo Diner • Cranks

China City • Poons, Lisle St

Charing Cross Road

Mr Kong •

Craterbourn St

Wong Kei • Fung Shing •

Pret A

Manger

Gerrard St

Warbour St

• Golden Drason

PizzaExpress •

Beotys •

St Martin's Lane

• Manzi's Cork & Bottle • Caffé Uno •

Chuen Cheng Ku • Häagen-Dazs •

LEICESTER

Jade Garden • • Poons

• Sheekey's

SQ

• China Court

Planet Hollywood • • Marché Mövenpick

Browns •

• Fashion Café

• TGI Fridays All Bar One • Sofra •

4

• Café Sogo

Haymarket

Café Fish • • Stock Pot

Woodlands • • Pierre Victoire

Wardour Street

MAP 4 – EAST SOHO, CHINATOWN & COVENT GARDEN

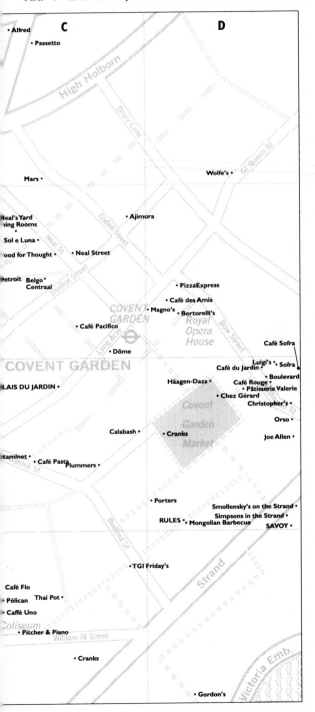

C

D

• Alfred

• Passetto

High Holborn

Drury Lane

• Wolfe's

Gt Queen St

Mars •

Neal's Yard
ning Rooms

Endell Street

• Ajimura

Neal St

Sol e Luna •

ood for Thought •

• Neal Street

Shelton Street

etroit Belgo •
Centraal

• PizzaExpress

• Café des Amis

*COVEN
GARDEN*

• Magno's
• Bertorelli's

*Royal
Opera
House*

• Café Pacifico

Long Acre

Bow Street

Café Sofra

• Dôme

COVENT GARDEN

Luigi's • • Sofra
Café du Jardin •

• Boulevard

Häagen-Dazs •

Café Rouge •
• Pâtisserie Valerie

LAIS DU JARDIN •

• Chez Gérard

Christopher's •

Covent

Orso •

Calabash •

• Cranks

Garden

Joe Allen •

Market

taminet •

• Café Pasta Plummers •

• Porters

Smollensky's on the Strand •

Simpsons in the Strand •

RULES • • Mongolian Barbecue

SAVOY •

Bedford St

• TGI Friday's

Strand

Café Flo

• Pélican   Thai Pot •

• Caffé Uno

Coliseum

• Pitcher & Piano

William IV Street

• Cranks

Victoria Emb.

• Gordon's

MAP 5 – KNIGHTSBRIDGE, CHELSEA & SOUTH KENSINGTON

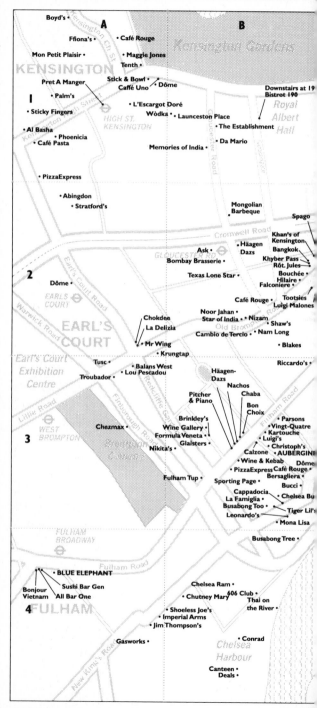

MAP 5 – KNIGHTSBRIDGE, CHELSEA & SOUTH KENSINGTON

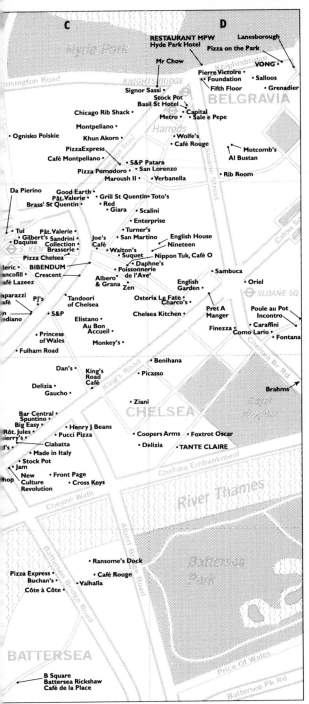

C

D

Hyde Park

RESTAURANT MPW
Hyde Park Hotel

Lanesborough

Pizza on the Park

Mr Chow

Knightsbridge

VONG •

ensington Road

KNIGHTSBRIDGE

Pierre Victoire •
• Foundation

• Salloos

Signor Sassi •

Fifth Floor

• Grenadier

Stock Pot
Basil St Hotel

BELGRAVIA

Chicago Rib Shack •

Metro •

• Capital
• Sale e Pepe

• Ognisko Polskie

Montpeliano •

Harrods

Khun Akorn •

• Wolfe's

• Motcomb's

PizzaExpress

• Café Rouge

Al Bustan

Café Montpeliano •

• S&P Patara

Pizza Pomodoro •

• San Lorenzo

Maroush II •

• Verbanella

• Rib Room

Da Pierino •

Good Earth •
Pât. Valerie •

• Grill St Quentin • Toto's

Brass' St Quentin •

• Red
• Giara

• Scalini

• Enterprise

• Tui

Pât. Valerie •

• Turner's

• Gilbert's Sandrini •

Joe's

• San Martino

English House

• Daquise

Collection •

Café

• Walton's

Nineteen

Brasserie

• Suquet

Nippon Tuk, Café O

Pizza Chelsea •

• Daphne's

BIBENDUM

• Poissonnerie

leric •

Crescent —

de l'Ave'

• Sambuca

ancofill •

Albero •

English

• Oriel

aparazzi

& Grana

Zen

Garden •

SLOANE SQ

afé

PJ's •

Tandoori

Osteria Le Fate •

of Chelsea

Charco's •

Pret A

Poule au Pot

n

• S&P

Chelsea Kitchen •

Manger

Incontro

ediano

Elistano •

• Caraffini

Au Bon

Finezza •

Como Lario •

• Fontana

• Princess

Accueil •

of Wales

Monkey's •

• Fulham Road

Dan's •

• Benihana

King's

Road

• Picasso

Café

Delizia •

Gaucho •

Brahms

• Ziani

CHELSEA

Bar Central •

Spuntino •

Big Easy •

• Henry J Beans

Rôt. Jules •

• Pucci Pizza

• Coopers Arms

• Foxtrot Oscar

ierry's •

d's •

• Ciabatta

• Delizia

TANTE CLAIRE

• Made in Italy

• Stock Pot

• Jam

hop

New

• Front Page

Culture

• Cross Keys

River Thames

Revolution

Cheyne Walk

• Ransome's Dock

• Café Rouge

Pizza Express •

Battersea

Buchan's •

• Valhalla

Park

Côte à Côte •

BATTERSEA

Price of Wales

• B Square
Battersea Rickshaw
Café de la Place

Battersea Pk Rd

MAP 6 – NOTTING HILL & BAYSWATER

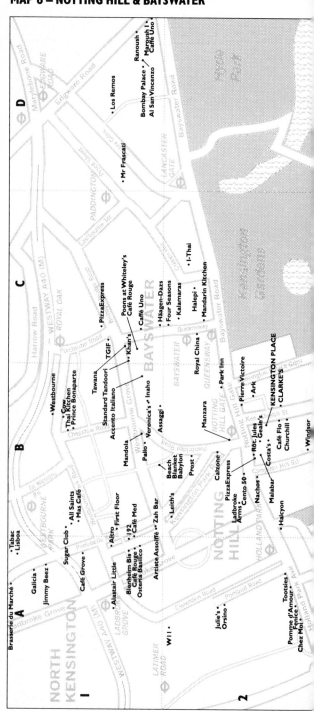

MAP 7 – HAMMERSMITH & CHISWICK

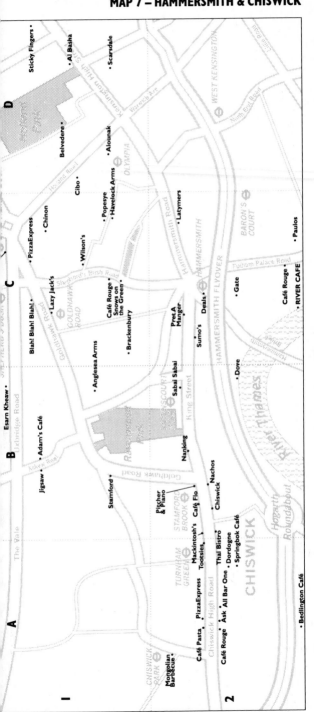

MAP 8 – HAMPSTEAD, CAMDEN TOWN & ISLINGTON

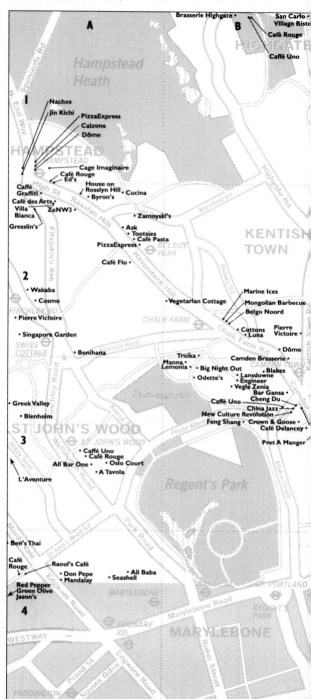

A

B

Hampstead Heath

HIGHGATE

Brasserie Highgate •

San Carlo •
Village Bistr
Café Rouge •

Caffé Uno •

I

Nachos
Jin Kichi
PizzaExpress
Calzone
Dôme

HAMPSTEAD
HAMPSTEAD

Cage Imaginaire
Café Rouge
Ed's

Caffé Graffiti •
Café des Arts •
Villa Bianca
Gresslin's

ZeNW3

House on Rosslyn Hill
Byron's

• Cucina

Rosslyn Hill

Mansfield Rd

KENTISH TOWN

• Zamoyski's

• Ask
• Tootsies
• Café Pasta
PizzaExpress •

BELSIZE PARK

Haverstock Hill

Café Flo •

2

• Wakaba
• Cosmo

FINCHLEY RD

• Pierre Victoire

• Singapore Garden

SWISS COTTAGE

• Benihana

Adelaide Road

• Vegetarian Cottage

CHALK FARM

Marine Ices
Mongolian Barbecue
Belgo Noord

Cottons
• Luna

Pierre Victoire

Chalk Farm Rd

• Dôme

Camden Brasserie •

Troika •
Manna •
Lemonia •

Big Night Out •
• Odette's

Blakes •
• Lansdowne
• Engineer
• Vegia Zenia
Bar Gansa •
Cheng Du

• Greek Valley
• Blenheim

ST JOHN'S WOOD

Prince Albert

Caffé Uno •
New Culture Revolution
Feng Shang • Crown & Goose

China Jazz

Café Delancey •

Pret A Manger •

3

ST. JOHN'S WOOD

Caffé Uno •
• Café Rouge
All Bar One • • Oslo Court
• A Tavola

L'Aventure

Regent's Park

• Ben's Thai

Café Rouge

Raoul's Café
• Don Pepe
• Mandalay

• Ali Baba
• Seashell

Red Pepper
Green Olive
Jason's

MARYLEBONE

Marylebone Road

GT. PORTLAND

REGENT'S PARK

4

EDGWARE RD.

MARYLEBONE

WESTWAY

PADDINGTON

MAP 8 – HAMPSTEAD, CAMDEN TOWN & ISLINGTON

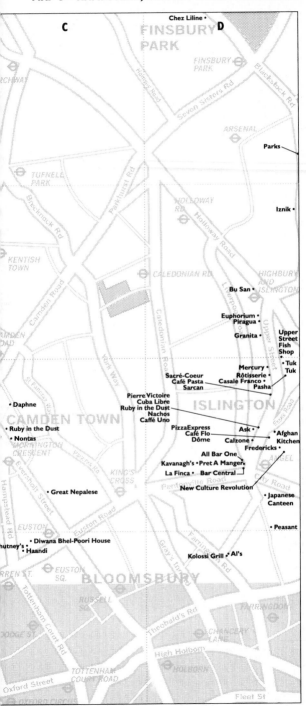

Chez Liline •

C **D**

FINSBURY
PARK

FINSBURY
PARK

Seven Sisters Rd

ARSENAL

Parks

TUFNELL
PARK

Iznik •

KENTISH
TOWN

HOLLOWAY
RD

CALEDONIAN RD

HIGHBURY
AND
ISLINGTON

Bu San •

Euphorium •
Piragua •

Granita •

Upper
Street
Fish
Shop

• Tuk
Tuk

Mercury •
Rôtisserie •

Sacré-Coeur
Café Pasta
Sarcan

Casale Franco •
Pasha •

Pierre Victoire
Cuba Libre
Ruby in the Dust
Nachos
Caffè Uno

ISLINGTON

• Daphne

CAMDEN TOWN

• Ruby in the Dust

• Nontas
MORNINGTON
CRESCENT

PizzaExpress
Café Flo
Dôme

Ask •

• Afghan
Kitchen

Calzone •

Fredericks •

All Bar One

Kavanagh's • Pret A Manger •

La Finca • Bar Central

Great Nepalese

New Culture Revolution

KING'S
CROSS

Euston Road

• Japanese
Canteen

EUSTON

• Peasant

utney's • Diwana Bhel-Poori House
• Haandi

Kolossi Grill • Al's

EUSTON
SQ.

BLOOMSBURY

RUSSELL
SQ.

FARRINGDON

Theobald's Rd

CHANCERY
LANE

High Holborn

HOLBORN

Oxford Street

TOTTENHAM
COURT ROAD

Fleet St

MAP 9 – THE CITY

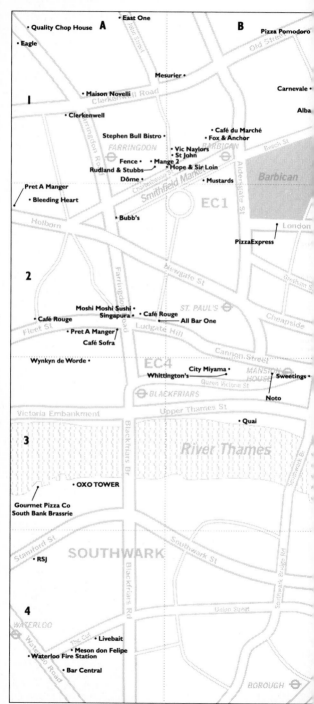

MAP 9 – THE CITY

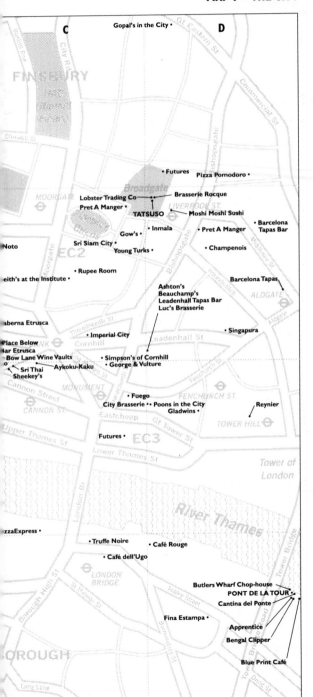

Gopal's in the City •

C

D

FINSBURY

• Futures   Pizza Pomodoro •

Broadgate

Lobster Trading Co ——   —— Brasserie Rocque
Pret A Manger •
TATSUSO ←——— Moshi Moshi Sushi
• Barcelona
Tapas Bar
Gow's •   • Inmala   • Pret A Manger
Sri Siam City •
Young Turks •   • Champenois
Noto

• Rupee Room

eith's at the Institute •

Barcelona Tapas

ALDGATE

Ashton's
Beauchamp's
Leadenhall Tapas Bar
Luc's Brasserie

aberna Etrusca

• Singapura

Place Below   • Imperial City
Cornhill   Leadenhall St
ar Etrusca
• Bow Lane Wine Vaults   • Simpson's of Cornhill
o •   • George & Vulture
• Sri Thai   Aykoku-Kaku
Sheekey's

MONUMENT

• Fuego   Reynier
City Brasserie •• Poons in the City
Gladwins •
Cannon Street   TOWER HILL
CANNON ST

Futures •   EC3
Lower Thames St

Upper Thames St

Tower of
London

River Thames

zzaExpress •
• Truffe Noire   • Café Rouge

• Café dell'Ugo

LONDON
BRIDGE

Butlers Wharf Chop-house
PONT DE LA TOUR •
Cantina del Ponte

Fina Estampa •
Apprentice

Bengal Clipper

Blue Print Café

OROUGH

MAP 10 – SOUTH LONDON (AND FULHAM)

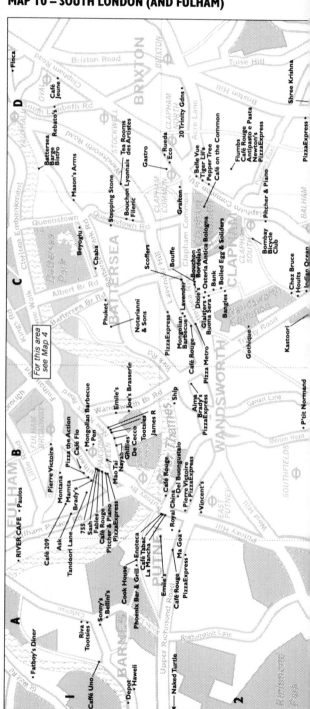

For this area see Map 4